CHRIST IN
THE AMERICAS
BEFORE
COLUMBUS

Unfamiliar Origins and Insights

*Spanish Translation and
Commentary by*

GARY BOWEN

"On the cover of *Christianity in The Americas Before Columbus* is the city Cholula, Mexico, surrounding an ancient pyramid with the Church of the Lady de los Remedios a top the pyramid with the volcano Popocatepetl in the background. The writings of Spanish conquistadors and early Catholic missionaries reference Cholula as the sacred city of the Americas."

TABLE OF CONTENTS

ACKNOWLEDGEMENTS

This book would not have been written without the encouragement of Dr. Paul Y. Hoskisson, appointed 2008 as Director of the Laura F. Willes Center for Book of Mormon Research, and the Foundation for Ancient Research and Mormon Studies (FARMS). I shared my research with Paul and his wife Joaquina at a 2009 luncheon meeting in Provo, UT with my wife Herlinda Briones Bowen. After the luncheon, Paul told me he knew of no one else who was studying the research sources I had shared with him. He said, "You need to get this written."

In 1967, visiting Herlinda's family in Los Mochis, Sinaloa, MX, she insisted I buy a book she had studied as a student, *Servando Teresa de Mier Escritos y Memorias* ("Servando Teresa de Mier Writings and Memoirs"). This was my introduction to 50 plus years studying Dr. Mier and his research sources on ancient Christianity in The Americas. Much of the book is translated from Spanish. Herlinda earned a Bachelor of Art in Spanish and a Teaching Licensure at the University of Utah. She is my Spanish Editor in Chief.

While writing, I came to know Deirdre Paulsen and Colleen Whitley retired Brigham Young University Professors of English, Writing, and Folklore. I was done writing when Deirdre Paulsen, Colleen Whitley and Paul Hoskisson recommended that I divide my writing into two books; an academic work, *Fray Servando Teresa de Mier, Writings on Ancient Christianity and Spain's Evangelizm of Mexico*, a translation of Fray Mier's defense of his December 12, 1794 Guadalupe Sermon, and *Christianity in The Americas Before Columbus, Unfamiliar Origins and Insights* that gives historical, geographic, and cultural authenticity to *The Book of Mormon*. Deirdre Paulsen and Colleen Whitley did the final editing, polishing my translation and writing to publishing standards.

Deirdre Paulsen, Colleen Whitley, and Paul Gardner coached me as I stumbled down the road to find a publisher. I finally contracted with Elite Online Publishing. I appreciate the work of Jenn Foster, Chief Executive Officer, and Melanie Johnson, Elite Online Publishing, for launching and publishing my books.

To all of you, *muchísimas gracias* (translation: "thank you very very much") for being my Author Mentor Team.

INTRODUCTION

The Tale of a Road Less Traveled and All the Difference It Made

Gary Bowen took the road less traveled, and that has made all the difference. In 1962, I earned a Bachelor of Science in Economics from the University of Utah. Not staying for the graduation ceremony, I left to serve two-plus years as a missionary in the West-Mexican Mission of the Church of Jesus Christ of Latter-day Saints. My mission was a post-graduate study in Spanish, Church scriptures, Church history, and everything Mexican. In 1964, my mission ended, and I married a West Mexican lady-missionary, Herlinda Briones-Vega. Herlinda was one of the first two converts to the Church of Jesus Christ in her hometown, Los Mochis, Sinaloa, Mexico. There is now a Church of Jesus Christ Latter-day Saints Stake in Los Mochis. The Briones-Vega family tradition is that when the Mormon missionaries first presented *The Book of Mormon* lesson in their home, Herlinda declared: "Oh, I learned that in school!" How is that possible? At that time, there were no Church of Jesus Christ of Latter-day Saints in Los Mochis.

Married three years, in 1968, Herlinda and I were browsing a bookstore in Los Mochis. Herlinda turned to me with a small paperback book in hand and said: "We have to buy this book. I studied Fray Mier in school." The book was *Servando Teresa de Mier escritos y memorias*, ("Servando Teresa de Mier, Writings and Memoirs"), Prologue and Selection, with footnotes by Edmundo O'Gorman, published 1945 by the Autonomous University of Mexico. Dr. O'Gorman (1906-1995) was a graduate in Law (1928), Doctor of Philosophy (1948), Doctor of Philosophy in History (1951), and General Director of Mexico's General Archive of the Nation from 1938 to 1952. *Servando Teresa de Mier escritos y memorias* cost 11 pesos, 92 U.S. cents. Published 1945, it had been on warehouse or bookstore shelves for 22 years. It is a little-known history even in Mexico. Evidence is the limited sales of Fray Mier's writings in his native Mexico. Chapters 4 and 5 are English translated letters found in *Servando Teresa de Mier escritos y memorias*, published by the Autonomous University of Mexico,

1

editor, Dr. O'Gorman, which gives authenticity to Mier's writings. *Christianity in The Americas Before Columbus* is my tale of a road less traveled, researching "unfamiliar origins and insights" on Mexico's ancient religious history.

How Herlinda learned of Fray Mier in school is unusual. The Los Mochis schools she attended in the 1940s and 1950s were private, non-religious, with very limited resources. Her father had a desk made for her to take to school. One year her school lacked a classroom for her grade, so classes were held outdoors beneath a tamarind tree. The school had no textbooks. Teachers taught English, Spanish, history, literature, typing, and mathematics classes from books a teacher purchased at Los Mochis bookstores. Her school had no required government or religious oversight or textbooks. The school's limited financial resources did not provide Herlinda with books to study. Teachers orally read books to the class or wrote book quotes on a blackboard for the students to copy and study.

Herlinda's study of Fray Mier in a Mexican middle school was more detailed and comprehensive than my university study of Fray Mier. It took me years to understand the historical significance of Fray Mier. My college study of Fray Mier was forgotten, so I began studying in Spanish, *Servando Teresa de Mier escritos y memorias*. I was then surprised to find Fray Mier referenced in a Latin America history textbook I had studied at the University of Utah and kept in my personal library, *A History of Latin America* by Hubert Herring, Second Edition, 1961, published by Alfred A. Knopf, New York. *A History of Latin America*, page 308, has a summary of Fray Mier's tragic life:

Fray Servando, a Dominican priest, had run afoul of the Inquisition in 1794 by preaching a sermon at the shrine of Our Lady of Guadalupe in which he suggested that the Virgin had arrived in Mexico on the cape of the apostle Thomas, who, he believed, was the first Christian missionary to the Indians. Fray Servando was punished for his doctrinal waywardness by commitment to a Spanish prison; he escaped, took part in various subversive movements looking toward the independence of Mexico, and was captured again by the Spaniards.

With an MBA from the University of Utah earned after my mission, I began my career in various businesses and became an amateur political enthusiast. Visiting Herlinda's family in Mexico, I also became a Mexican *politico*. The weekend before Memorial Day 1988, I received a phone call from a man who told me he was en route from Los Mochis to Salt Lake City to visit me. The gentleman's introduction was that Herlinda's Uncle Estanislao Briones had told him that I would be a reliable consultant on all things political, even in Mexico. The surprise visitor was a member of the Mexican National Congress, Chamber of Deputies, the same as the United States House of Representatives. The Deputy and I visited three days in Salt Lake City. We met again the following year in El Paso, Texas, and thereafter whenever I visited Los Mochis. Building a friendship, I shared with the Deputy my study of Fray Mier and the parallels I found between Fray Mier's religious history of ancient Mexico and *The Book of Mormon*. I was surprised to learn that this well informed Mexican Congressional Deputy did know of Fray Mier. Over the years, I have met few Mexicans who know of Fray Mier and his role in the history of their country. In 1990, the Deputy telephoned me to say that he had attended a conference in Monterrey, Nuevo Leon, Mexico, Fray Mier's place of birth and the constituency which elected Mier to the First Constituent Congress of Mexico in 1822. The Deputy had asked his Monterrey colleagues what they knew of Fray Mier. He was referred to a biography published in Monterrey, of which he purchased two copies, one for himself and one for me. Thus, I came into possession of *Biografía del Benemérito Mexicano D. Servando Teresa de Mier Noriega y Guerra*, ("Biography of the Distinguished Mexican Don Servando Teresa de Mier Noriega y Guerra") by Governor José Eleuterio González first published 1876. The "Commemorative Edition Facsimile of the Original" was published by the State of Nuevo Leon and the Autonomous University of Nuevo Leon on the sesquicentennial of the death of Father Mier 1827-1977. Only 1,250 copies were printed of the Sesquicentennial edition, June 30, 1978. A dozen years after the 1978 reprint, my Deputy friend found original copies of the *Biography* still available. There being few copies of Fray Mier's biography published by the State of Nuevo Leon and the Autonomous University of Nuevo Leon, exemplifies the esteemed, yet shrouded status of Fray Mier in his native Mexico. The *Biography* compiles Fray Mier's writings, memoirs, and speeches with a few biographical pages written by Governor González.

My Fray Mier research grew into a small library of books

mostly in Spanish, written by Spanish conquistadors, early Catholic Priests, historians, and anthropologists of Mexico's history, many cited by Dr. Mier in his writings. This book's bibliography lists that small library. Many of the library's authors are Catholic Fathers. Some of the books are English translations; most are in Spanish. Spanish editions are accessible and inexpensive paperback books published by Mexican universities or by classic publishing houses such as Mexico's Editorial Porrua, S. A. I found another very important reason for reading these histories in the authors' Spanish. Cross referencing English and Spanish editions of an author's writings, I chanced upon omissions in the English translations from the Spanish. I have come to believe that there is a prejudicial practice by English publications of omitting Fray Mier and other Spanish authors' writings on Fray Mier's core message of "the ancient preaching of the Gospel in America." Fray Mier and other Mexican and Spanish authors of the 16th to 19th centuries verify that Hebrew-Christian traditions were practiced in Mexico before Columbus. Sadly, the written history and scripture of Mexico's Christian religion were destroyed by the Spanish conquistadores as you will read later in the book.

The first time I read Fray Mier's "Farewell Letter to the Mexicans," Chapter 5, I wanted to translate and share the "Farewell Letter..." with members of the Church of Jesus Christ of Latter-day Saints. My first sharing of Fray Mier's "Farewell Letter" was forty-five years ago at a Church of Jesus Christ of Latter-day Saints, California Spanish Branch picnic, organized by LDS Church missionaries. The missionaries were thrilled to hear my brief testimony of Mier's "Farewell Letter..." as historical evidence of the practice of Christianity in ancient America and a witness to the history of *The Book of Mormon*. The missionaries wanted to know where they could buy a copy of Mier's "Farewell Letter to the Mexicans." I told them, "There is no English translation and it's rare to find it in Spanish even in Mexico."

Career and family obligations overrode my Fray Mier research for many years. In those years I had a chance encounter with Mexican Catholic Priests, which gave me a unique insight into Mexico's Catholic religion and the significance of Fray Mier in Mexican history. In 1992, I taught a seminar on United States finance at the Autonomous University of Baja California, Tijuana, Mexico. During the week, I was invited by a University English Instructor to attend an English class he taught across town at a

Catholic University. On the drive over, I told the English Instructor of my Fray Mier studies. The Instructor, a United States citizen, was incredulous. Arriving at the Catholic University, we went into a small room where the English Instructor introduced me in conversational English to the "students," the University's Provost, a Cuban, and a half dozen Mexican Jesuit Priest Professors. Unexpectedly, I became the subject of the English class when the English Instructor broached the topic of the day, his delirious tale of our drive to the University and my sharing a weird story about some guy, Father Mier, and his ridiculously silly ideas. The Instructor, rudely, asked the class, "Have you ever heard of Father Mier?" The response was unspoken. The Cuban Provost shook his head, signaling no, but the Mexican Priests all nodded their heads up and down, signaling yes. The Instructor was flabbergasted, as was I. The Instructor asked, "How do you know of Father Mier?" The Priests practiced their English responding; "We studied Father Mier and his writings in seminary while studying to become Priests." The Priests' nervous response to the ill-mannered questioning was a heads-up. The Instructor quickly switched the class conversation to another subject.

This chance meeting at the Catholic University was an eye opener for me. The Cuban Provost had no idea who Father Mier was, while the cautious response of the Mexican Jesuit Professors awakened me to the fact that while unknown to the average Mexican, Fray Mier is studied by Mexico's Catholics when preparing to become Priests. I pondered the question: Why do Mexican Catholic Priests study the writings of Fray Mier?

My classroom meeting with these Mexican Jesuit Priests reminded me of a chance encounter I had twenty-nine years earlier while serving as a missionary in Tepic, Nayarit, Mexico. The Church of Jesus Christ of Latter-day Saints' Tepic Branch was a small congregation, one of four missionaries served as branch president. We lived and held church services in a small rented home. Most of our time was spent knocking on doors throughout the city, introducing ourselves and our gospel message. Proselyting the city's neighborhoods, we saw a much beloved Catholic Father visiting homes throughout the week. He was known and loved throughout Tepic, as a true loving shepherd of the flock, visiting those in need. One afternoon crossing the plaza in front of Tepic's central Cathedral, my companion and I heard a man calling us: "*Hermanos, Hermanos*" ("Brothers, Brothers"). We turned around expecting to see a member of our church congregation. We were astonished to see Tepic's beloved Catholic Father calling us "*Hermanos.*" The Father greeted us with friendly handshakes, complemented us on our good-work, and encouraged us in our missionary labors. He counseled us: "Your task is not easy, but the residents of Tepic are good people. In time, many will join your church." We were speechless. We remembered our missionary role and asked the Father the "Golden Question:" "What do you know about the Mormon Church?" We were surprised when the Father told us he had read *The Book of Mormon* while studying to become a Catholic Priest. The Father bid us a kind farewell. Turning to leave, he called us back. "Brothers, please let me give you a bit of advice. Many will accept your message and become baptized in the Mormon Church, but do not deny or preach against the Virgin of Guadalupe to these people." This experience overwhelmed our hearts and minds and is unforgettable to me.

The Jesuit Professors and Priests I met in 1992 at a Catholic University, studied Fray Mier. A beloved Catholic Priest, I met in 1963, read *The Book of Mormon* and respected the LDS Church. His kind counsel: "Teach your Church's message, but do not deny the Virgin of Guadalupe" was a scene taken from the drama of Fray Mier's life. Mier was accused of denying the Virgin of Guadalupe in his December 12, 1794 sermon, which led to his being imprisoned, exiled, and subject to an Inquisition for the rest of his life. It is now too late to ask the kind Father if he had studied Fray Mier. I can only speculate upon the connection between Fray Mier's life and the Catholic Father's kind advice that the kind Father was very probably a student of Fray Mier's writings and history. Over many years of study and sharing my knowledge of Fray Mier, the only persons who have had any prior knowledge of Fray Mier's sermon and writings were my wife Herlinda and the Jesuit Professors of a Mexican Catholic University. My chance encounters with Mexican Priests gives me probable reason to speculate that the Mexican Catholic Church has connected the propositions of Fray Mier's 1794 Guadalupe Sermon to *The Book of Mormon*. Fray Mier's December 12, 1794 Guadalupe Sermon is the thesis of my two books *Christianity in The Americas Before Columbus, Unfamiliar Origins and Insights* and *Fray Servando Teresa de Mier: Writings on Ancient Christianity and Spain's Evangelism of Mexico.*

The English Instructor in Mexico thought my Mier study was ridiculous, but I discovered a year later that the English Instructor had begun his own Mier study. He gave me a copy of *Mi libro de Historia de México* ("My Book of Mexico's History"), a Fourth Grade, Primary Education textbook, published by Mexico's Federal Secretary of Public Education, First Edition 1992. Mexico's Fourth Grade history features Fray Mier as a fighter for liberty with a vague illusion to Mier's "New Ideas," but with no explanation of what his "New Ideas" were. This is truly a paradox! Fray Mier is honorably profiled while his message is hushed. This is a topic of Chapter 3, "The Mier Paradox." The English Instructor, also gave me a copy of *The Memoirs of Fray Servando Teresa de Mier*, translated from the Spanish by Helen Lane, edited with introduction by Susana Rotker, copyrighted 1998 by Oxford University Press, Inc. It is one of 29 books in Oxford University Press's Library of Latin America. The O'Gorman and González books, which are the Spanish sources of my Fray Mier translated works, are cited in the Oxford University Press bibliography. *The Memoirs*, "Note on the Text" states:

> For the present edition, the first in English, the area of the Memoirs most likely to interest the general reader has been chosen: the extraordinary tale of what the Europe of Napoleon Bonaparte was like, told from the point of view of a Mexican priest persecuted by the Inquisition, until his return to Mexico as a participant in the struggle for independence.

Sadly, *The Memoirs of Fray Servando Teresa de Mier* reduces his legacy to a travelogue of Napoleon Bonaparte's 19th Century Europe. Oxford University Press translates and publishes Fray Mier's memoirs, while knowingly omitting his writings in defense of his Guadalupe Sermon, which was the cause of his inquisition and European travels in forced exile. Fray Mier endured a labyrinth of persecutions for 28 years, December 1794 to March 1823, which I detail in my book, *Fray Servando Teresa de Mier: Writings on Ancient Christianity and Spain's Evangelism of Mexico*. There is no duplication of the Spanish to English translations of Fray Mier's writings published by Oxford University and my books of Fray Mier's writings: *Christianity in The Americas Before Columbus: Unfamiliar Origins and Insights* and *Fray Servando Teresa de Mier: Writings on Ancient Christianity and Spain's Evangelism of Mexico*. I cite this as an example of the myth cliché that masks Fray Mier's writings on

Mexico's ancient Christian religion. Why omit the reasons for a Mexican Priest's persecution by the Inquisition, while featuring his memoirs on travels in exile? This evidences my observation after many years studying histories written by early Catholic missionaries and Fray Mier that English translations of these Spanish writings on Mexican history are edited to knowingly and willfully omit evidence of Hebrew-Christian practices.

Mid-1990's, I met with an administrator at The Foundation for Ancient Research and Mormon Studies ("FARMS."). The FARMS's administrator brushed aside my study of Fray Mier with the comment: "FARMS is a Foundation for Ancient Research and Mormon Studies, not the 15th to 19th century writings you describe." The administrator was unwilling to continue a discussion on the findings of Fray Mier and early Catholic missionaries, even though those writings give historical authenticity to *The Book of Mormon*.

In 2009, I had the good fortune to meet with Dr. Paul Y. Hoskisson, Associate Dean of the Neal A. Maxwell Institute for Religious Scholarship, a successor to FARMS at Brigham Young University. At the end of our luncheon conversation on Fray Mier, Dr. Hoskisson shared these words: "No one I know of is working on the subject we have discussed." He encouraged me to push on. With his moral support, my intent was to translate and publish Fray Mier's "Farewell Letter to the Mexicans" in a pamphlet with an introduction and footnotes. While editing my translation of the "Farewell Letter. . .," I found an Internet Website, "The Book of Mormon Archaeological Digest II," with an article titled, "Christian Myths in Pre-Columbian Mexico," a redacted edition of Fray Mier's "Farewell Letter to the Mexicans," Chapter 5 of this book. "The Book of Mormon Archaeological Digest II" "Christian Myths" article concludes: "We can be sure, with *The Book of Mormon* as our faithful guide, that there is more to Mier than mere myth. . .without removing or adding anything to the truth." To title Fray Mier's "Farewell Letter to the Mexicans" as "Christian Myths," revives Fray Mier's Inquisition and is a further denial of Mexico's true history. As labyrinthine as are the writings of Fray Mier and the events of his life, I have concluded that Fray Mier's writings link Mexico's ancient Hebrew-Christian practices, history, culture, persons, and geography to *The Book of Mormon*.

The "Christian Myths" article was cause for me to question and research what is a "myth" and "mythology." Harvard University offers a degree in Folklore & Mythology which defines "myth" as;

"(1) The traditional beliefs, myths, tales, and practices of a people, transmitted orally, and [mythology as] (2) the comparative study of folk knowledge and culture." I concluded that if I did not document Fray Mier's life story and did not publish a wider sample of his writings, I would be asking the readers to accept Fray Mier's writings as mere mythology, feeding the flames of Fray Mier's ongoing *postmortem* Inquisition. Hence, my "Farewell Letter to the Mexicans" pamphlet grew into two books: *Fray Servando Teresa de Mier: Writings on Ancient Christianity and Spain's Evangelism of Mexico* and *Christianity in The Americas Before Columbus: Unfamiliar Origins and Insights*. Without Dr. Hoskisson's kind encouragement, this work would not have been completed.

Fray Mier's writings are not read in Mexico's public or religious elementary and secondary schools, leaving him largely unknown. He is studied in Mexican Universities and in Mexican Catholic seminaries by men preparing for ordination as priests. Fray Mier abridged pre-Columbian religious history found in the writings of Spanish Conquistadors, early Catholic missionaries, surviving Anáhuacans, and their succeeding Mexican historians and anthropologists. His writings planted seeds of dignity and pride in Mexico, contributing to Mexico's Revolution of Independence. *Christianity in The Americas Before Columbus* is dedicated to bringing Fray Mier's message from the shadow of censorship and alleged Christian myth to the light of truth.

Fray Mier was not an archaeologist. He studied written folios and codices of 15th to 18th century Catholic missionaries, Spanish conquistadors, anthropologists, and Mexican scholars. Pre-Columbian Mesoamerica was the only place in all of America now known to have a written language. The written language was not alphabetic writings but was hieroglyphic symbols. Some of the early Catholic priests learned to speak and read the native languages of Mexico. Most of the ancient folios and codices surviving the conquest and collapse of Mexican civilization were destroyed by the Spanish conquistadors and the Catholic Church. Fray Mier did not give a speech, write a letter, or a text without citing the sources for his postulations on Mexico's ancient religious practices. As such, Fray Mier provides a synopsis of Mexico's libraries of ancient religious practices. From my research, I also learned that the cities of Mexico's ancient culture lie not in uninhabited forests, but under today's streets and buildings of Mexico's modern cities.

Fray Mier's "Apologia" describes parallels between his travails and those of Don Quixote. The sorrows of Fray Mier, a light to the world in the face of inquisition, imprisonment, exile, and deprivation, has made him the subject of satirical disbelief and accusations that he is the inventor of Christian myth in ancient America. Fray Mier reached for the stars of truth only to become imprisoned and exiled. Miguel de Cervantes Saavedra describes Don Quixote as: "One man scorned and covered with scars who still strove with his last ounce of courage to reach the unreachable stars; and the world was better for this." My hope is that *Fray Servando Teresa de Mier: Writings on Ancient Christianity and Spain's Evangelism of Mexico* and *Christianity in The Americas Before Columbus: Unfamiliar Origins and Insights* will bring Fray Mier's writings to the reachable light of day and make the world better for this. Let us now take Fray Mier's less traveled Quixotic Road.

TRANSLATING FRAY MIER'S WRITINGS

Fray Mier's Spanish is very dignified and formal in its literary style. But it is also pompous and stilted, making it difficult to translate. My wife, Herlinda, is a gifted translator of Spanish and English, a certified teacher of her native Spanish language and French, and editor of my translations of Fray Mier's writings to English. Herlinda agrees Fray Mier's writings are difficult works to translate. Why, I asked her, is his writing style so complex? She couldn't give me a quick answer. Spanish writings of 16th century missionaries and conquistadors are easier to read and translate than the 19th academic writings of Fray Mier. My, "Aha moment" was a rereading of José Eleuterio González's Fray Mier biography. González points out that the root of Servando Teresa's Latin study began as a small child when he first learned to read and write. He was enrolled in a private elementary school in Monterrey, Mexico. A wealthy woman had died granting an endowment for the founding of a Latin elementary school. Servando Teresa born and raised in Monterrey spoke Spanish as his natural language. Nevertheless, Servando Teresa's first years of elementary school deeply embedded him in the Latin language. By the age of fifteen, he continued his studies at the Porta Coeli College, under the tutelage of the Dominican Friars in Mexico City's Santo Domingo Convent where was ordained a priest. He earned a Doctor of Theology and was a highly respected preacher. He wrote and preached in the Spanish language, but in a Latin grammar style. In his writings and speeches, he frequently quotes scriptures in the Latin Vulgate Bible, and other Latin sources without translating to Spanish. Clearly, he read and studied the scriptures and numerous authors in the Latin language throughout his life.

Having studied Latin in high school, I was suddenly struck with the thought: Fray Mier wrote in Spanish, but his grammar style is Latin. If you find the English translation stilted, be aware that I have purposely retained a little of Dr. Mier's stilted style in the English translation.

DUE DILIGENCE

I worked thirty-three years as a financial advisor with New York Wall Street firms and as a securities examiner with the State of Utah. Though unrelated to the religious-historical thesis of *Christianity in The Americas Before Columbus*, my professional experience taught me very important principles. One was before investing your time and money, do your "Due diligence!" Due diligence is a term used in the securities industry to describe the process of making sure a financial investment and the persons managing your investment are legitimate. Who are these persons? Can they do what they claim? Can they be trusted? What are the risks? Is this a scam? Do not invest your time and money until you have carefully studied the facts! Applying the due diligence process to Fray Mier and his thesis you should read this book with this check list in mind:

- What were Fray Mier's qualifications? His curriculum vitae: academic education, an ordained Priest of the Roman Catholic Church, Fray of the Dominican Order, Doctor of Theology, Papal Domestic Prelate, Mexican, Anáhuacan, and elected Deputy to the First Constituent Congress of Mexico; these give his writings credibility. And at the end of a life of persecution, Guadalupe Victoria, President of the Republic of Mexico, assigned Fray Mier living quarters in the National Palace, where he lived the remaining years of his life.

- What were the documents and sources of his writings? Evidence that others also had access to these sources and referenced them in their historic writings must be provided with transcripts of some of his most important writings. Fray Mier's writings translated in *Christianity in The Americas Before Columbus* are published by the National Autonomous University of Mexico; government and educational entities. The editor of the Fray Mier book from which the writings of this book are translated was General Director of the Mexican National General Archive, Dr. Edmundo O'Gorman.

- <u>Conflicts of interest exist.</u> Fray Mier was an ordained Catholic Priest, exiled to Europe, who became a recognized revolutionary leader of Mexico's struggle for independence. Returning to Mexico after twenty-two years in exile, he was in and out of jail multiple times. While in jail, he was elected a Deputy to the First Mexican Constituent Congress. Fray Mier's message was consistent throughout his prolonged inquisition, exile, secularization, multiple imprisonments by Church and State, and election to Mexico's Congress. He never wavered from his core message even under the most rigorous scrutiny of Church, State, Judicial Courts, public media, and constituents. He was severely tested in his life for his beliefs, which he never denied.

- <u>Fray Mier disclosure issues:</u> Dr. Mier was subjected to State and Church inquisitions, defamation, imprisonments, and exile. This tags him with a criminal record, not an uncommon happening to those who protest an established authority of rule and belief. Fray Mier survived with a legacy of esteem. Church leaders objected to his Guadalupe Sermon, but not unanimously. There was no finding during his life that he was the creator of myth or invented history.

- <u>Sources:</u> Fray Mier's thesis sources are well known authors and scholars of Mexican history, Roman Catholic missionaries, and ecclesiastic leaders of Mexico. A list of these sources is in: *Fray Servando Teresa de Mier: Writings on Ancient Christianity and Spain's Evangelism of Mexico.*

- <u>Censorship:</u> Censoring and suppressing a set of facts does not make them false. Fray Mier's sermon became a driving force in Mexico's battle for independence and liberty. Mier's defense of his Inquisition is in: *Fray Servando Teresa de Mier: Writings on Ancient Christianity and Spain's Evangelism of Mexico.*

- Secrecy Issues: Discomfort over Fray Mier's writings continues evidenced by the veil of secrecy that makes him and his legacy largely unknown. Why is the theme of his Guadalupe Sermon hidden even today? Chapter 3, "The Mier Paradox" travels the labyrinth of "Secrecy Issues."

- Insights: *Christianity in The Americas Before Columbus* includes two of Fray Mier's letters with annotated commentary. His letters provide unfamiliar origins and insights to history, geography, culture, and language recorded in *The Book of Mormon.*

- Conclusion: Fray Mier's writings merit study.

PROLOGUE

"It is one thing to write like a poet, and another like a historian: the poet can count, or chant things not like they were, but like they should be; and the historian has to write them not like they should be, but like they were, without removing or adding anything to the truth."
El Ingenioso Hidalgo Don Quijote de la Mancha
—Miguel de Cervantes Saavedra—

Servando Teresa de Mier (1763-1827) was an ordained priest of the Dominican Order of the Roman Catholic Church. In Spanish he was addressed as Señor, Don, Padre, Doctor, and more commonly as Fray. Fray is Spanish for the English title, Friar. Both English and Spanish publications refer to him as Fray Servando or Fray Mier. Out of respect and admiration for the man and his writings, this book shall address him as Fray Mier, and where translation requires as Father Mier or Dr. Mier.

Fray Mier was 31-years old with a Doctor of Theology when he was invited by Mexico City's Council to deliver the annual December 12, 1794 sermon at the Collegiate Church of Guadalupe, honoring the tradition of the Virgin of Guadalupe, Mexico's Patron Saint. His Virgin of Guadalupe Sermon caused a notorious scandal. Fray Mier's Sermon put forth two propositions: 1st that the Gospel of Jesus Christ was first brought to the Americas by the Apostle Saint Thomas; and 2nd was a complex explanation of how the Virgin of Guadalupe came to Mexico. The outcome was that he was accused of denying the tradition of the appearance of the Virgin of Guadalupe triggering an ecclesiastical suspension of his license to preach, imprisonment, exile, and Inquisition investigations for the next 27 years of his life.

Gary Bowen has authored two books based on the scholarly research and writings of Fray Mier published by Elite Online Publishing, titled *Christianity in The Americas Before Columbus: Unfamiliar Origins and Insights,* and *Fray Servando Teresa de Mier: Writings on Ancient Christianity and Spain's Evangelism of Mexico.*

Christianity in The Americas Before Columbus translates Fray Mier's: "Farewell Letter to the Mexicans." There is no known text of Mier's Guadalupe Sermon, but it is believed that Mier's "Farewell Letter..." is his writing that most closely summarizes the

15

theme of his Guadalupe Sermon. A footnote by Edmundo O'Gorman to the "Farewell Letter. . ." states:

> Fray Mier's "Farewell Letter" is the shortest and most focused writing on the Gospel in America before the Conquest, as a compendium of his forty years of researching, writing, and persecutions for his preaching on Christianity in Ancient America. He wrote in the despair of prison with every expectation of further persecutions and sufferings in the belief that this was his last will and testament of the truths he spent his lifetime advocating.

Fray Servando Teresa de Mier: Writings on Ancient Christianity and Spain's Evangelism of Mexico translates Mier's "Apologia," his academic and legal defense of the theses of his Guadalupe Sermon, with his writings and speeches to Mexico's Constituent Congress. A short extract from his "Apologia" is an insight into the depth of Dr. Mier's research. Dr. Mier wrote:

> And, who does not know of the blasphemies of the incredulous against the Christian religion, whose Divinity, they say, was testing them for sixteen centuries, up to crushing their bones, with its expansion into all the world by only twelve men, and with the universality of the Church; and in the end a New World was discovered where nothing was known of it? It is false. Throughout America, monuments and vestige evidences of Christianity were found, according to the unanimous testimony of the missionaries. . . .What was the Mexican religion, but Christianity confused by time, and the mixed-up nature of the hieroglyphics? I have made a great study of their mythology and in its depth; it comes down to God, Jesus Christ, his Mother, Saint Tomé, his seven disciples called the seven Tomés chicome-cohuatl and the martyrs that died in the persecution of [the Aztec King] Huémac. The Spaniards, because they did not recognize it in another language and liturgy and had introduced enormous abuses, destroyed the same religion that they were professing and replaced the same images that they burned, because they were under different symbols. What an immensity of things I have to say about this!

Fray Servando Teresa de Mier: Writings on Ancient Christianity and Spain's Evangelism of Mexico is a translation of Dr. Mier's research and conclusions which he wrote in an academic Latin language style. It is the first publication in English of these writings.

Christianity in The Americas Before Columbus takes the reader through a labyrinth study of ancient American Christianity and the conundrum—Are Mier and his writings "the truth?" His work reveals why and how ancient American Christianity was hidden by the Spanish conquest of America. It includes Fray Mier letters, anthropology, early Catholic missionary diary notes, and links Mexican geography, history, religion, and culture to geography, history, religion, and culture recorded in *The Book of Mormon*, bringing historical authenticity to *The Book of Mormon*.

SECTION I

The Road Less Traveled

THE ROAD NOT TAKEN

Two roads diverged in a yellow wood,
And sorry I could not travel both
And be one traveler, long I stood
And looked down one as far as I could
To where it bent in the undergrowth;

Then took the other, as just as fair,
And having perhaps the better claim,
Because it was grassy and wanted wear;
Though as for that the passing there
Had worn them really about the same,

And both that morning equally lay
In leaves no step had trodden black.
Oh, I kept the first for another day!
Yet knowing how way leads on to way,
I doubted if I should ever come back.

I shall be telling this with a sigh
Somewhere ages and ages hence:
Two roads diverged in a wood, and I—
I took the one less traveled by,
And that has made all the difference.

—Robert Frost—

CHAPTER 1

Delirium or Bliss?

If these things appear deliriums,
they do not appear so much to those who have studied our
antiquities.

—Fray Servando Teresa de Mier
In defense of his Guadalupe Sermon recited in the Sanctuary
of Tepeyacac, the 12ᵗʰ day of December 1794.

Robert Frost's poem, *The Road Not Taken*, reads like a summary of the travails of Fray Servando Teresa de Mier: "Yet knowing how way leads on to way," he took the road less traveled; and sadly, he "shall be telling this with a sigh somewhere ages and ages hence." Fray Mier took a rebellious road, grassy and wanting wear, yet still passed there by Catholic priests and scholars who have and still do research and write of Mexico's ancient history. Mier took the way to learn of Mexico's ancient Christianity lost in the passage of time. Fray Mier's legacy is his endeavor to restore the sequestered history of Mexico's ancient Christianity. In one of his memoirs Fray Mier wrote: "A Jesuit in Rome told me all religion is politics." Fray Mier was not a politician, so the writings of Fray Mier are a forthright road less traveled, and sadly less read. Before beginning to study Fray Mier's writings with any hope of belief, one needs to look down one road and then the other road as far as one can see. Researching the historical writings of his Catholic predecessors and colleagues bears witness to Fray Mier's thesis: "that the ancient preaching of the Gospel in America is beyond doubt."

Fray Mier leaped from the precipice of accepted Catholic doctrine with his infamous December 12, 1794 Virgin of Guadalupe Sermon. The Guadalupe Sermon earned Fray Mier free exile from Mexico and rich investigations by the Spanish Inquisition. Mexico's 1820 Revolution of Independence freed Mexico from Spain, and Fray Mier from twenty-six years of inquisition, incarceration, and exile. After Mexico's Revolution of Independence from Spain, Fray

Mier came at the end of his life to be known as the most popular man in Mexico. Yet, Fray Mier closes his "Apologia," defense of his Sermon, with his fear of ruin, writing: "I have now announced the infernal machine that his [Bishop Haro] hate constructed for my perdition. It remains to be told how his agents, enabled with his letters, caused it to explode, to obstruct, to corrupt the channels of justice, to stop me from its achievement, and to complete my ruin."

Why and who instigated Fray Mier's infamous Inquisition for his Guadalupe Sermon is the thesis of *Fray Servando Teresa de Mier: Writings on Ancient Christianity and Spain's Evangelism of Mexico*. Fray Mier's writings evidence the ancient preaching of the Gospel took place in Mexico. His writings are not his unique invention. Alarms went off, only because he was the lone voice to step up to a public pulpit to declare known but suppressed history. Dr. Mier compiled and digested his writings from reputable, well-known authors of Mexican history. Even so, Dr. Mier's preaching was extremely disturbing to Mexico's Catholic hierarchy; resulting in his being severely berated, jailed in Mexico, and then deported and jailed in Spain. He lived twenty-two years as a political exile and prisoner in Mexico, Spain, Portugal, France, Italy, England, the United States of America, and again in Mexico. From 1794 until his death in 1827, he was the perpetual subject of State and Church Inquisitions. The man's lifetime legacy of suffering firsthand prejudicial judgements lives on. Fray Mier and his writings are hidden in the closets of modern-day scholars, religious and political authorities. There is an ambivalent pattern in Mexico of honoring Fray Mier while shrouding his teachings, thus adding to his sorrowful legacy. Why was Fray Mier a target of the Inquisition? Why is his legacy shrouded and dismissed? This volume sets forth theories on why Fray Mier suffered decades of Inquisition, and why his writings are even today veiled in secrecy.

Driving north to Zocalo, the heart of Mexico City, you will cross Fray Servando Teresa de Mier Boulevard. Mexico's strict religious laws separating church and state renders the use of the reverential Catholic title of Fray on a public boulevard very surprising. Equally surprising is the prominent placement of Fray Servando Teresa de Mier Boulevard. Most Mexicans in the 21st Century have little idea of who he is and no knowledge of his teachings. Fray Mier has gone from being the "most popular man in Mexico" at end of his life to now being almost unknown in Mexico. An inquisitional prejudice still hides Fray Mier's writings from the light of truth.

Fifteen-year-old Servando Teresa de Mier went from his native city, Monterrey, Nuevo Leon, to the National capitol, Mexico City where he enrolled in the Saint Dominic Convent and Porta Coeli College as a student of philosophy and theology. Earning his Doctor of Theology, he returned to the Saint Dominic Convent, where he served as Professor of Philosophy, gaining great acclaim as a Gospel preacher. His preaching fame earned him the honor of being asked to give a December 12, 1794 commemorative sermon honoring Mexico's Patron Saint, the Virgin of Guadalupe. December 12 is still a national celebration in honor of the Virgin of Guadalupe. After preaching his Guadalupe Sermon, Fray Mier was accused of denying the tradition of the appearance of the Virgin of Guadalupe, turning his fame to infamy, and thus began the Inquisition, which defines his legacy. Fray Mier spent the rest of his life defending the thesis and motives of his December 12, 1794 sermon, which caused him to be accused of disloyalty to the Kingdom of New Spain and to the Catholic Church. Fray Mier's *Apologia*, written over decades gives his detailed defense of his Guadalupe Sermon. No transcript of his Guadalupe Sermon is known to exist. However, Edmundo O'Gorman writes a footnote on the Guadalupe Sermon: " His *Farewell Letter to the Mexicans* in this selection deals with this matter." From O'Gorman's research on Mier, "Farewell Letter to the Mexicans" finds that in length and topic it is the closest surviving record of Fray Mier's Guadalupe Sermon. Chapter 5 is a translation of the "selection" Dr. O'Gorman references.

Fray Mier defends his 1794 sermon as a lesson to his fellow countrymen to be proud of their ancient religious history— to have them know that Christianity was preached in ancient Mexico before Columbus, before Spanish conquistadors, and before Catholic missionaries came to America. His "Apologia" speaks to what he calls the "Two Probable Propositions" of his Guadalupe Sermon. His two propositions are likely a summary of his sermon.

The First Proposition was that the Gospel had been preached in America centuries before the arrival of Catholic missionaries by Saint Thomas, one of the biblical apostles of Jesus Christ. The sermon's proposition that Saint Thomas brought Christianity to America caused barely a ripple in the waters of Anáhuac. It may have been the center of the storm, if the sermon had been preached in 1594 when the Catholic Church was less well established in

Mexico.

The Second Proposition, the most complex of the two, is that Mexicans came to know of the Mother of the true God, known as *Tonantzin*, through the preaching of Saint Thomas. To convey a sense of the complexity and controversy of his Second Proposition, know that it takes up two-thirds of Fray Mier's "Apologia." His short defense of the First Proposition conveys the sense that his Saint Thomas thesis was accepted by his inquisitors. The massive amount of his *Apologia* dedicated to defending his Virgin of Guadalupe Proposition suggests this was the trigger for the outrage of Church and State. In summary, Fray Mier's Second Proposition argues that the ancient Mexican Christian religion of Saint Thomas was melded into the Catholic Church through the persona of Spain's Virgin of Guadalupe. Guadalupe is an Arabic-Latin origin compound-word. The Arabic word *guadi*, in English wadi, is a riverbed. The Latin word *lupa* is a she-wolf. *Guadalupe* translates to *Wolf-river*. Guadalupe is not a Native American Indian word. The original dark-faced Virgin of Guadalupe image is found in the Monastery of Guadalupe, Cáceres, Extremadura, Spain, homeland of many of the early Spanish explorers. To demonstrate the uncertainty of the origin of Spain's Lady of Guadalupe, the tradition is cited as commencing in the 4th, 8th, 13th, and 15th centuries. What is certain is that the tradition and image of the Virgin of Guadalupe originated in Spain before the European conquest of America. The Cáceres Monasterio de Guadalupe was founded according to legend when a shepherd discovered an image of the Virgin Mary in Cáceres buried on the banks of the Guadalupe River, Spain, in the early 14th century.

The Mexican Virgin of Guadalupe appeared to a native Mexican Juan Diego December 1531 at the hill Tepeyac within modern Mexico City. The parallels between the Spanish and Mexican traditions of Our Lady of Guadalupe clearly manifest the Mexican tradition mirrors the image and tradition of Spain's Extremadura Virgin of Guadalupe.

The Anáhuac tsunami which befell Fray Mier was his sermon's proposition on Our Lady of Guadalupe, but, why? To give a modern cultural *salsa savor* to Fray Mier's sermon, Google an Internet Spanish language Website translated it as: "Mexico, why I can't help loving you?" The Website lists Mexico's top 100 reasons for loving Mexico, beginning with #1 the image of Mexico's Catholic faith—the Virgin of Guadalupe. Following are #2 The

National Seal on Mexico's Flag, #3 The Colors of the National Flag, and #4 The National Hymn. This is not a surprise to anyone familiar with Mexican culture and traditions. The core Catholic faith in Mexico is the Virgin of Guadalupe.

Fray Mier identifies his sources primarily as anthropologists and Catholic priests. Their writings were based upon observed practices and native Mexican hieroglyphic writings on paper folios extant at the start of Spain's conquest of Mexico. Fray Mier read their Spanish and Latin works in the libraries of Mexico City where he studied and earned his Doctor of Theology. Most native hieroglyphic folios had been destroyed before his time. Fray Mier's writings merit a comparative study of folk knowledge and culture. An aura of skeptical disbelief surrounds Fray Mier to the present time. He was not the originator of the Saint Thomas theory on how Christianity came to America. The scandal he caused was not the invention of a myth. It was his publicly preaching a sermon, in a Catholic pulpit, on a national religious holiday, of an iconic Mexican religious image. The American writer Joseph Campbell has a one sentence definition of mythology: "Mythology is what we call someone else's religion." Fray Mier's 12th of December 1794 Guadalupe Sermon introduced his Catholic congregation to "someone else's religion," the religion of ancient Mexican Christians. Fray Mier died in 1827, but the prejudice toward his propositions on native Mexican Christianity never died.

FRAY MIER'S WRITINGS AND LETTERS

Chapter 4, "Eleventh Note of the Second Letter from an American to the Spanish," and Chapter 5, "Farewell Letter to the Mexicans," were written by Fray Mier in support of the theme of his Guadalupe Sermon. They are translated from *Servando Teresa de Mier, Escritos y Memorias* edited by O'Gorman. Extensive footnotes are added to provide detailed information on the facts and ideas set forth.

My translation of Fray Mier's writings is published in a separate volume titled: *Fray Servando Teresa de Mier: Writings on Ancient Christianity and Spain's Evangelism of Mexico.* It includes Fray Mier's *Apologia* with scholarly details not found in his letters. Also translated are "Dr. Mier in Portugal, Spain, England, and America," a collection of other Fray Mier writings, speeches he delivered to the Mexican Constituent Congress, and Governor José Eleuterio González's memorial writings of Fray Mier. These are more detailed Fray Mier writings translated from González's *Biografía del benemérito mexicano D. Servando Teresa de Mier Noriega y Guerra* ("Biography of the Distinguished Mexican Servando Teresa de Mier Noriega y Guerra, Esq. ")with fewer footnotes. Fray Mier's writings are his comprehensive defense of his Guadalupe Sermon. In "Farewell Letter. . ." Fray Mier writes that he commenced writing his lengthy *Apologia* soon after his December 12, 1794 Guadalupe Sermon. *Apologetic Manifesto* was not ready for printing until August 1820, after 26 years of writing and editing. The first publication of *Apologia* was the book titled: *Vida, aventuras, escritos viajes del Dr. Servando Teresa de Mier*, ("Life, Adventures, Writings, Travels of Dr. Servando Teresa de Mier"), by Manuel Payno, Mexico D.F., Imprenta Abadiano 1865, published 38 years after Fray Mier's death. Fray Mier's "Apologia" was republished 1876 in Dr. González's Mier Biography in Monterrey, Nuevo Leon, Mexico with a Commemorative Edition, Facsimile of the Original, published by the State Government of Nuevo Leon, Mexico and the Autonomous University of Nuevo Leon upon the Sesquicentennial of the Death of Father Mier, 1977.

The thesis of Fray Mier's "Apologia" is that the Gospel of Jesus Christ was preached in America before Spain's conquest of America. He abridges the few surviving records of the ancient people of Anáhuac (Mexico), and the many records of the Catholic missionaries who followed the Spanish conquest of New Spain. Apologia has the same spelling and meaning in Spanish and English: derived from apology, a Greek origin word, defined as "speaking in defense." The common English usage of apology would lead one to think that Mier's "Apologia," is his plea for forgiveness for a wrongful act. In fact, it is his written "defense" and declaration of his innocence of the Inquisition's false accusations and judicial proceedings, which his December 12, 1794 Guadalupe Sermon fomented. His "Apologia" reads like a legal deposition, written in stilted Latin grammar, as if it were to be filed with a Court of Justice for legal judgement. Neither the Spanish nor the translated English text is a quick read. Dr. Mier wrote of how he came to know the propositions of his Guadalupe Sermon, which provide due diligence to Mier's "Apologia." It is a well- studied historical restoration of Mexico's hidden ancient history. Sadly, it was still hidden almost two centuries after his death. It is a truthful and well researched history that opens a gate to a down-to-earth study of the geography, history, culture, religion, and people recorded in *The Book of Mormon.* There is no record of Dr. Mier's "Apologia" or "Apologetic Manifesto," ever being previously translated and printed in English. *Fray Servando Teresa de Mier: Writings on Ancient Christianity and Spain's Evangelism of Mexico* is the first English publication of Mier's "Apologia" in defense of his December 12, 1794 Guadalupe Sermon.

FRAY MIER'S CONTRIBUTIONS TO MEXICAN ANTHROPOLOGY

In 1797, Fray Mier fled from Spain to France, arriving in Paris in 1801. In Paris, he founded a Spanish language academy and was active in religious discussions and councils where he continued to share the propositions of his Guadalupe Sermon. His shocking message spread to Europe. He writes in his Paris Memoir: "Also, Baron von Humboldt told me in Paris: 'I believed that it was an invention of the friars, and thus I said in my statistical essay; but after I have seen your curious dissertation, I see that it is not so'."

After meeting Fray Mier, Alexander Humboldt traveled to Mexico in 1803; where he lived and studied the anthropology of Mexico for a year. Humboldt resided in Mexico City on Republic de Uruguay Street half a block from a National Library where he is memorialized by a bronze statue in front of the Library, which was a short walk from the Porta Coeli College where Fray Mier studied and lectured after earning his Doctor of Theology. Connecting dots gives cause to believe that Humboldt's study of Mexican anthropology was motivated by his Paris discussions with Fray Mier. Humboldt's *Voyage aux régions équinoxiales du Nouveau Continent* ("Voyage to the Equinox Regions of the New Continent")was published in thirty volumes between 1810 and 1813. In 1974, Mexico's Treasury and Public Credit Department published a complete version of Humboldt's work titled, *Vues des cordillères et monumens des peuples indigènes de l'Amérique* ("Views of the Mountain Ranges and Monuments of the Native Peoples of America"). From this work, Jaime Labastida translated to Spanish and published in 1986 those chapters which referred to Mexico, titled, *Aportaciones a la Antropología Mexicana,* ("Contributions to Mexican Anthropology"). Chapter 6, "Alexander von Humboldt's Contribution to Mexican Anthropology," lists some of Humboldt's discoveries. Humboldt did not endorse the idea of ancient Christianity in America, but his anthropological study of Mexico adds credibility to Fray Mier's writings on the ancient religious culture of Mexico; and most significantly, attests to the existence of ancient Mexican paper folios written in hieroglyphics.

FRAY MIER ABRIDGES THE SURVIVING RECORDS OF ANCIENT MEXICO

Fray Mier was not the only Mexican Catholic Priest studying Mexico's ancient religious traditions. Another chastised priest was Father Francisco Javier Clavijero (1731-87); born in Veracruz, Mexico. As a child he learned to speak the native Náhuatl, Otomí, and Mixteca languages. He entered the Society of Jesus (Jesuits), 1754. In 1767, the Jesuits of New Spain were subject to an eviction order by Carlos III, King of Spain who believed that the Society of Jesus had acquired too much wealth and influence over Spanish affairs. Father Calvijero fled to Italy in 1767, where he lived until his death. He began his study of Aztec codices and the writings of the early Spanish conquistadors and missionaries before he was exiled from Mexico. In Italy, he wrote in his native Spanish *Historia Antigua de México* ("Ancient History of Mexico") with limited research resources he had brought from Mexico. He translated his book to Italian, its First Edition, published 1780, as *Storia Antica del Messico* ("Ancient History of Mexico"). The book was translated from Italian to English, published First Edition 1787, London, England; Second Edition 1806, Richmond, Virginia; Third Edition 1807, London, England; and Fourth Edition 1817 Philadelphia, Pennsylvania. Father Clavijero's book was translated from Italian to Spanish for its First Spanish Edition 1826, London, England; and Second Edition 1844, Mexico City, Mexico, with numerous other Spanish Editions since then published in Mexico. Father Clavijero's *Historia Antigua de México* ("Ancient History of Mexico") includes many details on the ancient religious practices of Mexico. The story of Clavijero's History publication shows a pattern. A history on ancient Mexico written by a Mexican Catholic Priest in Spanish could be published in Italian, German, and English, before a First Spanish Edition was published in Mexico, sixty-four years after the original Italian Edition. Father Clavijero's life in exile and his written "Ancient Mexican History," epitomizes the politics of religion in Mexico, which swept over Fray Mier. Father Clavijero is cited in footnotes as collaborative evidence of the details of Fray Mier's writings.

Fray Mier took up the banner of Bishop Bartolomé de las Casas, an antecedent quixotic traveler in the Mexican labyrinth. Bishop de las Casas (1474-1566) born in Sevilla, Spain, had arrived on the Island of Hispaniola in 1502. He traveled between Europe and Latin-America for 46 years, living in various Spanish colonies before retiring and dying in Madrid, Spain. He became a friar of the Saint Dominic Order in 1523 and the first Catholic Bishop of Chiapas, Mexico from 1545 to 1546. Bishop de las Casas was an outspoken critic of the horrific cruelty of the Spanish conquistadores toward the Native Indians, and their enslavement in Spain's encomienda system. Encomienda is "a grant by the Spanish Crown to a colonist in America conferring the right to demand tribute and forced labor from the Indian inhabitants of an area." In Spanish "encomienda" means "assignment." Encomienda is found in *Random House Dictionary of the English Language*, defined as: "1. the system instituted 1503 under which a soldier or colonist was granted a tract of land or a village together with its Indian inhabitants." Encomienda is discussed in detail later in this book. Bishop Bartolomé Father de las Casas writes that he was granted an encomienda as a young priest, when he came to see an encomienda, very simply, as slavery! Father de las Casas frequently traveled between Spain and the Americas as an advocate of Native Americans earning him the titles of "Attorney and Universal Protector of All the Indians," and more commonly as, "Protector of the Indians." Bishop de las Casas's advocacy of humane treatment of Indians made him very much despised by Spain and New Spain rulers, politicians, entrepreneurs, conquistadors, and Church officials. About 1536-37, Bishop de las Casas wrote in Latin, later translated to Spanish, *Del único modo de atraer a todos los pueblos a la verdadera religión,* ("The Only Way to Draw All People to the True Religion") with the principal theme being "free will." He wrote and preached against the forced conversion of Native Indians. About 1552, he wrote a historical work titled *Los indios de México y Nueva España,* ("The Indians of Mexico and New Spain"), which references the images of Saint Thomas, the Apostle, and the virgin Mother of the Son of the Great Father existing in the Americas prior to the arrival of the Europeans, the very theme of Fray Mier's Guadalupe Sermon. Bishop de las Casas cites early Catholic missionaries as the source of his history, as does Fray Mier.

The French Hispanist, Marcel Bataillon, published a book in French, translated to Spanish in 1976 as *Estudios sobre Bartolomé de Las Casas,* ("Studies on Bartolomé de Las Casas"). Bataillon's Bishop de las Casas biography repeats Spain's political problems with the discovery of pre-conquest Christianity and Saint Thomas, the Apostle, in its conquest of the New World. From various sources, Spain's King Carlos V and the Spanish colonists' encomienda enslavement of the Native Indians of the New World violated existing Roman Catholic edicts if the native people were Christians. Therefore, because Native Americans were found to be Christians, they were re-branded as cannibals, idolaters, heathens, and demons to hide their Christianity giving Spanish colonists encomienda rights and Catholic missionaries the duty to evangelize these non-Christian Indians. There was a two-hundred-year time span between Bishop de las Casas and Fray Mier; but there was a parallel in that both were ostracized. Bataillon refers to Fray Mier as an admirer of Bishop de las Casas. By 1794, two-hundred-fifty years after Bishop de las Casas outraged Church and State, the native people of America were solidly converted to Catholic Christianity, and their memory of ancient Christianity was lost. The anger Fray Mier fomented was his alleged denial of the piety of Mexico's Virgin of Guadalupe, introduced to Mexico during the life of Bishop de las Casas.

Fray Mier abridges ancient Hebrew-Christian religious practices found in pre-Columbian Mexico. Fray Servando Teresa de Mier: Writings on Ancient Christianity and Spain's Evangelism of Mexico and *Christianity in The Americas Before Columbus: Unfamiliar Origins and Insights* opens a new gateway to studying the history of The Book of Mormon. From the beginning of Spain's invasion of America, the Catholic Church evangelized New World heathens to embrace Catholic Christianity. Fray Mier threatened this apologist excuse by openly preaching to the Mexican people that we already had knowledge of Christianity before the Europeans arrived. If Fray Mier's Propositions were accepted, how could the conquest's encomienda slavery, the pillaging of natural resources, implied racial superiority, forced conversion, and brutal dictatorial rule be permitted? But, Independence from Spain succeeded in Mexico. Why, then, is Fray Mier's Guadalupe Sermon hushed up, even today? Shrouding, jesting, and prejudice cloud the legacy of Fray Mier, opening a labyrinth of speculations. Fray Mier preached and wrote of the fusion of ancient America Christianity into the Catholic Church by means of the Virgin of Guadalupe, the Patron Saint of the Catholic Church in Mexico and the icon of Mexican culture. My studies and encounters with Mexican Catholic Priests give reason to believe that there is still a fear that Fray Mier's writings could harm the Catholic Church.

Fernando de Alva Cortés Ixtlilxóchitl, a direct descendant of the kings of Mexico, wrote a history in 1640, telling how the conquest of Mexico brought about an implosion of its civilization by pandemic European diseases. Bishop de las Casas describes arriving in Mexican cities to find mounds of bodies lying unburied in the streets.

Ixtlilxóchitl writes how in 1520 the conquistadors burned the written royal archives of New Spain. Ixtlilxóchitl describes this catastrophe as a major loss. These records were the repositories of religious and historical writings of ancient Mexico. European diseases killed the keepers of ancient Mexican history and the conquistadors burned the keepers written memories. The largest surviving link to ancient American Christianity referenced by Fray Mier, are the writings of the early Catholic missionaries. Even Ixtlilxóchitl, with inherited historical records from his Aztec ancestors, cites the Catholic Fathers as important sources in his histories.

Archeologists and anthropologists study ancient Mexican ruins and artifacts but will not study a classical history book on pre-Columbian America. These histories were written in plain 16th, 17th, 18th, and 19th century Spanish by Catholic Fathers. Even authors, who are members of the Church of Jesus Christ of Latter-day Saints, commonly claim there is no surviving evidence of Hebrew-Christian practices in pre-Columbian America. Fray Mier's compilation of Mexican history bears witness to ancient Hebrew-Christian history and culture in Mexico. Everyone and especially members of the Church of Jesus Christ of Latter-day Saints with a firm belief in *The Book of Mormon* must overcome a prejudice against historical records written by Catholic Fathers. They are the most credible historical records of ancient Christianity in America.

WHY HONOR THE MAN AND SUPPRESS HIS MESSAGE?

It is hard to grasp the contradiction between the respectful publication of Fray Mier's Memoirs and Writings by modern Mexican universities, while his legacy is not taught in Mexico's schools, leaving him totally unknown to most modern Mexicans. His Guadalupe Sermon was cause for state and church authorities to imprison and exile Fray Mier. He endured a life of persecution to become, at the end of his life, a Domestic Prelate of the Supreme

Pontiff and an elected member of the First Constituent Congress. Quoting from Eleuterio González's *Biografía de Mier*, "(H)e became at this time [the time of his death] the most popular man in Mexico." He gained this popular acclaim from the people of Mexico with scant knowledge of the message of his Guadalupe Sermon abridged in his "Farewell Letter . . . ." Mier's "Farewell Letter. . ." ends with the declaration—"The Deists themselves today confess that the ancient preaching of the Gospel in America is beyond doubt."

School textbooks, historical writings, and novels tell of Mier's life and memoirs while suppressing, censoring, dismissing, or hedging as myth his Guadalupe Sermon message. The goal of this book is to increase the profile and study of Fray Servando Teresa de Mier's writings on Mexican antiquities so that you, the reader, can come to know the truth of Christianity's existence in the ancient Americas, so that these things no longer appear to be delirium! Fray Mier gives verifiable, truthful, recorded history that the Gospel of Jesus Christ was known and practiced in Mexico before the arrival of Catholic missionaries in 1520, thereby delivering spiritual bliss! There is authentic American history, a witness to Jesus Christ's testament recorded in The New Testament, Saint John 10:16—*And other sheep I have, which are not of this fold: them also I must bring, and they shall hear my voice; and there shall be one fold, and one shepherd.*

CHAPTER 2

Biography of the Mier Family and Dr. Mier

The Biographies of "The Mier Family" and "Dr. Mier" are translations of pp. 5-9, *Biografia del benemérito mexicano D. Servando Teresa de Mier Noriega y Guerra*, ("Biography of the Distinguished Mexican Servando Teresa de Mier Noriega y Guerra, Esq. ") author, José Eleuterio González, editor, Juan Peña, publisher José Saenz, Monterey, MX 1876. Commemorative Edition, Facsimile of the Original, Government of the State of Nuevo Leon, MX, Autonomous University of Nuevo Leon, Sesquicentennial of the Death of Dr. Mier, 1827-1977, 1977. Governer José Eleuterio González wrote:

> In antiquity, noble titles were no more than the instruments of clever governments and good connoisseurs of the human heart for exploiting the vanity and arrogance of mankind, driving these ruinous passions that came to produce heroic actions to the good of the native land and of humanity. Today philosophical reason justly condemns the chimeric privileges of ancestry in the same manner that it condemns the vanity and arrogance of mankind; but as these have not been left behind for that of being as vain and arrogant as their superiors, they appreciate as much as they appreciated the privilege and nobility of their origin, even when they may be well persuaded that they themselves are insubstantial and void of reason in these things. In addition to the old parchments also belonging to history, and the opinions of men, however futile and frivolous that they may be, when they have influenced something in their actions, they ought to find a preferential place in the narration that they do of themselves. These things heeded it will not appear strange that I commence by giving a slight idea of the illustrious family from which the hero of our history descended.

In a place called Buelna belonging to the principality of Asturias, there is an ancient Solariega family, from which the Dukes of Granada and the Marquis of Altamira boast they are descended; and which gave some Abbesses the Huelgas Convent, an honor that was only granted to women who had a blood kinship with the kings. From this illustrious family at various times, some men of merit came to Mexico, like the Judge Don Cosme de Mier y Trespalacios, and the famous Inquisitor Don Juan de Mier. Also, to Monterrey in 1710 came two personages from this distinguished family; one was Don Francisco de Mier y Torre, Governor and Captain General of the New Kingdom of Leon, and the other was Don Francisco de Mier Noriega, Notary Public and Monterrey Councilman, a seat which he bought in a public auction in Mexico City before coming, and that he also served as Secretary to the first one. The Governor, concluding his governance, returned to Mexico City in 1714. The Notary settled in Monterrey, marrying Doña Margarita Buentello, descendent of Juan Buentello Guerrero, one of the first conquistadors of this land and Head Constable before Zavala came. To this matrimony were born two children, who were Doña Antonia Margarita and Don Joaquin.

A brief time later, Don Francisco de Mier Noriega died. Doña Antonia Margarita married Captain Don Santiago Fernandez de Tijerina, from who descends the family that carries this last surname. The widow Doña Margarita Buentello, even though the Jesuits then had a college face to face with her house, sent her son Don Joaquin to study in Mexico City. This one came back from his studies in 1744, according to a document that I have in sight, and from then until the year 1790 in which he died one finds in the archive his signatures, first as a witness in attendance, later as Alderman and Mayor and afterwards as Lieutenant Governor and interim Governor. In the provincial military that was then what is today, the National Guard, he obtained all the military ranks up to General. Don Joaquin de Mier Noriega was married two times, first with Doña Antonia Guerra and later with a Señora Garza, both descendants of the first conquistadors. From these marriages Don Joaquin had many children, of which the following arrived at adulthood: Doña Josefa, married to Don Juan Rosillo, from which the Canales family comes that today occupies a distinguished place in Tamaulipas; Doña Adriana, wife of Don Joaquin Ugartechea, from where the family of this surname descends; the celebrated Doctor Don Servando and Don Vicente, who followed the ecclesiastical career; Don Froylan, from whom are descended the Mier's who live in Cadereyta and the Morales who are in Monterrey; Don Joaquin and Don Antonio, fathers of the Miers that are in this city and in other towns; and another Doña Josefa, married with Don Marcos de Ayala, from where the family of this name comes that today we know in Monterrey.

The house that Don Francisco de Mier Noriega built, that his son Don Joaquin inherited, and in which his children were born, is number 26 Comercio Street in front of the Government Palace, which was previously the Jesuit College.

The Mier family has always been very distinguished. Many of their members have held high positions in the State: Don Froylan was Governor in 1815, his son Don Francisco de Mier held it in 1823, and the Licentiate Don Francisco Morales, grandson of Don Froylan, held the same position in 1846. Many have always appreciated their antiquity and their status as descendants of the first conquistadors of this land; and most of all the nobility of their origin by way of Mier. Some have conserved with much appreciation the shield of arms of their Solariega family.

DR. MIER

This Gentleman [Dr. Mier] was born in Monterrey, Mexico, the 18th day of October 1763 and was baptized the 26th day according to what appears in a parish baptism book of this city. In the margin there is a note that says:

"José Servando de Santa Teresa; Spaniard. On the 26th of October of [one thousand] seven hundred and sixty and three years in this Monterrey Parochial, the Priest Don Juan Bautista Baez Treviño baptized by Parish license and placed the Holy Oil and Chrism onto José Servando de Santa Teresa nine days from birth, Spaniard, legitimate son of Don Joaquin Mier Noriega and of Doña Antonia Guerra, Spaniards and residents of this city. His Godfather was Don Salvador Lozano, resident of this said city, to whom I warned of his obligation and kinship, and in order that it may be evident we sign it. — Br. Bartolomé Molano. — Br. Juan Baez Treviño."

It is of much worth to the man to encounter, when he begins to feel the first glimmers of reason, good teachers who inculcate in him wholesome principles, and that the first knowledge that they may give him should be sound and good. This good luck touched the child Servando, since in the year 1767 Don Francisco de Cuevas, a very good man, a native of Mexico City, came and founded in Monterrey a school similar to those that were in the capital of the Viceroyalty, that was the best that could have been in that period: in the same year Doña Leonor Gomez de Castro left upon dying six thousand pesos in order that a Latin Grammar Professorship could be founded, which was established in the following year under the Mastership of Br. Don Juan José Paulino Fernandez de Rumayor and under the care and direction of Dr. Don Antonio Martinez, then the Priest of this city. In these schools, the child Servando Teresa de Mier learned the first letters and the Latin grammar, in which he was very gifted. Next, he went to Mexico City to continue his studies in the college of the Dominican Friars; his father recommended them to him, very amply defraying his costs. In little time, he took the Holy Order in the Santo Domingo Convent; but from what happened to him in Mexico City, Señor Rivera Cambas gives us more circumstantial news, from which I will quote here the part that suits my purpose, from his beautiful and well written biography of Dr. Mier, read in the Lyceum Hidalgo says that:

"Since Servando entered the novitiate, 'his soul eager for freedom' was continually submerged in misgivings, his inclinations clashing with the observance of the rules under which he was to protest; notwithstanding the young age of the novice, as he was only fifteen-years-old, he held back for two days the time set for the taking of vows; but urged by the Schoolmaster Father Leon, who assured him that soon there was to be a reform, he pledged under this concept at the age of sixteen-years, binding himself with eternal ties when he did not have sufficient deliberation. Since then he passed on to the Porta Coeli College, where he studied philosophy with Father Arana and Schoolmaster Barreda, and Theology with them and the Fathers Moreno and Pina. He was there about seven years and he received the confirmation from the Archbishop Haro, his patron being the Lecturer Father named Palero, and at the same time they gave him the lesser orders, of sub-deacon and of deacon, leaving Porta Coeli already as Regent of studies for the large convent where he stayed for about five months."

"The pressure exercised upon his spirit by such a such a tight circle and marked by the miserable rules, Father Mier fell ill, so that he needed to go find free air, withdrawing to the Convent of La Piedad, his soul full of the grief arising from the constant contradictions in which he was condemned to live, deceived while he was still a child."

"As he often lamented of having taken vows, feeling belonging to a community that he had so many motives to be released, his superiors sought to isolate him each time more to achieve the submission of that inflexible spirit. Mier maintained that among the professed: "His vows were impracticable, the temptations many, and the bad example ended up dragging down the best."

"In retreat he had the moral patent of Lecturer of Theology and he returned to the large convent at eight months, already an ordained Priest. Named *Concluder*, and recently Master of Studies, he graduated with a Bachelor in Philosophy and Theology, and as a Doctor in this Faculty, when he was barely 27 years old."

"The Doctor remained devoted to study, when six years later he was commissioned by the Capitol Municipality to deliver the famous 12th of December 1794 Sermon."

The Doctors Orellana and Benavides confirmed that Dr. Mier took the Holy Order of Santo Domingo in 1780, that in the Porta Coeli College he sustained with great brilliance five Philosophy and Theology public actions, that in 1787 he opposed the Chair of the Department of Arts; and before preaching the ill-fated December 12, 1794 Sermon, he had preached the honors sermon of the famous conquistador Hernan Cortez.

I will put forward here a notice, even though it is found in the case documents that they have published, because it explains, in some way, the true cause of the persecutions of which Dr. Mier was the object and puts forth a manifesto of his sincere and candid character: it is the case that two times they took him down, by order of the Government, secret inquiries on Fray Servando's conduct and way of thinking, and this was because, as the Inquisitor Peredo later said: "His strength and his dominant passion is revolutionary independence." It is very natural that Father Mier seeing consummated the independence of the United States, could feel the desire that in Mexico another such event could take place. Very many Mexicans, without doubt, thought in the same way; but they had the malice necessary to hide their thoughts, and Father Mier manifested them everywhere, without imagining that the expression of a desire so just could ever cause him any harm. Ah! The innocent Doctor, for his fault of malice, could not understand the many miscarriages political passions are capable of, irritated by the insane desire to command.

Moreover, it is now time that the reader has the satisfaction of knowing through the same pen of the naive, candid and most wise Mier the interesting tale of his adventurous pilgrimages.

EVENTS IN THE LIFE OF SERVANDO TERESA
DE MIER

Events in the Life of Servando Teresa de Mier is an amended translation from *Servando Teresa de Mier Escritos y Memorias* ("Servando Teresa de Mier, Writings and Memoirs") by Edmundo O'Gorman, Ediciones de la Universidad Nacional Autonoma, Mexico, D. F., 1945.

1763
October 18, Servando Teresa de Mier Noriega y Guerra born in Monterrey, New Kingdom of Leon, New Spain (state of Nuevo Leon, Mexico). His childhood and elementary education is in Monterrey.

1779
The young, 15-year old, Servando Teresa de Mier enters the Dominican Convent in Mexico City.

1780– 1790
Mier takes the vows of the Roman Catholic Dominican Order, becoming Fray Servando Teresa de Mier, and is quickly admitted to Porta Coeli College, Mexico City, where he studies philosophy and theology, graduating as a Doctor of Theology. Fray Mier returns to the Dominican Monastery in Mexico City as a Professor of Philosophy. He acquired great fame as a preacher.

1794
November 8—Fray Mier preaches at a memorial service honoring Hernán Cortés, which earns him great applause and fame, and an invitation from the Mexico City Council to deliver the annual December 12 sermon at the Collegiate Church of Guadalupe, honoring the tradition of the Virgin of Guadalupe, the Patron Saint of Mexico.

December 12—Fray Mier's Virgin of Guadalupe Sermon causes a notorious scandal. He is accused of denying the accepted tradition of the appearance of the Virgin of Guadalupe.

December 13—Mier's His Guadalupe Sermon is cause for an ecclesiastical process with suspension of his license to preach.

1795

January 2—Mier is imprisoned in his cell in the Santo Domingo Monastery.

February 21—The Dominican Canons Uribe and Omaña issue a judgement condemning Fray Mier's Guadalupe Sermon.

March 21—Archbishop Alonso Núñez de Haro y Peralta sentences Father Mier to ten years-imprisonment in the Convent of Our Lady de las Caldas, Diocese of Santander, Spain; and perpetual loss of all his authorities to publicly teach, preach, or take confessions. He is taken to prison in the San Juan de Ulúa Castle, Mexico.

June 7—Mier is sent from Veracruz, Mexico, aboard the frigate La Nueva Empresa to Cádiz, on the south coast of Spain.

The end of July—Mier arrives in Cádiz, where he is imprisoned in the Santo Domingo Monastery of Cádiz until the end of November.

December 25—Mier is transferred and imprisoned in the Convent de las Caldas, Santander, on the northern coast of Spain, where he escapes. Apprehended, he is again sent to prison.

1796

After three months Mier is moved from the Convent de las Caldas to San Pablo Convent in Burgos, Spain, where he remains a prisoner until the end of the year. He negotiates and is granted a transfer back to Cádiz.

1797

June or July in route to Cádiz, he is arrested in Madrid, where he petitions for a hearing to obtain justice. He fails and is ordered to go to a convent in Salamanca, Spain. He escapes, fleeing to Burgos, where he is captured and locked up in the San Francisco Convent. He escapes and flees from Spain to France.

1801

Mier arrives in Bayonne, France, the Friday before Palm Sunday. In Bayonne, he visits a synagogue where he holds theological debates with the rabbis. He rejects an offer of marriage to a beautiful, rich Jewish woman.

June or July—Mier goes to Bordeaux, France, and from there he leaves for Paris, France, with the Spanish Count of Gijón. In Paris, he meets Simón Rodríguez, teacher to Simón Bolívar; together they open an academy to teach Spanish. In Paris, Fray Mier translated the *Atala* writing of François Chateaubriand. He, also, wrote a dissertation against Count de Volney, which earns him the protection of the Grand Vicar of Paris, who entrusts to him the Santo Tomás Parish. He decides to leave for Rome to obtain his secularization.

1802

July—Mier arrives in Rome, Italy, where he seeks a Papal Brief of Secularization. He boards a ship for Naples with the aim of traveling to Spain in the entourage of Princess Isabella, who goes to marry Ferdinand II of Aragon, Spain.

September—Mier arrives in Naples, Italy, too late to join the Princess's entourage. He stays for three months in the Naples Rosario Convent. He returns to Rome to negotiate a favorable expedited execution of his Brief of Secularization.

1803

July 6—Dr. Mier is granted perpetual secularization retaining some dispensations and honors.

The middle of July—Dr. Mier leaves Rome for Florence. Italy, and from there goes on to Barcelona and Madrid, Spain.

August—Dr. Mier arrives in Madrid; where, he is again apprehended and sent to Los Toribios, Spain, a detention home in Seville, Spain.

1804

June 24—Dr. Mier flees from Los Toribios. He ships out and arrives in Sanlúcar de Barremeda. Spain; from there he goes to Cádiz, Spain. Re-apprehended he again is sent to Los Toribios, from where he again flees.

1805

October—Dr. Mier arrives in Cádiz, where he boards a ship for Ayamonte, Spain on the border of Portugal. He is an eyewitness to the October 12, 1805 Battle of Trafalgar, the famous sea battle fought between the British Royal Navy and the combined fleets of the French and Spanish Navies during the Napoleonic War. Dr. Mier lands in Portugal, lives in Lisbon, where he finds work as the secretary in the Spanish Consulate.

1807

Living in Portugal, Dr. Mier is named a Domestic Prelate of Pope Pius VII for having converted two Portuguese Jewish Rabbis to Christianity, which entitles him to wear the red-trimmed black cassock with purple sash of a Papal Prelate for the rest of his life.

1808

Dr. Mier lends a helping hand to the Spanish prisoners of war held by the French General Jean-Andoche Junot, Commander of the Napoleonic Army occupying Portugal and northern Spain. He is offered, as a reward, the position of Army Chaplain to a volunteer battalion from Valencia, Spain, which opposes the occupying French Army.

October 2—He leaves for Catalonia, Spain, to join the Valencia Volunteer Regiment.

1809

June 18— Dr. Mier falls prisoner in a defeat of the Valencia Volunteers at Belchite, Spain. With others, he is sent as a prisoner to Zaragoza, Spain. He escapes.

1810

At the end of the year, he and the Valencia Volunteers are ordered to go to Cádiz.

1811

The Regency of Spain grants Fray Mier an annual pension of 3,000 pesos upon accepting the office of Archbishop of Mexico City. Mier declines the offer. He decides to go to London to propagate, as he later affirms, the idea of independence of Mexico.

October—Mier arrives in London, where he meets Joseph Blanco White, editor of the Spanish magazine, *El Español*, an advocate for the independence of Mexico. Fray Mier writes and publishes his two *Cartas de un Americano al Español,* ("Letters from an American to the Spanish").

1813

In London, Mier writes and publishes, under the pseudonym José Guerra, *Historia de la Revolución de la Nueva España*, ("History of the Revolution of New Spain").

1814

Mier travels to Paris where he meets Lucas Alamán. They become close friends. Alamán, a student in Spain and France from 1814 to 1820, witnessed the 1810 sack of Guanajuato, Mexico, by rebels under the command of Father Miguel Hidalgo y Costilla. After twenty years in exile, this was a rare opportunity for Fray Mier to be brought current on the political climate in Mexico. Alamán became a Mexican statesman, the leading spokesman and theorist for the Mexican Conservative Party, and one of Mexico's major historians of the 19th century.

1815

March 19—Napoleon Bonaparte returns to France, which causes Fray Mier to return to London. In London he meets the Spanish insurgent Francisco Javier Mina.

1816

May 15—Fray Mier embarks with other volunteers commanded by Mina aboard the frigate Caledonia, which sails from Liverpool, England, bound for America.

June 30—The ship arrives in Norfolk, Virginia, where they are transferred to Baltimore, Maryland. In Baltimore, Mina begins to organize his military expedition to Mexico.

1817

April 6—Mina's expedition leaves the island of San Luis in Galveston Bay, Mexico, with Fray Mier in the company.

April 21—The expedition arrives in Soto la Marina, Mexico, where Mina's volunteers construct a fort.

May 24—Mina departs with the bulk of his forces, leaving Fray Mier and a small garrison behind in the Soto la Marina fort.

June 17—The Spanish Brigadier General Joaquín Arredondo takes control of the   fort. General Arredondo denies the terms of surrender, imprisoning Fray Mier and stripping him of his books and other possessions. He is sent under escort to Mexico City. In transit, Fray Mier breaks his right arm.

August 14—Mier arrives in Mexico City where he is incarcerated in the Inquisition's jails. Charges are filed against Fray Mier. During his incarceration, he begins to write his *Apología* and *Memorias*.

1820

May 30—Notice had already been given that the Inquisition Tribunal in

Mexico was to be abolished. So, to assure his detention, Fray Mier is transferred from the jails of the Inquisition to the jail of the Royal Court.

June 14—The Inquisition Tribunal is shut down.

July 18—The Court rules that Fray Mier be deported to Spain.

July 19—Fray Mier is escorted to a prison in Veracruz.

August 3 or 4—Fray Mier is locked up in the San Juan de Ulúa Castle. Fray Mier later affirms that while in prison he maintains communication with Vicente Guerrero, revolutionary general, and prepares to meet with Agustín de Iturbide, Emperor of Mexico, (1822-1823). In prison he continues writing *el Manifiesto Apologético*.

December 9—Fray Mier sends a message that he has been shipped aboard the schooner La Galga to Spain.

1821

February 3—It appears that in fact this was the date Mier shipped out. He arrives in Havana, Cuba, and is locked up in the fortress La Cabaña. He escapes.

The end of May—Mier ships out aboard the frigate Robert Fulton bound for the United States. He stays in the United States for about eight months living in Philadelphia, where he writes and publishes his *Memoria Política Instructiva*, ("Instructive Political Memoir"). The independence of Mexico had been consummated September of this year. Wanting to return to his new homeland, Fray Mier sets sail for Veracruz, Mexico.

1822

February 23—Mier falls as prisoner of General José García Dávila, Royal Commandant of San Juan Ulúa Castle, Veracruz, Mexico. While a prisoner in the Castle, he writes *Exposición de la persecución que he padecido desde el 14 de junio de 1817 hasta el presente de 1822*, ("An Exposition of the Persecutions I Have Suffered from June 14, 1817, to the Present, 1822").

March 5 and 15—Mexico's First Constituent Congress discusses and votes to demand that General Dávila release Fray Mier.

May 21—Agustín de Iturbide is declared Emperor of Mexico, and Fray Mier is released from San Juan de Ulúa Castle and immediately leaves for Mexico City. A short time later Fray Mier meets with Emperor Iturbide in Tlalpan, a borough of Mexico City. Fray Mier later recounts how he frankly expounded his republican sentiments to Iturbide.

July 15—Fray Mier is seated as a Deputy representing Monterrey in the Mexican Constituent Congress. As a member of Congress, he immediately intervenes in the ongoing Congressional discussions opening a debate on his anti-Iturbide sentiments.

August 26—He and other Deputies are incarcerated by Iturbide in the Santo Domingo Monastery, Mexico.

1823

January 1—Father Marchena helps Fray Mier escape from the monastery. Re-apprehended, he is sent to the Royal Court's prison, and later to the Inquisition's ancient prison.

February 23—The remains of Revolutionary Infantry Regiments 9 and 11 that are in Mexico City, rise-up against Emperor Iturbide freeing Fray Mier and other prisoners taking them to Toluca outside of Mexico City.

March 7—Fray Mier is reinstated as a Deputy of the First Mexican Constituent Congress, taking back his seat from the substitute deputy, Attorney Juan Bautista Arizpe.

In the March 29 session—Congress declares the government of Mexico has been dismissed and declares Executive Power shall be passed to persons named by Congress. Fray Mier now figures as the representative of his Province.

May 21—The Constituent Congressional edict is resolved by common consent.

October 30—The First Mexican Constituent Congress has its closing session, and The same day celebrates the first preparatory meeting for the installation of the Second Constituent Congress. Fray Mier presents his credentials as Deputy to the Second Constituent Congress from the Kingdom of Nuevo León. Mexico.

November 7—The Second Mexican Constituent Congress convenes.

December 13— Fray Mier asks Congress to extend his time to speak by one hour and delivers his famous "The Prophecies" speech, in which he attacks the adoption of a federal system of government.

1824
February 3—The Constitutional Act of Federation is adopted. In contradiction to his "Prophecies" speech, Fray Mier signs the Act of Federation.

April 1—Fray Mier debates the proposed Constitution.
October 4—Fray Mier signs the Federal Constitution of the Mexican United States.

December 23 —A decree is announced granting Fray Mier an annual pension of 3,000 pesos. The decree is issued the same day. In addition to the pension, Guadalupe Victoria, President of the Republic of Mexico, assigns Fray Mier living quarters in the National Palace, where he lives the remaining years of his life.

December 24—The Second Mexican Constituent Congress has its closing session.

1827
November 17–Fray Mier receives last rites by the hands of Father Ramos Arizpe, Justice Minister to Mexico's President Guadalupe Victoria.

President Victoria was present with a large audience of dignitaries. Fray Mier delivers a speech in defense of several charges brought against him during his life.

December 3—Fray Mier dies in his private quarters at the National Palace at the age of 64 years, 1½ months. He was entombed at the Santo Domingo Monastery. The Vice President of the Mexican Republic, Nicolás Bravo, presides at the interment.

CHAPTER 3

The Mier Paradox

Miguel de Cervantes Saavedra's *El Ingenioso Hidalgo Don Quijote de la Mancha* ("The Ingenious Hidalgo Don Quixote de la Mancha") has Don Quixote tongue lashing Sancho Panza near the end of his knight's quest. "Oh, hardened soul!" "Oh, squire without respect!" ". . that post tenebras spero lucem," translating the Latin Vulgate Bible Job 17:12 – "after darkness, I hope for light." "Post tenebras spero lucem" was the motto of the French Wars of Religion (1562-98), later Protestant movements, and was on the title page of first editions of Cervantes's tale of the hapless Knight Don Quixote who tilts with windmills, rights wrongs, and comes to the aid of the hopeless where e'er he be. In his "Apologia," Fray Mier quotes Don Quixote in parables of his own quixotic quest for truth of all things. Fray Mier lived a quixotic life.

Don Quixote is a tragic comedy sadly reflecting Fray Mier's real life travails. The allegorical Don Quixote is driven by a crazed madness for truth in words and deeds. The real-life Fray Mier was driven by a fervent desire for truth in all things, not a history invented by Spain, but the real history of Mexico. The fallout of Fray Mier's 1794 Guadalupe Sermon gave his life a quixotic stamp of comical allegations of myth and a hopeless sequestration in darkness. In truth, Fray Mier provides historicity to the words of Jesus Christ that were fulfilled in Mexico: King James Bible; John 10:16 – "And other sheep I have which are not of this fold: them also I must bring, and they shall hear my voice; and there shall be one-fold, and one shepherd." Holy Scriptures witness the persecutions of divine prophets. Fray Mier's steadfast devotion to the theme of his Guadalupe Sermon and the depth of his research testify that he was a divinely inspired prophet of Mexico.

July 2013, vacationing in Mexico, I visited historical sites in Puebla, Teotihuacan, Mexico City, and Cholula. Entering Mexico City by bus from the south we crossed "Avenida Fray Servando Teresa de Mier," part of a 42-kilometer Circular Loop surrounding Mexico City's Central Zone. It was a joyful surprise. Despite Fray

Mier's inclusion in the Circular Loop, most citizens of Mexico know little about him. Fray Servando Teresa de Mier Avenue validates the honor in which Mexico quietly enfolds him. But equally surprising was the inclusion of the title "Fray" in the Avenue's name. Many of Mexico's Revolution of Independence heroes were Catholic Fathers. They are honored throughout Mexico with streets and monuments named after them, but never with religious titles such as Fray, Father, or Bishop. Mexico City's Fray Servando Teresa de Mier Avenue near the Palacio Nacional, the offices of Mexico's National Government, silently evidences a veiled respect for Fray Mier and his religious sermon. Mexico City's National Museum of Anthropology and History displays the Aztec Calendar and artifacts of José Ignacio Borunda, which Fray Mier's "Apologia" references as resources he used in preparing his Guadalupe Sermon. In Chapultepec Castle hangs a portrait of Bishop and Viceroy Alonso Núñez de Haro, Fray Mier's archenemy, but no portraits of the rebellious Fray Mier. These preserved traces of Mexican history in Mexico City Museums give credence to Fray Mier, who unveiled Mexico's ancient Christian history.

The "Mier Paradox" needs to be defined. Originally a paradox was merely "a view which contradicted accepted opinion." About the middle of the 16th century the word had acquired the commonly accepted meaning it now has: "An apparently self-contradictory (even absurd) meaning, which, on closer inspection, is found to contain a truth reconciling the conflicting opposites."[1] The "Mier Paradox" embodies a multiplex of paradoxes. When he returned to Mexico from his European exile, Fray Mier was imprisoned on-and-off during the years 1817 to 1823. He wrote his "Farewell Letter to the Mexicans" while in prison, published in 1821. The brevity and thesis of his "Farewell Letter..." even though written some twenty-seven years after his December 12, 1794 sermon, is likely a rewrite of his Guadalupe Sermon. His inquisition by Church and Government authorities for preaching the Guadalupe Sermon, his "Apologia" defense, and his memoirs meet the definition of a paradox—absurd statements, which upon close inspection contain the true history of Mexico. The ultimate paradox is the Fray Mier enigma. Why is the person, Fray Mier, still sequestered in the darkness of a censured and edited Mexican history? Why is his Guadalupe Sermon on ancient Christianity in America still hidden two hundred twenty-five years after the scandal of 1794? To bring the light of truth to darkness, Chapter 3,

"The Mier Paradox," sets forth Spain, New Spain, and Mexico religious and state political patterns from the 1400's to our present time—patterns of avoiding open study and discussions of Mier for fear that the light of truth will be unveiled.

ARE YOU SMARTER THAN A 4 TH GRADER?

Mexico's 4th Fourth Grade History Book illustrates a parable of "two roads diverged in a wood:" One, the road of recognized Mexican history and Two, the road of the "Mier Paradox." *Mi libro de Historia de México*, (*"My Book of Mexico's History"*), "Fourth Grade Primary Education," published by "The Secretary of Public Education, in compliance with the National Constitutional mandate to impart free primary education, hands over to the children of our Country this textbook;" distributed by the "National Commission of Free Textbooks" with this counsel: "This copy stays under your responsibility. Study it, take care of it, and enjoy it." The textbook's 1992 first edition has 79, 8 by 10 ¾ inch, pages. Half of each page is printed text, the other half colored icons, maps, and pictures. The following is a translation from *Mi libro*'s Lesson 10, "The XIX Century Revolution of Independence," a history and pictures of three heroes of Mexican Independence: Fray Servando Teresa de Mier; the priest of Dolores, Guanajuato, Father Miguel Hidalgo y Costilla; and the priest Father José María Morelos y Pavón.

The following pages 51-54 are a translation and images from Mexico's 4th Fourth Grade History Book.

Mi libro de Historia de México, Fourth Grade, Lesson 10
THE XIX CENTURY — Revolution of Independence

THE NEW IDEAS

During the XVIII Century there arose in Europe **enlightened** and **liberal** ideas in favor of the liberty and equality of all men, and against the privileges of the Church, the nobility, and the kings.

• These ideas of liberty and equality were also known throughout America. They were in support of the struggles for independence and against the privileges of the few.

Fray Servando Teresa de Mier Fought for Liberty

THE SHOUT OF DOLORES

In the early morning of September 16, 1810, the Priest Miguel Hidalgo called the people ringing the bell of his Dolores parish and gave the **shout** of liberty that started Independence.

• Some Creoles and many Indians, Mestizos, and Castes followed Hidalgo. Some 600 men left Dolores armed with sticks, spears and machetes. On the way the people joined them. Quickly they totaled almost 80,000. The insurgents shouted "Viva the Virgin of Guadalupe! Death to the Spaniards!"

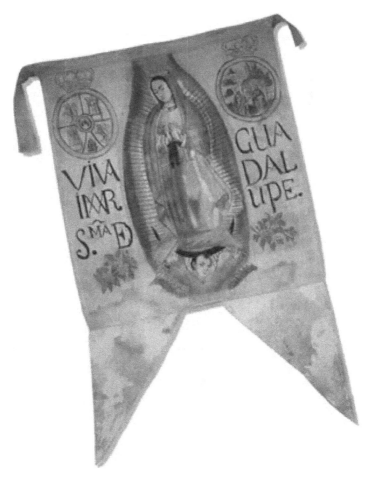

Miguel Hidalgo's Banner

HIDALGO'S CAMPAIGN

At the beginning, the **insurgents** won battles in San Miguel, Celaya and Guanajuato. But they decided to not take Mexico City for lack of arms and of military preparation.

• Even though they were many, the insurgents were not well organized, nor did they have good weapons. Some Creoles who supported them withdrew from the movement, astonished by the violence against the Spaniards.

• The Spanish troops, called Royalists, defeated the insurgents. Hidalgo was captured and executed in 1811.

Miguel Hidalgo y Costilla Initiated Independence.

MORELOS' CAMPAIGN

Hidalgo dead, the Mestizo Priest José María Morelos y Pavón organized another people's army. He won battles in Cuautla, Oaxaca and Acapulco. He dominated the south of New Spain.

• In the Congress of Chilpancingo, Morelos clearly defined the will to make the country independent from Spain. He expressed his ideas of liberty and justice in the **Sentiments of the Nation** that he read in the Congress.

• The Royalist army captured Morelos, who was executed in 1815. The insurgents continued the guerilla war.

José María Morelos Continued the Fight.

SENTIMENTS OF THE NATION

Mi libro, Lesson 10, quotes "Sentiments of the Nation," Article 1. José María Morelos authored and presented "Sentiments of the Nation" September 14, 1813 to the Congress of Chilpancingo, Mexico. There are 23 Articles demonstrating a blending of Mexico's Church and State authority, which help to understand why Mexico's ancient religious history is hidden and takes a step further down the road of the "Mier Paradox." Note: Articles 2, 3, and 4 establish the Catholic Church as Mexico's national religion; while Article 19 requires legislation that shall establish by constitutional law the celebration of December 12 in honor of Our Most Holy Lady of Guadalupe, patroness of our liberty. These four Articles bolded for emphasis are clues to why Fray Mier is shrouded in darkness. At the time of Fray Mier's December 12, 1794 Guadalupe Sermon and into the 21st Century, the Virgin of Guadalupe is the central icon of Mexico's Catholic Faith. This gives insight to the reason for Fray Mier's Guadalupe Sermon Inquisition, and his apologetic rewrite of the history of the Virgin of Guadalupe.

José María Morelos, "Sentiments of the Nation," Chilpancingo, Mexico (1813); reprinted in *Colonial Spanish America: A Documentary History*, ed. Kenneth Mills and William B. Taylor, (Wilmington, DE: A Scholarly Resources Inc. Imprint, 1998), pp. 341–44, Articles 1 through 23.

1. That America is free and independent of Spain and every other nation, government, or monarchy, and thus it shall be proclaimed, informing the world why.
2. That the Catholic religion shall be the only one, without tolerance for any other.
3. That the ministers of the Church shall live only from the tithes and first fruits, and the people shall not be required to pay for services, except as true offerings and expressions of their devotion.
4. That the dogma of the religion shall be upheld by the Church hierarchy, consisting of the Pope, the bishops, and the parish priests, because every plant that God did not plant should be weeded out. . .Matthew 15.
5. That sovereignty flows directly from the people, and they wish it to be lodged only in the Supreme National

American Congress, composed of representatives of the provinces in equal numbers.

6. That the legislative, executive, and judicial powers shall be divided among those bodies that are established to exercise them.

7. That the representatives shall serve for four years in rotation, the old ones leaving office so the newly elected can take their places.

8. The representatives shall be paid a sufficient but not excessive salary. For now, it shall not be more than 8,000 pesos.

9. Government posts shall be held only by Americans.

10. Foreigners shall not be allowed to enter the country unless they are artisans who can instruct others and are free of all Suspicion.

11. States alter the customs of the people; therefore, the Motherland will not be completely free and ours until the government is reformed, replacing the tyrannical with the liberal, and, also expelling from our soil the enemy Spaniard who has so greatly opposed our Motherland.

12. Since the good law is superior to any man, those [laws] that our Congress issues shall be so, and shall promote constancy and patriotism, and moderate opulence and poverty so that the daily wage of the poor man is raised, his customs improved, and ignorance, preying upon others, and thievery removed.

13. That the general laws shall apply to everyone, including privileged corporations except as applies directly to their duties.

14. To draw up a law, there shall be a gathering of the greatest number of wise men possible, so that the deliberations may proceed with greater certainty. [These men] shall be exempt from some of the duties that might otherwise be demanded of them.

15. Slavery shall be forever forbidden, as shall caste distinctions, leaving everyone equal. One American shall be distinguished from another only by his vices and virtues.

16. That our ports may admit [the ships of] friendly foreign nations, but they cannot be based in the kingdom no matter how friendly they are. And only designated

ports—ten percent of those that exist—shall be used for this purpose. Disembarkation in any other is forbidden.

17. The property of every individual shall be protected, and their homes respected as if they were a sacred asylum. Penalties shall be assigned for violators.

18. That the new legislation shall not allow torture.

19. That the new legislation shall establish by constitutional law the celebration of December 12 in every community of the land in honor of Our Most Holy Lady of Guadalupe, patroness of our liberty, and every community is to practice monthly devotions to her.

20. That foreign troops or those from any other [Spanish] kingdom shall not set foot on our soil unless it is to come to our aid, and then only with the authorization of the *Suprema Junta*.

21. That no expeditions outside the limits of the kingdom shall be made, especially not overseas expeditions; but others not of this kind are to be encouraged in order to propagate the faith among our brothers in the interior [inland or northern Mexico and the American Southwest].

22. That the plethora of tributes, fees, and taxes that weigh us down shall be eliminated. A five percent charge on grains and other produce, or a similarly light tax, shall be levied on every individual. It shall not oppress us like the alcabala, the tobacco monopoly, the tribute, and others. With this light contribution and good administration of property confiscated from the enemy, the cost of the war and the salaries of employees can be paid.

23. That equally we will honor the day of Sept. 16th every year, the day on which the voice of independence was raised, and our miraculous liberty began, because this day the lips of our nation were unfurled to reclaim its rights, with sword in hand, to be heard, remembering always the merit of our grand hero, Señor Miguel Hidalgo and his companion Ignacio Allende.

NOTES ON THE 4TH GRADE MY BOOK OF
MEXICO'S HISTORY,

LESSON 10 | THE XIX CENTURY
REVOLUTION OF INDEPENDENCE

The inclusion of Fray Mier, in "THE XIX CENTURY Revolution of Independence, Lesson 10," evidences Mexico's respect for him; and even more noteworthy, authenticates the credibility of his translated writings in *Fray Servando Teresa de Mier: Writings on Ancient Christianity and Spain's Evangelism of Mexico* and his translated letters in *Christianity in The Americas Before Columbus*. The picture titled: "Fray Servando Teresa de Mier Fought for Liberty," with the text, "The New Ideas—in favor of liberty and equality for all men, and against the privileges of the Church, the nobility and the kings" reveals the paradox of Fray Mier in Mexican history. "The New Ideas" he truly taught were that the Gospel of Jesus Christ was known in America before its discovery and conquest by Spain, and that Mexico's Virgin of Guadalupe was a substitute for the ancient Mexican Tonantzin, Mother of God, the Christian Virgin Mary. The audacity of Fray Mier's December 12, 1794 Guadalupe Sermon was to publicly reveal history hidden for three centuries by Mexico's Church and State hierarchy. The retaliatory consequences of his sermon forced him to fight for his own rights of liberty and equality, which lead to his fight for all Mexicans' liberty and equality. Sadly, Fray Mier and the theme of his Guadalupe Sermon are still hidden by Mexico's Government and Catholic Church authorities.

Ascribing "New Ideas" to Fray Mier without disclosing the theme of his Guadalupe Sermon is curious. Fray Mier's propositions seem absurd, but they are ancient truths discovered and documented by the early Catholic missionaries to the Americas. His propositions are so contrary to our commonly accepted history of America that they fit the definition of a paradox only because of a knowing and willful hiding of ancient Christianity in The Americas by Spain's monarchy. The inclusion of Fray Mier in *Mi libro*, Lesson 10, while withholding his true Mexican legacy is an invented paradox:

Mier, Hidalgo, and Morelos are all Catholic clergy. Fray Mier's portrait includes him dressed in clerical cap, collar, and cassocks with the monastic title Fray. Both Hidalgo and Morelos are identified as priests, but they are not clothed in religious garb.

Hidalgo and Morelos became revolutionary warriors, Mier did not. Hidalgo's shout and Morelos's battles are listed with no mention of Fray Mier's indiscreet blunder, his preached sermon. Hidalgo and Morelos were captured and executed. Mier was captured, imprisoned, but not executed. What was the difference? Hidalgo and Morelos organized armed revolution against Spain. Mier unveiled Mexico's true religious history aggravating Catholic Church hierarchy, but not New Spain's Viceroy. Fray Mier preached and stirred up Mexico's sense of religious equality. Fathers Hidalgo and Morelos shouted and fought for civil liberty and national independence.

Hidalgo and Morelos are celebrated heroes of Mexico, while Fray Mier and his "Guadalupe Sermon" are largely unknown by the citizenry of modern Mexico. *Mi libro*, Lesson 10, illustrates how he is clothed in a veil of ignorance in modern accounts of Mexico's revolutionary history. Each year Mexico's Independence Day is celebrated beginning at midnight, the eve of September 16 by the President of Mexico standing on an upper balcony of Mexico City's National Palace where he rings a bell, waves the Mexican flag, and shouts out to the crowded Zócalo the names of the heroes of Mexican Independence: "Viva Hidalgo! Viva Morelos! Viva Mexico!" The Shout of Dolores by Father Miguel Hidalgo, his revolutionary leadership in northern Mexico and Father José Morelos taking revolutionary leadership in southwest Mexico after the death of Hidalgo are commemorated and highly esteemed by Mexico. But, no "Viva Mier" Is ever shouted out.

Why then, does *Mi libro*, Lesson 10, list Mier in the company of Hidalgo and Morelos? Fray Mier had no known allegiance or contact with Hidalgo or Morelos, having been exiled to Europe. Fray Mier did foment independence from Spain while in Europe. Hidalgo and Morelos led the common people of New Spain in military campaigns, while Mier used Europe's and America's printing press and Council media to teach hidden "New Ideas." He was an activist on behalf of Mexico's poor and humble masses. Exiled in 1795, Fray Mier returned to Mexico in 1817, where he was jailed for deportation under the jurisdiction of the Catholic Church, not the Viceroy of Spain. Fray Mier's exile to Europe and his imprisonment by the Catholic Church evidences that his ideas were threatening to the Church, but not so to the nobility, the King, nor the Viceroy of Mexico. Fray Mier was a revolutionary of new religious ideas. He was not a Hidalgo or Morelos guerrilla. *Mi libro*,

Lesson 10, includes Hidalgo's Virgin of Guadalupe banner. The Virgin of Guadalupe was and still is the icon of Mexico's civil and religious culture! The Inquisition accused Fray Mier of denying the Virgin of Guadalupe. The politics of Mexico's blending of Church and State is the heart and soul of the "Mier Paradox."

Mier's Guadalupe Sermon conflicted with Mexico's Catholic Church and still bears that dark cloud. Fray Mier was an idealist with a romantic love for Mexico. He did not actively contribute to the revolution while exiled in Europe until he met the Spaniard Francisco Javier Mina in London; whom he accompanied to the United States and New Spain where Mina did battle with royalist forces. Fray Mier never engaged in warfare nor incited violent action in his writings. His controversial Guadalupe Sermon and his many years defending the propositions of his sermon is his contribution to Mexico. Fray Mier's shout in his "Farewell Letter to the Mexicans" was: "My fellow countrymen stop howling and go study this issue. The Deists themselves today confess that the ancient preaching of the Gospel in America is beyond doubt."

Mi libro, Lesson 10, "The New Ideas" of Fray Mier in Spanish in part reads: "*y contra los privilegios de la Iglesia, los nobles, y los reyes;*" translated "and against the privileges of the Church, the nobility and the kings." Note, "*Iglesia*" ("Church") is capitalized. Capital letters are rare in Spanish. Spanish does not capitalize the first letter of a title of honor or respect of nobles or kings. Book titles only capitalize the first word of the title. The capital "*I*" of "*Iglesia*" in Spanish implies a specific church, the Catholic Church. Fray Mier was deemed to be a rebel against Mexico's Catholic Church, even though he lived throughout his life as a faithful religious regular of the Catholic faith. Fray Mier requested and was granted perpetual secularization in Rome, 1802-1803, retaining some dispensations and honors. Nevertheless, he lived a monastic life until the day he died.

In 1807, as an exile in Portugal, Fray Mier was named a Domestic Prelate of Pope Pius VII, entitling him to wear the red-trimmed black cassock with purple sash of a Papal Prelate for the rest of his life, which he wore even while imprisoned by the Catholic Church in Mexico, periodically from 1817 to 1820. He identified himself by the titles of Fray and Bishop upon returning to Mexico. His conflicts appear to have been with Mexican Church hierarchy, not with the Church hierarchy of Rome or Spain. A conjecture is that the Catholic Church at large is not concerned with

Fray Mier's account of Mexican history, but the Catholic Church in Mexico is very concerned. To capitalize "*Iglesia*" is a typo disclosing the concern "of the Church," meaning the Catholic Church of Mexico.

Reading Fray Mier's "Apologia," defense of his proposition two, the Virgin of Guadalupe is complex and confusing. The Virgin of Guadalupe is a respected icon to most parents and 4th grade students using the textbook. *Mi libro*, Lesson 10, is truly a paradoxical puzzle. Given Fray Mier's 18th and 19th Century conflict with Mexico's Catholic Church and today's strong Virgin of Guadalupe culture in Mexico, why did Mexico's Secretary of Public Education choose to include Fray Mier in a public Fourth Grade history textbook, while deleting his true message? Fray Mier is little known in modern Mexico. Why not simply delete him from *Mi libro*? The answer may be that it was not until 1860, when Mexico's President Benito Juarez passed the Reform Laws that established the liberty of cultures and the separation of Church and State. The Reform Laws authorized the nationalization of Church property and abolished many clergy privileges. The inclusion of Fray Mier, in *Mi libro* by the Secretary of Public Education, is so out of context with the theme of the Lesson, even though he fits the time line, that there is reason to speculate that there is an implied political message to the Catholic Church in Mexico. Which is: Do not use Hidalgo, Morelos, or "Sentiments of the Nation" to negate the 1860 separation of church and state; or we could unleash Fray Mier's enlightened and liberal "New Ideas" on the ancient preaching of the Gospel in America.

Fray Mier researched and restored lost truths that with the lapse of time have again been lost in archives until they have become seen as myths by the clueless who do not know the true history of ancient and modern Mexico. Until Fray Mier's writings are published in an unsuppressed and uncensored format to be studied in the light of day, the significance of his writings will remain in darkness. Adding Fray Servando Teresa de Mier to *Mi libro*'s 4th Grade History of Mexico, even without the full disclosure of his masqueraded "New Ideas," Mexico's Secretary of Public Education has done its due diligence and decided upon close inspection that there is truth in the conflicting opposite theological thesis of Fray Mier. That said, Mexico's Secretary of Education is not yet ready to reconcile those opposites with the Catholic Church. Thus, Fray Mier's resurrected history is still veiled and hidden in the academic closets of the Secretary of Public Education.

LIBERTY AND EQUALITY OF ALL MEN AGAINST THE PRIVILEGES OF THE CHURCH, THE NOBILITY, AND THE KINGS

Mi libro, Lesson 10, profiles Fray Mier as he might be scripted by Octavio Paz, (1914-1998), Mexican author, poet, and diplomat. Octavio Paz was awarded the 1990 Nobel Prize for Literature. At the time of the Prize announcement, *El laberinto de la soledad* (*"The Labyrinth of Solitude"*) was credited with being the prime work for which he was awarded the Nobel Prize. The book offers an odd cultural and historical insight of what it is to be a Mexican. His language can be crude, but good-hearted as he astutely analyzes expressions, attitudes, the distinctive values at the heart and soul, and the origin of all the fragmented attributes contributing to being Mexican. In the past and today, a Mexican as described by Paz is burdened by tradition and racial castes that bind a Mexican to his and her culture; which guide their reactions and sustain the framework of the Mexican spirit that is definitively engraved in the intellectual conscience of Mexico's history and universal values.

Spain's conquest and rule of New Spain imposed a very prejudicial European caste system on the colonial people. Eighteenth century caste paintings profile sixteen different racial castes. New Spain castes can be grouped into four categories: Peninsulares, Creoles, Indians, and Mestizos. The high and mighty "Peninsulares" were the nobility of New Spain, a Spaniard born in Spain's Iberian Peninsula. The second class were "Creoles" who were born in New Spain of Spanish parents. Creoles had little power and authority in the governance of church and state. The "Native Indian" population were enslaved with little humanity, no power nor authority in New Spain. "Mestizos" were a varied mix race of Indian and Spanish ancestry. The Castes were a mix of racial ethnicities, which made up rest of the 16 racial castes system. Indians, Mestizos, and Castes were low-class, well below Creoles, with diverse classifications of racial and social standing depending upon the racial mix. Fray Mier was a proud Creole with a noble Spanish heritage, a Doctor of Theology, very much respected for his knowledge of Mexican history and culture. Nevertheless, as a Creole he was denigrated by the ruling Spanish Peninsulares who were the Church and State hierarchy. We read in his "Apologia" and his letters of the pain and humiliation he suffered physically and mentally from the dismissive attitude of the Peninsulares toward his Creole status. From his writings, it is easy to see that Fray Mier was not a humble person. But as a Creole he was harnessed by the Peninsulares with a yoke of humility, which gave him cause to reach out to New Spain's masses, its Indian and Mestizo populace. His 1794 sermon was not a shout of revolution. It was a public statement to the Indian and Mestizo classes: Know and be proud of your Christian faith and traditions, which you had before the arrival of Spain to America! For the first time recorded, he publicly preached a sermon on a secret history known by Mexican scholars. In exile, his letters to the Indians and Mestizos of Mexico always embraced the message, love thyself, be proud of your ancient Christian heritage. Fray Mier's Guadalupe sermon was a gospel message of ethnic pride and equality. It was not the shout of Miguel Hidalgo and José Morelos for revolution and liberty from Spain.

Octavio Paz's book: *Sor Juana Inés de la Cruz o Las trampas de la fe*, ("*Sister Juana Inés de la Cruz or the Traps of the Faith*") is a biography of Sor Juana a Hieronymite nun, poet, and native of New Spain, who lived from 1651 to 1695. His *Sor Juana* biographical Prologue and First Part, "The Kingdom of New Spain" makes a brief reference to Fray Mier. Paz's *Sor Juana* introduction offers an essential insight to understanding the Mier Paradox, describing the pre-revolutionary culture Fray Mier confronted in 1794, a hundred years after Sor Juana. *Sor Juana* profiles the New Spain Empire in these words:

> The key word that defined and justified the historical action of Spain and the existence of its Empire was *evangelism*.[2] Other theologians, among them the majority of the Jesuits, maintained that the Indians' ancient beliefs already had glimmers of the true faith, be it by natural grace or because the Gospel had been preached in America before the arrival of the Spaniards; and the Indians still kept confused memories of the doctrine. In the 17th century this last belief was extended and affirmed. It was an opinion as seen later in the argument of Fray Servando Teresa de Mier in favor of Independence that implicitly undermined the fundamental principle of Spanish domination in America: evangelization."[3] "In the changed circumstances of the second half of the 17th century, the apparition of the Virgin of Guadalupe, precisely in the

sanctuary of an Indian goddess, was a confirmation of the unique and singular character of New Spain. A true *sign,* in the religious sense with which this word was used in the 17th century, insinuates a mysterious connection between the Pre-Columbian and the Christian World. This apparition was a consecration of the destiny of North America and of its metropolis, the imperial city of Mexico. I will not extend myself on the Guadalupe worship: it is an immense theme. The figure of Guadalupe-Tonantzin is engraved on the heart of Mexico and it is impossible to understand our country and its history if one does not understand what has been and what Guadalupe worship is.[4]

In El laberinto de la soledad, Octavio Paz writes:

All the history of Mexico, since the Conquest until the Revolution, can be seen as a search of ourselves, deformed, or masked by foreign institutions, and in a Way that defines us. The pre-Cortés societies achieved very rich and diverse creations, according to what one sees from the little that the Spaniards left in place, and by the revelations that each day the archeologists and anthropologists hand over to us. The Conquest destroyed those ways and superimposed the Spanish way. In 'The Spanish' culture two directions lie hidden, reconciled but not entirely merged by the Spanish State: the medieval tradition, of a noble descent, lives on in Spain until our days, and a universal tradition that Spain appropriates and makes its own before the Counter Reformation.[5]

Fray Servando Teresa de Mier fits the model of 20th century civil right activists Mahatma Gandi and Martin Luther King, Jr. much better than he does that of his 19th century contemporaries Miguel Hidalgo and José Morelos. His Guadalupe Sermon, like Martin Luther King's 20th century speech, "I Have a Dream," awakened the passions of the audience. Fray Mier's speech alarmed church hierarchy to enforce his inquisition and exile. His "Apologia's" short defense of the sermon's proposition that Saint Thomas brought Christianity to ancient America is reason to believe this was not the scandal. The Saint Thomas theory was accepted by Mexican clergy and scholars since the discovery of

America, though unknown by the Mestizo and Indian populace. Judging from his detailed defense of his Virgin of Guadalupe proposition, this was the cause of the Church's outrage. Octavio Paz's 20th Century characterization of the Virgin of Guadalupe mirrors the image at the time of Fray Mier: "The figure of Guadalupe-Tonantzin is engraved on the heart of Mexico and it is impossible to understand our country and its history if one does not understand what has been and what Guadalupe worship is." When I served as a Mormon missionary in Mexico, 1962-64, Father Barajas, a Catholic priest, counseled me and my missionary companion: "Preach your Mormon religion, many people in our city will join your church." Then pausing, he said: "Do not preach this people against the Virgin of Guadalupe." Fray Mier in his "Apologia" adamantly claims that he did not deny the Virgin of Guadalupe. He questioned how the Virgin had appeared in Mexico and the source of the cloth on which the image was painted. His defense was that the Virgin of Guadalupe was a mixing of the images of the ancient Indian goddess Tonantzin, Mother of the true God, with Spain's Virgin of Guadalupe to evangelize Mexicans of ancient Christianity to Catholic Christianity. Octavio Paz verifies Fray Mier's proposition by linking the names Guadalupe-Tonantzin. Fray Mier's Guadalupe Sermon revealed to the Mexican people a hidden history, which overtime contributed to the revolutionary call for Mexico's liberty from Spain. Sadly, after his death in 1827, Mexico's heroic Fray Mier and his sermon were again shrouded in darkness.

ST. THOMAS, THE ULTIMATE PARADOX

Fray Servando Teresa de Mier was commissioned to preach a sermon in the Basilica of Our Lady of Guadalupe, December 12, 1794, the Day of the Virgin of Guadalupe, a religious festival still celebrated in Mexico every year on the 12th of December. The congregants crowding the Basilica would have been admiring believers of the tradition of the apparition of the Virgin of Guadalupe to Juan Diego. A summary of Mier's Guadalupe sermon is most probably his "Farewell Letter to the Mexicans." There is no known transcript of the sermon, so we must rely upon Fray Mier's "Apologia," his Letters, and other writings in defense of his sermon. His sermon had two propositions: One, the Gospel of Jesus Christ was first preached in the Americas by the Apostle Saint Thomas; and Two, Spain's Virgin of Guadalupe was introduced into Mexico by the Catholic Church to hasten the evangelism of Mexico's native population. The congregation's heart felt adoration of the Virgin of Guadalupe may have caused them to interpret Fray Mier's theological story of Guadalupe-Tonantzin as a denial of the Guadalupe tradition and worship.

On the other hand, the congregation did not adore St. Thomas as they did Our Lady of Guadalupe, daily in their homes. The St. Thomas legend was a theory of early Catholic missionaries to explain how the Christianity they found came to America. The St. Thomas sermon proposition would have raised the congregation's curiosity but not anger. The questions raised would be such as: Who is St. Thomas? Oh, the doubting Apostle St. Thomas appointed by Jesus Christ. How did St. Thomas get to Mexico, and what does he have to do with the Virgin of Guadalupe? By December 12, 1794, the St. Thomas legend had been suppressed for 240 years. "St. Thomas, the Ultimate Paradox" sets forth a theory that Spain and Portugal conspired to conceal traces of Christianity and the St. Thomas legend to make lawful the conquest and enslavement of the Americas and its native people. The political scheme was to bring the conquest in compliance with Catholic Papal Bulls, which prohibited the enslavement of Christians. The political scheme, also, included proactive evangelism. The widespread belief of early Catholic missionaries in the St. Thomas proposition has evolved in the 21st century to where St. Thomas in America is no more than a myth. Rather than a myth it should be classified as misinterpretation of indigenous culture that Spain and Portugal discovered in America. Classification as a myth gives a right to the assertion that there is no evidence of Judeo-Christian practices or beliefs in ancient America. So today, Fray Mier can be classified as a myth builder and pushed away into darkness. To such an assertion, Fray Mier declared in his 1820 "Farewell Letter. . ." that: "The Deists themselves today confess that the ancient preaching of the Gospel in America is beyond doubt."

Another missionary, also 300 years before Fray Mier, wrote extensively on Saint Thomas and Christianity in The Americas. April 15, 1502 Bartolomé de las Casas landed on the island of Hispaniola where he lived until 1506. He returned to Spain in 1507, then to Rome where he was ordained a priest. Returning to Hispaniola in 1511, he bounced back and forth between Spain and the Americas for 37 years. Participating in the conquest of Cuba, serving as a Catholic missionary to Venezuela, Mexico, Peru,

Nicaragua, and Guatemala, he took his vows as a Dominican Friar in 1523 and as the first Bishop of Chiapas, Mexico in 1545. During those 37 years he was a strong advocate on behalf of the American Indians to the hierarchy of Spain and the Catholic Church for which he was designated "Universal Procurator and Protector of all the Indians." After serving as Bishop for two years, he returned to Spain about 1548, to never again return to the Americas. Between 1555-1559, Bishop de las Casas wrote and redacted a history of the Americas from his experiences and documents accumulated while living in the New World. His work is titled: *Apologética historia sumaria cuanto a las cualidades, dispusición, descripción, cielo y suelo destas tierras, y condiciones naturales, policías, repúblicas, maneras de vivir e costumbres de las gentes deestas Indias Occidentales y Meridionales, cuyo imperio soberano pertenece a los reyes de Castilla:* ("*Apologetic Summary History as to the Qualities, Disposition, Description, Heaven and Earth of These Lands, and Natural Conditions, Politeness, Republics, Ways of Life and Customs of the Peoples of These Western and Southern Indies, Whose Sovereign Empire Belongs to the Kings of Castile.*") *Los indios de México y Nueva España*, ("*The Indians of Mexico and New Spain*") is an anthology of the *Apologética historia* ("*Apologetic History*").[6]

Marcel Bataillon, a renowned French Hispanist, in 1965 published *Études sur Bartolomé de las Casas*: ("*Studies on Bartolomé de las Casas*),[7] in which he refers to the Mexican Fray Servando de Mier as a great admirer of Fray de las Casas, which Fray Mier notes in his *Historia de la revolución de Nueva España*: ("*History of New Spain's Revolution*"), published 1813 in London. Bataillon states Fray Mier's early study of Fray de las Casas pertained to slavery in Hispaniola.

The Spanish encomienda system, founded 1503 in the Americas, granted Spanish soldiers, colonists, and Catholic priests a tract of land or a village with ownership of the land's natural resources and feudal authority over the Indian inhabitants living on the land or in the village. Fray de las Casas was granted an encomienda on Hispaniola. His personal experience while a Catholic priest as an encomendero, feudal slave holder, was his introduction and cause for his agitation over the enslavement of the native Indians. In Madrid, Spain, 1516, Fray de las Casas presented to church and state hierarchy two memorandums in favor of the Indians and in condemnation of Spain's encomiendas. Fray de las Casas declared that on this occasion he was appointed "Universal Procurator and Protector of all the Indians," devoting the rest of his life as protectorate of the native people of the Americas.

December 12, 1794 Fray Mier took the road less traveled, 278 years earlier, by his admired Dominican brother Bishop de las Casas on behalf of Mexico's native people. Bataillon credits Professor Juan Manzano with the discovery of surprising instructions for the new world, given by His Majesty the King of Spain, May 1, 1543. Manzano made his discovery known in an article published 1941 by the *Revista de Estudios Políticos ("Magazine of Political Studies"*) of Madrid.[8] His Majesty sent a spiritual message to the unknown heathens beyond the oceans. His instructions included credentials of the envoys, who were to deliver the King of Castile's message. The named envoys were Fray Juan de Zumárraga, Mexico's first Bishop; Fray Domingo de Betanzos, founder of Mexico's Dominican Province; and Fray Juan de la Magdalena, also of Mexico's Dominican Province.

Bataillon says: "The documents, finally, clarify a riddle that for a long time was bothersome in Zumárraga's history and of his relationship with Las Casas." The pieces of the riddle were that Fray de las Casas was to be one of the three envoys designated by Bishop Zumárraga until Fray de las Casas opted out to become the Bishop of Chiapas. The envoys' mission was to evangelize China. Even 51 years after the discovery of America, Bishop Zumárraga still thought he presided over the territory of east India where China lay to the north. By his understanding, China was geographically attached to the north of his Catholic Diocese of New Spain. Fray Betanzos and Martin de Valencia had been profoundly disappointed by the Mexican Indians who spoke without illusion of their heritage, for which their penalty was the gigantic epidemics, a fulfilment of a prophecy by a Dominican Father "the end of this (Mexican) nation." Their plan was that the Gospel of Jesus Christ was to pass through the Antilles to New Spain and Peru, on to China. Their image was that the Asian people of China were not idolaters, since their ancestors had been converted to Christianity by the Apostle Saint Thomas, an original disciple of Jesus Christ. Fray Zumárraga even dates one of his letters thus "Eve of the Indian Apostle Saint Thomas." An added footnote says Fray de las Casas in his *Apologética historia ("Apologetic History"*) speaks of the evangelization by Saint Thomas of India and of Saint Bartholomew in the furthest extremes of India" that by luck was near that of our Indies."

It was a known fact by the Catholic Church that the Apostle

Saint Thomas preached the Gospel of Jesus Christ in India. Columbus and Spanish conquistadores had a confused perception of the geographic proximity of India to Mexico on the maps of their time. This was their explanation for the traces of Christianity they found in New Spain. Bataillon states that his text is not the time or place to analyze the Christian preaching by Saint Thomas, the memory of which could have been deleted. He footnotes a quote from Manzano's works, ". . . or by luck through the neglect or weakness of their ancestors the memory of the preaching of his Name and Faith has been lost as it was done in the past." These are the same arguments Fray Mier puts forth in his "Apologia" to explain Mexico's lost memory of its Christian heritage prior to the conquest. Bataillon speculates that the motive of Fray de las Casas for propagating the Saint Thomas legend was to assure a peaceful evangelism in the sphere of the new world.

In *Los Indios de México y Nueva España* ("*The Indians of Mexico and New Spain*"), Chapter XV, "The Mayan Gods," Bishop de las Casas tells of a letter he received, 1546, from one of his clergy, which he kept among papers that he carried with him when he returned to Spain. Bishop de las Casas writes:

> I will refer to another matter, a lot of news in all the Indies, and until today nowhere has it been found, and it is that as that kingdom also came, for proximity, within the limits of my Chiapas Bishopric, I went there to land on so healthy a land and port. I found there a clergy, good, of mature age and honest, who knew the Indians language for having lived in it several years; and because to move forward to the head of the bishopric it was necessary for me set up my vicar and I begged him and I charged him that he should go around visiting the Indians within the land, and that I told him, preach to them in a true way. Which, at the end of some months, and I even believe that of one year he wrote me that he had found a Lord Chief that, questioning him about their belief and ancient religion they used to have for that kingdom, he said to him that they knew and believed in God who was in the heaven, and that this selfsame God was Father and Son and Holy Ghost, and that the Father is named Izona, that he had created man and everything: the Son had Bacab for a name, who was born of a maiden still a virgin, named Chibirias who is in the heaven with God. They named the Holy Ghost, Echuac. They say that

Izona means the Great Father; of Bacab, who is the Son, they say that Eopuco killed him, and had whipped and put a crown of thorns on him, and that he put him with arms stretched out on a post, not understanding that he was nailed, but tied (so for him to mean he extended the arms), where he finally died; he was dead three days, and on the third, that he returned to life and he rose to the heaven, and that there he was with his Father. After this, later came Echuac, who is the Holy Ghost, and that he filled the earth of all that it needed. Asked what Bacab or Bacabab meant, he said that Son of the Great Father, and of this name, Echuac, that means merchant. And the Holy Ghost brought good merchandise to the world, since he filled the earth, that are mankind's terrains, of his gifts and graces, so divine and abundant. Chibirias sounds like Mother of the Son of the Great Father. He added more: that at some time all the men had to die, but of the resurrection of the flesh he knew nothing.

Asking how he had notices of these things, he responded, the men taught it to their children, and so it descended from hand to hand. And he said more: that anciently twenty men came to that land (of those he pointed out fifteen of their names, that because it is bad lettering and because it makes no difference here I don't put them down, of the other five the clergy says that he found no trace). The principal one of them was called Cocolcán; this they called god of the fevers or temperatures; two of the others, of the fish; another two, of the farms or estates; another, that thunders, etc.; they wore long clothes, sandals for footwear, long beards, and they wore no hats upon their heads; who ordered that the people confess and fast, and that some fasted Friday, because Bacab had died that day; and that day has by name, Himis, which they honor and have a devotion for the death of Bacab. The men know all these peculiarities, but the common people only believe in the three persons Izona, and Bacab, and Echuac, and Chibirias, the Mother of Bacab, and in the mother of Chibirias, named Hischen, who we say to have been Saint Anna.

All the above thus said that clergy, named Francisco Hernández, who wrote to me, and among my papers I have his letter. He said more: that he took that Lord before a friar of Saint Francis who was over there, and he repeated everything again before the monk, of which both were amazed. If these things are true, our holy faith appears to have been known in that land; but however in no part of the Indies do we happen to find such news, as in the land of Brazil, that the Portuguese possess, they imagine to have found traces of Apostle Saint Thomas, but as that news did not fly ahead, yet, certainly, the land and kingdom of Yucatán is given to understand more peculiar things and of greater antiquity, for the great and admirable and exquisite manner of very ancient buildings and inscriptions of certain characters than in any other part. Finally, these are secrets things that only God knows. [9]

O'Gorman adds a footnote to Fray de las Casas' reference to the Apostle Saint Thomas: "The belief in this legend persisted throughout the Colony and was used as an argument against the rights that Spain claimed over its American possessions."[10]

And thus, we come to a discussion of the politics of Jesus Christ's Apostle Saint Thomas in America; a very controversial discussion that began in 1492, becoming with the passage of time no more than a myth, largely unknown today. Here is how history created the St. Thomas myth: Europe errored early on the discovery of America in believing that Christopher Columbus had discovered a new route to East Asia, India, China, the surrounding territories, and islands. Europeans crossed the Atlantic Ocean in the early decades after 1492, ignorant of the fact that this new-found western route to Asia included the discovery of western continents that became known as America. Early European explorers believed the people inhabiting this New World to be natives of India, so they were called Indians. We continue the error even today by calling the descendants of America's native people, Indians.

Bishop de las Casas, the first Bishop of Chiapas, Mexico, had earlier earned the title, Protectorate of the Indies, describes the territory of his Chiapas Diocese as including Yucatán in the north, and the southern border territory of modern Mexico, and Guatemala; surrounded on the north by the Gulf of Mexico and the Caribbean Sea, and on the south by the Pacific Ocean. Citing the 1546 letter he received from Father Hernández, fifty-four years after the discovery of the New World, he notes traces of Christianity, such as the Holy Trinity, the Holy Virgin, and the Apostle Saint Thomas in this land he called the Indies. About 1543, just before being named Bishop of Chiapas. Fray de las Casas and other missionaries, based upon maps of their time, were to travel north of what is now the modern Republic of Mexico, to evangelize China. Bearing witness to these errors of geography is our common identity even to the present time of the Caribbean Sea and its islands as the West Indies.

It is accepted Christian tradition that the Apostle Saint Thomas took the Gospel of Jesus Christ to the east, founding Christianity in India where he was killed and buried circa 72 A.D. Fray Mier declares in his "Apologia": "Throughout America, monuments and vestige evidences of Christianity were found, according to the unanimous testimony of the missionaries." These early Catholic missionaries to the West Indies believed they had encountered vestige evidences of Christianity planted fourteen hundred years earlier by the Apostle Saint Thomas. St. Thomas did not cross the Pacific Ocean to preach Christianity in The Americas, but the European explorers and missionaries believed they had crossed the Atlantic Ocean to arrive in India. Nevertheless, St. Thomas was the theoretical missionary who the early Catholic missionaries credited with having brought Christianity to America, which they discovered already existed in this New World.

The vestiges of ancient Hebrew-Christian practices in America were preserved by the early Catholic missionaries in their writings on the religious beliefs and practices of the native peoples. What happened to those vestiges? How did they come to be destroyed and hidden after the discovery of the New World by Spain? The answer can be summarized in three hypotheses: 1. The Catholic Church vs. The Eastern Orthodox Church, 2. The Catholic Church on Christian Slaves, and 3. The Catholic Church Evangelizes the American-Indians.

THE CATHOLIC CHURCH VS. THE EASTERN ORTHODOX CHURCH

Christianity in the newly discovered West Indies, now the American continents, could have caused conflict between the Eastern Orthodox Church and the Roman Catholic Church. The Spanish missionaries flooding into the New World were clergy of the Catholic Church, based in Rome. The Catholic Church's discovery of Christianity in this World was new to them; and the theory that the origin of Christianity found in the New World was the missionary work of St. Thomas, and their believing they were in India, could arguably have brought these New World Christians under the jurisdiction of the Eastern Orthodox Church, based in Constantinople. The Roman Catholic and Eastern Orthodox Churches shared a history of contentiousness. A final schism between the Roman Catholic and Eastern Orthodox Churches took place in 1054 A.D. A reunion failed in 1274 A.D. at the Second Council of Lyon, and again at the 1439 A.D. Council of Florence. The Council of Florence did establish an amiable agreement between Orthodox and Catholic Church hierarchies, only to be rejected by local congregations of the Eastern Orthodox Church. The Florence Council, also, became politically more difficult to implement after Constantinople fell to Ottoman rule. The Council of Florence agreement and then the failure to implement it, just fifty-three years before 1492, had to be an on-going friction between the Orthodox and Catholic Churches. Fray Mier does not specifically address this controversy; however, in his "Apologia" he references an "Eastern Council" that described how the Virgin was to be painted, "Eastern rites and customs" practiced by the ancient Christians of Mexico, and an "Eastern Apostle," which evidences a belief by some Catholic clergy that the Christian practices of the native American Indians were of Eastern Orthodox origins. The Catholic evangelization of a people in a territory that they believed to have been proselyted by Apostle Saint Thomas, which after his death came under Eastern Orthodox ecumenical jurisdiction could not be ignored. The St. Thomas theory had to be suppressed, kept quiet, and hidden if the evangelization and conquest of the Americas by Spanish and Portuguese Catholic missionaries were to continue. If not, there was the possibility of open conflict between the Roman Catholic and Eastern Orthodox Churches.

THE CATHOLIC CHURCH ON CHRISTIAN SLAVES

There are numerous Papal edicts that Christians are not to be enslaved. The enslavement of American Indians, if they were Christians, would have been strictly prohibited by the Catholic Church. In 1503, Spain established a system of land ownership in the Indies known as an *encomienda*. Spain's encomienda system was a restoration and transplant of medieval Europe feudalism to

America. The encomienda system was simply ownership of land and natural resources with the land's Native-Indian inhabitants as virtual slaves, granted to a Spanish colonist, known as an encomendero. The encomienda could include entire villages. The encomendero was also charged to bring the Indians on his land to Christianity. Fray de las Casas resided on the island of Hispaniola 1502-1506. In 1507, de las Casas returns to Spain where he is ordained a Catholic priest. In 1511, he is again on Hispaniola, where even as a Catholic priest, he is granted an encomienda, which he renounces in 1515. Fray de las Casas returns to Spain in 1516, where he argues that an "encomienda" is no more than slavery. His declaration earned him the titles "Universal Procurator and Protector of all the Indians," and "Protectorate of the Indies." Even with these titles Fray de las Casas does not get encomiendas outlawed.

A review of Catholic Papal Bulls regarding slavery in the decades preceding and following the discovery of America, and Spain's royal edicts in response to these Papal Bulls, is insightful to understanding the scandal that Fray de las Casas unleashed regarding encomiendas and the enslaving of the native people of America. Modern history denies the slavery of American Indians in histories of the Spanish conquest. Catholic Church edicts prohibiting enslavement of Christians disclose why the denial and hiding of ancient Hebrew-Christian practices in America was enforced to allow Spain's granting of encomiendas in America. A synopsis history, *Slavery and the Catholic Church,* by John Francis Maxwell, summarizes Church and Royal edicts on slavery from 1434 to 1526.[11] "It was a custom of war in Christendom that no Christian prisoner of war should ever be enslaved."[12]

During the 1430's, the Canary Islands had many converts to Christianity, while Spain and Portugal made numerous raids on the Islands to capture slaves. Pope Eugene IV issued Papal Bull *Creator Omnium*, December 17, 1434, that threatens excommunication of anyone who enslaves any Canary Islander Christian convert. Canon Law had previously sanctioned slavery only in the case of just war and pagan captives. But *Creator Omnium* allowed slavery in all wars, of any person; except, exemption from slavery was any Christian. Further raids, of the Canary Islands gave cause for Pope Eugene IV to issue his Bull *Sicut Dudum*, January 13, 1435; which again affirmed his prohibition against enslaving Canary Island natives who had converted to Christianity. *Sicut Dudum* was amended by another Papal Bull, September 15, 1436, that agreed to Portugal's conquering and enslaving non-Christian territory and people of the Canary Islands with a mandate prohibiting enslaving Christians.

Pope Nicholas V issued his Papal Bull *Dum Diversas*, June 18, 1452, giving King Alfonso V of Portugal the right to "attack, conquer, and subjugate Saracens, Pagans and other enemies of Christ wherever they may be found." Control of the Canary Islands was a source of animosity between Spain and Portugal. Pope Nicholas was asked to settle the conflict. He did, at last, in favor of Portugal. *Romanus Pontifex*, Pope Nicholas's January 8, 1455 Papal Bull, reaffirms the sanctions of *Dum Diversas* for the purchase of black slaves, and gives Portugal the right to conquer the lands between Morocco and the East Indies with the duty to convert the inhabitants to Christianity. And, in a 1454 edict issued to King Alfonso V, Pope Nicholas extended those rights to all who may be taken as prisoners in future wars. These rights were confirmed by subsequent Bulls of successor Popes Callixtus III, Pius II, Sixtus IV, Leo X, and Alexander VI. These Papal Bulls became the basis for the rights and limits to slavery in the new-found Americas.

Pope Callixtus III assumed the Papal Chair in 1455. He issued his Papal Bull, *Inter Caetera* in 1456 reaffirming the right of Portugal to enslave infidels, Africans, and Moors based upon his interpretation of prior Bulls, *Romanus Pontifex* and *Dum Diversas*. However, his Bull of 1456 was in direct opposition to the stance taken by Pope Eugene IV in his 1435 Bull, *Sicut Dudum*. There was a contiguous back and forth debate over who could, or could not be enslaved, or even if anyone could be enslaved by Christian Canon. Pope Pius II, in his October 7, 1462 speech, Apud Raynaldum in Annalibus *Ecclesiasticis ad ann n. 42*, to the ruler of the Canary Islands, condemned slavery of newly baptized Christians. Pope Pius II instructed Bishops to penalize those who violated his edict. Later interpretations were that his condemnation applied only to new converts being enslaved. Pope Sixtus IV in his June 21, 1481 Papal Bull, *Aetmi Regi*, confirms Pope Nicholas's Papal Bulls *Dum Diversas* of 1452, and *Romanus Pontifex* of 1455, which granted Portugal the right to take slaves from Africa. Pope Sixtus in an earlier 1476 Bull, *Regimini Gregis*, threatens the excommunication of all who enslave Christians. These ecclesiastic penalties were specifically directed toward those who enslaved recent converts to Christianity in the Canary Islands and Africa.

These Papal Bulls set the standards for commerce and evangelism along the coast of Africa and were soon to be practiced in the discovery and conquest of the New World.

Following the discovery of the West Indies in 1492, Queen Isabella I of Castilla and King Ferdinand II of Aragon were prescient in realizing these Papal Bulls would apply, as well, to the New World. They understood that if they did not receive Papal authority equal to that granted to Portugal in the preceding decades; then, they would be hampered in their exploitation of the people and resources of the West Indies. Therefore, they petitioned Pope Alexander VI for a Papal Bull. Pope Alexander VI immediately responded with three Papal Bulls, *Eximiae devotionis*, May 2, 1493; *Inter Caetera*, May 4, 1493, and *Dudum Siquidem*, September 23, 1493. The three Bulls granted Isabella I and Ferdinand II rights with respect to the newly discovered West Indies equal to what Pope Nicholas V's Bulls had previously bestowed upon Portugal in its exploitation of the Canary Islands and Africa.

Demonstrating a conflict of interest and probable prejudice is the fact that Pope Alexander VI was Spanish with complex family roots in Spain and personal connections to Queen Isabella I of Castilla and King Ferdinand II of Aragon. Alexander VI served as Pope August 11, 1492 to August 18, 1503. This was only the second time that a Spaniard had been Pope. The first time was Alexander VI's uncle Calixtus III who served as Pope April 8, 1455 to August 6, 1458. Both are authors of Papal Bulls on slavery. Pope Alexander VI issued two Papal Bulls May 2 and May 4, 1493 less than two months after Christopher Columbus arrived in Portugal, March 4 and Spain March 15, 1493, a very short time to research, write and review a Papal Bull. Pope Alexander VI's 1493 Bulls granted territorial sovereignty of the western half of the New World to Queen Isabella if the lands were not ruled by Christian princes. Alexander VI's *Inter Caetera* included the mandate "that barbarous nations be overthrown and brought to the faith," in other words converted to Christianity.

November 3, 1514, in his Papal Bull, *Praecelsae Devotionis*, Pope Leo X repeated verbatim all these documents and approved, renewed and confirmed them. In summary, the Catholic Church vacillated on its acceptance of slavery in the decades immediately preceding and following 1492, while firmly holding to the principle that enslavement of Christians was not allowed.

Queen Isabella issued a Royal decree in 1503, at the request of Christopher Columbus, that the "Carib" Indians be known as cannibals, and hence be enslaved. The Spanish word "Carib" at that time became synonymous with "cannibal," or an "inhuman person." There is no documented evidence that the native peoples of the West Indies practiced cannibalism. Most likely, it was a myth fabricated to justify Queen Isabella's 1503 decree and the launch of the encomienda system in the Indies to enslave those terrible "Caribs." Fray Bartolomé de las Casas designated "Protectorate of the Indians" argued in 1516 and for the rest of his life that slavery was at the heart of Spain's conquest of the New World. Fray de las Casas wrote a handbook on slavery in 1547. A Royal edict was issued November 28, 1548, which ordered that his handbook be confiscated and destroyed, which was enforced in both Spain and the Americas.

King Ferdinand II of Aragon issued the Laws of Burgos, December 27, 1512. The Laws were written as a sham to create the appearance of improved treatment of Indians, but they legitimized encomienda slavery and allowed forced relocation of Indians to church missions where they would be evangelized.

King Charles I of Spain issued the Royal Provision of Granada, November 17, 1526, regulating expeditions in the West Indies to prevent the Spanish settlers' abuse of native Indians. Maxwell states: "The Provision of Granada was an application in practice of the common Catholic teaching concerning the title to slave-ownership of non-Christians captured in a just war; whereby, King Charles V, Holy Roman Emperor, the same person, different title, authorized the enslavement of Indian prisoners captured in just warfare."[13]

From 1513 to 1556 the Spanish conquest used the *Requerimiento* ("Requirement"), a written declaration of Spain's sovereignty over the Americas. Written by Doctor of Law Juan López de Palacios Rubios in 1513, it asserted that God through Saint Peter and his Papal successors held authority over the whole Earth, and that the Papal Bull, *Inter Caetera*, of Pope Alexander VI conferred title over the Indies to Spain's monarchy. It was demanded that the *Requerimiento* be read to the native Indians under the control of the conquistadors. It was read in Spanish to Indians of New Spain who spoke no Spanish. It was finally banned by the Spanish monarchy in 1556. The *Requerimiento* likely came from the tradition of the wars between the Moors and Christians of Spain and from the moral debates in Spain over the rules and regulations governing the colonization of the New World and associate problems such as war, encomiendas, slavery, forced conversions, relocations, and war crimes. Its use was criticized by many early Catholic missionaries, and especially by Fray Barolomé de las Casas.

This was a harbinger to the discovery and conquest of the people and riches of the Americas that had to have exerted influence on the Papal Bulls and Spain's Royal decrees regarding slavery. With the Ottoman Turks successful 1453 capture of Constantinople, the Roman Catholic kingdoms of Western Europe battled, traded, and reached diplomatic treaties with a powerful Muslim empire. The Muslim Ottomans were at the center of the Eastern and Western Worlds. They controlled the nations of the Eastern Orthodox Church. The elite corps of the Ottoman army were the Janissary, New Soldiers, who were mostly Christian draftees. Experiencing Portugal's capture of lands and peoples in West Africa and the Canary Islands with their small number of Christian converts; now, when the Catholic nations battled the Muslim Ottoman Empire, the enemy soldiers they fought and captured were often Orthodox Christian Janissary soldiers. Janissary prisoners of war, when captured by Catholic nations, were not to be enslaved pursuant to Papal Bulls.

The conquistadors arrogantly avowed that the native people of the New World were cannibals, idol worshipers, engaged in human sacrifice, heathens, savages, etc.; to endow Spain with the right to argue that these New World natives were not Christian, and, thereby empower Spain with the authority to enslave the pagan Native-American Indians pursuant to Papal Bulls. If the conquistadors admitted that the people of the New World were Christian, then Spain and Portugal were in violation of these Papal Bulls and would have been subject to severe ecclesiastical penalties for the enslavement of Christians. The quandary the conquistadors stumbled upon was pervasive evidences of Christianity in the New World. Such as, the 1546 letter Bishop de las Casas received from Father Hernández, which the Bishop linked to the teachings of St. Thomas. Bishop de las Casas's reference to St. Thomas two and a half centuries before Fray Mier's Guadalupe Sermon demonstrates that Fray Mier did not invent the St. Thomas theory; nor his declarations that: "Throughout America, monuments and vestige evidences of Christianity were found, according to the unanimous testimony of the missionaries." And, "The Indians had in their power (as the missionaries in Veracruz gave in written testimony to the celebrated Fray Gregorio García) the entire Bible in images and hieroglyphic figures, they confused them with the passage of time, they put into practice the Scripture's histories, and confused their own history and their religion."

How were Spanish and Portuguese royalty, and Catholic Church hierarchy to deal with this Christian enigma? The enmity toward Bishop de las Casas, during the 1500's, was resurrected in the attacks against Fray Mier for his 1794 Guadalupe Sermon. Fray Mier unveiled suppressed history of ancient American Christianity in the personas of St. Thomas and Guadalupe-Tonantzin.

Papal Bulls of 1434 to 1514 prohibiting the enslavement of Christians, whether Catholic or Eastern Orthodox, with missionary testimonies of Native-American Christianity gives reason to hypothesize that a political travesty was crafted. Had the conquistadors of America admitted that Indians were Christian, Catholic Canon Law would have forbidden them to enslave, to unjustly wage war, or to ravage the land and wealth of America that flowed to greedy Spain and Portugal. The brutal conquest of the Americas was legalized in blatant violation of the Catholic Church's Papal Bulls on slavery by obliterating and hiding the ancient Christianity of the Americas.

THE CATHOLIC CHURCH EVANGELIZES THE AMERICAN-INDIANS

The anthropologist, Baron von Humboldt, does not use the word evangelize, but he does describe the beginning of the process of evangelism of native Christians to convert to the Catholic Church. "By the time, in which the calendar was composed, Christianity was confused with Mexican mythology; the missionaries not only tolerated they even assisted, up to a certain point, the mix of ideas, symbols, and worship. They persuaded the indigenous people that the Gospel, in the most remote times, had already been preached in America; they sought its signs in the Aztec ritual with the same ardor that the learned suppose, in our days, in devoting themselves to the study of the Sanskrit, or in discussing the extensive analogy between Greek mythology and that which originated on the borders of the Ganges and the Bourampouter."[14]

The mix of ideas, symbols, worship, the overlay of Spain's Virgin of Guadalupe on the Native-Mexican tradition of Tonantzin, and the belief that the Gospel of Jesus Christ had already been preached in the West Indies (Americas) by the Apostle St. Thomas, were the propositions of Fray Mier's December 12, 1794 Guadalupe Sermon. Mixing ideas, symbols, worship, the St. Thomas tradition, and overlaying Spain's Virgin of Guadalupe image on the Mexican Tonantzin hastened evangelization by Catholic missionaries of Mexican's who practiced a different Christian faith to become Roman Catholic Christians.

THE MIER PARADOX SUMMARY

The self-contradictory propositions of Fray Mier's Guadalupe Sermon seem absurd to believe that a New World isolated from the Old World had Hebrew-Christian principles of faith practiced by pagan Indians before the arrival of the Roman Catholic missionaries; however, when investigated and explained his statements and writings prove to be well founded and true. The following incidents corroborate the hypothesis of a political travesty by the royalty of Spain and Portugal and Catholic Church hierarchy of New Spain to wipe out and hide Mexico's pre-Cortés Christian history, giving historicity to the paradox.

- The writings of Fray Mier, Bishop de las Casas, and many other early Catholic scholars and missionaries, evidence roots of Christianity in The Americas before 1492. Fray Mier states: "The Deists themselves today confess that the ancient preaching of the Gospel in America is beyond doubt." The inquisition of Fray Mier during his life, his defense, and Mexico's modern esteem for Fray Mier; even though hidden, is a paradox bearing witness to the political labyrinth of religion in Mexico. The scandal Fray Mier caused was to raise his voice with the shout (a closing comment at the end of his "Farewell Letter to the Mexicans): "My fellow countrymen stop howling and go study this issue." In short, Be proud of your ancient Christian heritage. A heritage suppressed at the time of Fray de las Casas to quiet the conflict over slavery. To be suppressed again more than 250 years later, to silence Fray Mier's cry for equality of all Mexicans; which became the first shout leading to revolution and Mexico's Independence from Spain.

- Mexico's native people had massive libraries of hieroglyphic written paper folios. Fernando Ixtlilxochitl writes that in 1520

Hernán Cortés ordered the royal archives of all New Spain burned—"in such a way that the entire royal archives throughout New Spain were burned, that was one of the greatest losses this land had, because with this all memory of their antiquities and other things that were like scriptures and memories were lost from this time: the books from the homes were the best and the most ingenious that there was in this land."[15] Fray Mier writes in his "Apologia" that beginning in 1526 Bishop Juan Zumárraga, Mexico's first bishop, made it his religious duty to exterminate with the help of the missionaries the hieroglyphic manuscripts of the Indians for being witchcraft and demons. He raised the Aztecs' libraries into mountains of manuscripts, which he threw to the flames. And as the Indians redid their manuscripts or hid them to conserve the history of their nation, the missionaries made use of converted Christian children, in whom were invested a mistaken zeal, to rob their parents' manuscripts. Fray Mier's writes in his "Apologia": "Thus this Bishop caused a loss, as irreparable as immense, to the Nation and to the Literary Republic."[16]

- Fray de las Casas's 1547 handbook on slavery was confiscated and destroyed by a Royal edict issued in both Spain and New Spain. The content of the handbook is unknown. However, to have provoked such universal enforcement Fray de las Casas had to have documented violations of Papal Bull prohibitions against enslavement of Christians.

- The Virgin of Guadalupe was a transplant vital to the success of Catholic evangelism in New Spain. Ancient Mexican Christianity had fallen into idolatry, illustrated by the Mexicans idol worship of Tonantzin, Mother of the true God. Spain transplanted to the heart of Mexico their Virgin of Guadalupe in the amended image of Mexico's ancient native goddess Tonantzin. From the writings of Fray Mier, one can speculate that this was one piece of a conspiracy to hide Mexico's Christianity and to convert its disciples to the Catholic Church. Spain's dark-faced Virgin of Guadalupe was a natural substitute for Mexico's ancient Tonantzin. Fray Mier's "Apologia" has a summary history of Mexico's Virgin of Guadalupe and its origin in Spain. Further study of the

Virgin of Guadalupe's roots in Spain, beyond what Fray Mier wrote, adds credence to his Mexican Guadalupe conspiracy. According to Spain's legend, circa 1326, a herdsman, Gil Cordero, found buried on the banks of Spain's Guadalupe River a wooden image of the Virgin Mary. The image was black, stained by the earth in which it had been buried for hundreds of years by Visigoth Christians escaping the Moorish invasion of Spain. Spain's Virgin of Guadalupe is now enshrined in the Guadalupe Monastery of Cáceres, Extremadura, Spain. Extremadura was the birthplace of many early Spanish conquistadors and emigrants to Mexico. The legend includes stories that Christopher Columbus visited the Virgin of Guadalupe shrine before leaving to discover the New World and again upon returning from his first voyage of discovery; and, also that he carried a replica of the image on his voyages. At that time, Spain's Cathedral of the Virgin of Guadalupe was second only to Santiago de Compostela as a pilgrimage destination. Queen Isabella I of Castile visited the Virgin of Guadalupe Cathedral most years of her sovereign reign as Queen of Spain from 1474 to 1504. The black face of Spain's Virgin of Guadalupe was painted in Mexico with a brown face likely to fit the Virgin of Guadalupe to the racial profile of native Mexicans. The parallel between the Virgin of Guadalupe discovery stories of herdsman Gil Cordero, 1326, in Spain and the Mexican shepherd Juan Diego, 1531, is more than coincidental. The black face and the root of the Virgin of Guadalupe in Extremadura, homeland of the Spanish conquistadors contributed to the common-sense transplant of the image from Spain to Mexico. Fray Mier wrote in his "Apologia": "The monks of Our Father Saint Francis, who were the first who came to prune this vineyard for the Lord, determined to substitute analogous images to their name or history so that they were more suitable to their fiestas and motifs, though not idolatrous in abuse or intention." A perfect model, of the first Catholic missionaries pruning and analogous substituting of images, is the testimony of Fray Mier on the grafting of the Spanish Virgin of Guadalupe onto the Mexican Tonantzin, Mother of the true God. The outcome was a success to Catholic evangelism. Vestiges of ancient Mexican Christianity became invisible, and the Virgin of Guadalupe is today the most visited religious shrine in Mexico.

- Savage meets civilization and kindness. Fray Bartolomé de las Casas in his work, *Brevísima relación de la destrucción de las Indias*, ("A Very Brief Account of the Destruction of the Indies"), first published 1552, turns upside down our understanding of Europe's conquest of the Americas. His account begins by profiling the native Americans as Christians who serve the God who created them: "(M)ore humble, more patient, more peaceful, and quiet; without grudges nor hustles, not lustful, not complaining, without rancor, without hatred, without coveting vengeance that there is in the world." And, "Into these gentle sheep and of the aforementioned qualities thus endowed by their maker and creator: entered the Spanish since then they knew them as most cruel wolves and tigers and lions of many hungry days."[17] To Fray de las Casas the Spanish were savages, while the Indians were their sheep to feed upon. He estimates that 15 million native peoples died within the first forty years of the Spanish conquest of the Americas. The "Very Brief Account" by Fray de las Casas reads like a historical holocaust. The acts of genocide he describes wiped out a civilization, ravaged the culture, and erased vestiges of Christianity. In addition to the Spanish savages described by Bishop de las Casas, the introduction of common European diseases into the Americas killed millions of people, destroying the culture, the civilization, and eradicating memories of ancient Christianity.

THE MIER PARADOX CONCLUSION

Catholic Papal Bulls on slavery, the burning of written records destroying Mexican historicity, the loss of the record keepers and millions of other inhabitants to infectious European diseases, and the political charade of substituting Spain's Christian images to replace preexisting New World Christian images leaves us with the writings of the early Catholic missionaries as the only surviving historical evidence of Christianity in ancient America outside of *The Book of Mormon*.

CHAPTER 3 NOTES

1. Cuddon, J.A., *A Dictionary of Literary Terms*, 3rd ed. Blackwell, 1991.

2. Paz, Octavio. *Sor Juana Inés de la Cruz o Las trampas de la fe.* Barcelona: Editorial Seix Barral, S. A. 1982, p. 48.

3. Ibid., p. 58.

4. Ibid., p. 63.

5. Paz, Octavio. *El laberinto de la soledad.* Mexico, D. F.: Fondo de Cultura Economica, First Edition 1950, 1983, p. 148.

6. de las Casas, Fray Barolomé, ed. Prologue, Appendices, and Notes by Edmundo O'Gorman, with collaboration of Jorge Alberto Manrique. *Los indios de México y Nueva España, Antología.* Mexico, D. F. Editorial Porrua, S. A., Sixth Edition 1987.

7. Bataillon, Marcel, trans. by J. Coderich and J. A. Martínez Schrem. *Estudios sobre Bartolomé de las Casas*, Serie Universitario, Historia/Ciencia/Sociedad 127. Barcelona: Ediciones Península, First Edition: 1976. The original French edition, *Études sur Batolomé de las Casas*, published by Centre de Recherches de l'Institut d'Études Hispaniques, Paris, 1965.

8. Bataillon, op. cit., 218-227.

9. de las Casas, op. cit., 56-57.

10. de las Casas, op. cit., 57.

11. Maxwell, John Francis. *Slavery and the Catholic Church.* Chichester & London: Barry Rose Publishers in association with The Anti-Slavery Society for the Protection of Human Right, 1975, pp. 51-66.

12. Ibid., p. 52.

13. Ibid., p. 58, 59, and 60.

14. Humboldt. op. cit PLATE XXXVI, 311-313.

15. de Alva Cortés Ixtlilxóchitl, Fernando. *Historia de la nación chichimeca.* Linkgua ediciones S.L., Barcelona, 2008. Original written circa 1611, p. 226-227.

16. González, José Eleuterio. Juan Peña, ed. *Biografia del benemérito mexicano D.Servando Teresa de Mier Noriega y Guerra.* Monterey, Mexico: José Saenz, published, 1876. Commemorative Edition, Facsimile of the Original, Government of the State of Nuevo Leon, Autonomous University of Nuevo Leon, Sesquicentennial of the Death of Father Mier, 1827-1977, 1977., p.40.

17. de las Casas, Bartolomé, Prologue Olga Camps. *Brevísima relación de la destrucción de las Indias.* Mexico, D. F.: Editorial Fontamara, S. A., 1984. First edition 1552, Sevilla; p. 33-34.

SECTION II

FRAY SERVANDO TERESA DE MIER'S LETTERS & ALEXANDER VON HUMBOLDT'S CONTRIBUTION

"Eleventh Note of the Second Letter from an American," written 1811, when Mier lived in London, England, is a defiant political treatise on Spain's brutal conquest of Mexico, forced slavery, dictatorial governance and degeneration of Mexico's population and culture.

It is believed that "Farewell Letter to the Mexicans," written 1820 while Mier is imprisoned in San Juan de Ulúa Castle, expecting deportation to Spain, without access to a library nor research notes, is a revived version of his December 12, 1794, Guadalupe Sermon. Mier reveals the roots of ancient Christianity in Mexico and the evangelism of Mexicans under the guise of Extremadura, Spain's, Our Lady of Guadalupe. Mier's Guadalupe Sermon earned him a lifetime of Inquisition, incarceration, and exile.

Fray Mier writes in his Paris Memoir: "Also, Baron von Humboldt told me in Paris: 'I believed that it was an invention of the friars, and thus I said in my statistical essay; but after I have seen your curious dissertation, I see that it is not so.' "

SECTION II

CHAPTER 4

Eleventh Note of the Second Letter from an American, On the Representation to the Courts from the Consulate of Mexico [1]

FOREWORD BY EDMUNDO O'GORMAN

"Next, we give the complete text of the "Eleventh Note of The Second Letter from an American," written by Father Mier, in London, and published in *El Español*, in 1812."

"This "Note" can be considered as a small independent essay in which Father Mier takes up with the motive of the Representation sent to the Courts of Cádiz from the Consulate of Mexico, on the grand theme that in another occasion I have called the calumny of America.[2] The Consulate echoes the tendency then very generalized in Europe of considering all that is American as congenitally degenerated. To said tendency belonged Paw [sic], Buffon, Raynal, and Robertson, to mention only the most notable, without need to forget Hegel, whose participation in this movement I have underlined in the previously cited book. Father Mier summarizes the writers that, like Calvijero, Feijóo, and Carti, opposed the thesis of the degeneration of America, as can be appreciated by the text here published.[3] But what is interesting is that Mier with other polemicists of American origin are placed in an intermediate situation, because even when he rejects with violence and indignation the thesis of the degeneration by nature of what is American; he accepts to a good degree the culpable degeneration due to the Spanish conquest and colonization. The polemic has clearly converted to a political subject. The Consulate of Mexico, in one way, wields the thesis to avoid conceding equality of political representation of the Colonies with the Metropolis, and Father Mier, in another way, uses it as proof and justification for independence. Such, in the end, is the great interest that this short treatise has."

ELEVENTH NOTE OF THE SECOND LETTER FROM AN AMERICAN BY FRAY SERVANDO TERESA DE MIER

This consists of the Court's Diaries from the month of September; but the Americans could not declare in them all that they knew, so as not to risk an inevitable persecution of their correspondents or of those who might believe such things. By letters received on the same Miño ship, that had arrived much before this business, they had been instructed that the Representation (from the Consulate of Mexico) was the work of the European Corps with only the names of the three completely illiterate entities of the Consulate, and that from these same was the money sent to gain votes in the Courts and to give a salary to a journalist who works to make his opinion be that of the public. Hence the difference of conduct in the Courts the 15th and the 17th days and hence having commenced Cancelada,[4] a journalist worthy of them, to write without subscription or earnings as he says, his *Telégrafo Americano* with more lies, than words, as a Deputy of the Courts is demonstrating in the *Censor*, from Number 18. The only truth is the confession made there that the Representation was from all the patriots, a name that in Mexico the Europeans profane by taking it on themselves.

I did not need such notices, because all that they accumulate are old Spanish calumnies against their victims who they hate like all tyrants. They are the same species that the Prussian Paw [sic] has divulged with so much pomp of erudition,[5] who, when he found himself repeatedly confused by various European scholars, gave as a final response that his Spanish correspondent had deceived him. Muñoz in his 1st Book on the *Historia del Nuevo Mundo*[6] adopted that doctrine, even though convinced by a letter from the Paraguayan Iturri,[7] he thought to retract it: the traitor Estala repeated it in his *Viajer*[8] with more acrimony to take revenge upon Dr. Mier who had impugned him. At the beginning of the Courts, they reproduced the same insults in the *Observador* and Deputy Feliu refuted them there and in the *Cosmopolita*, No. 1. The damage was already done by the Italian, Carli in his *Cartas Americanas*[9] and in these notes by the French Langles;[10] and finally by the Veracruzano Clavijero in Volume 4 of his *Storia del Messico Antico*, [sic][11] and the Anglo-

American Jefferson.[12]

Indeed, what other thing, does the Representation suppress? They began weaving the *History of the Conquest of Mexico*, to the discredit of Solís[13] and the rest of the Spanish historians; the Indians appear equal to the brutes: hordes of savages, wandering tribes without cities, without stability, without agriculture, without arts; therefore, all these advances are due to the old and new Peninsular Spaniards. This is all the consequence of an atmosphere that stupefies, degenerates, and degrades, so that the Europeans thereby bastardize themselves.

The best proof of this would be their Representation. But is not all this already refuted, even the evidence? Can anyone believe four Tobacconists who speak of that which they did not see against the testimony of more than a hundred Spaniards of every exception, who wrote the opposite, going into a thousand details, exhibiting the designs of the temples, informing the Emperor himself, such as Cortés[14] and even sending him the plans of the cities? Why if the land is so bad, so hard to stay in it and so much effort to go there illegally, does one expose themselves to the penalties if the laws prohibit their emigration? I will bet that of the 74,000 Europeans that are in New Spain, 70,000 deserve to be allotted to the military for ten years according to those warnings. They will not tell me how the Spanish, who had seen nothing but Gothic cities and temples in their land, tortured drain boards for the streets, birds' nests or pigsties with roof-tiles for houses, suddenly built magnificent cities and temples, very wide and level streets, and beautiful houses without roof-tile? They learned it from there, since they have only stolen and made others better a long time later in the Spanish ports of Cádiz, Barcelona, Bilbao, etc. that traded with America.

Have these men not read that all this is what Cortés does not stop pondering in his *Cartas al Emperador*?[15] Was he by chance a prophet for already saying that which then did not exist? It is true that he tore it down and burned everything to capture Mexico, but he writes to the Emperor in 1525 that to rebuild it he returned the government of the two districts of San Juan de Tenochtitlan and Santiago de Tlaltelolco[16] to the Indians, which he crowded with so many people that in a year the city was already rebuilt with many thousands of homes. He does not say it, but other historians yes, that by attending to this, to which Cortés gave the highest urgency the Indians neglected their seed sowing and there followed such hunger that 24,000 perished. Other Spaniards did not oppress any less the Indians in other parts, where they worked for nothing without giving them anything, says Torquemada,[17] and that this hard labor, *operibus duris luti et lateris* ("hard bondage, in mortar, and in brick"),[18] caused them such mortality in 1540, that of the four parts of the Indians three perished.[19] What will I say of the immense work of draining Mexico? These Indians, who had no arts, but who had built seven cities in a lagoon of 52 square leagues, knew how to drain Mexico City with only the engineers that the King of Texcoco sent them. And the Spaniards could not do it in 1630 not even after bringing from Paris the Engineer Boot and the King ordered the City moved to the heights of Santa Fe. Fortunately, it did not rain in five years and an earthquake dispersed the waters. The Spaniards tried to divert the waters of seven rivers, that entered the lagoon to prevent another flood, to raise the Guadalupe and Mexicaltzingo causeways, and to raise the floor of Mexico on the bed of Lakes Texcoco and Zumpango; and to shorten the contoured heights of Mexico's slopes opening the Huehuetoca precipice, drilling through the mountains and making a larger reservoir than those made by the monarchs of Babylon and Egypt. The Indians did all this, 30,000 of the 200,000 that worked daily dying in these works, shifting by week. This consists of printed judicial pieces printed in Mexico in the history of the drainage.[20]

And that after all this, the Europeans have the nerve to say that all this is owed to them? At the least they will say that some of these places did not exist at the time of the Indians. Yes: these having an appropriate distance where the artisans and rich lived, they were scattered in country homes to look after the agriculture, to which they were so dedicated that Cortés did not cease from highly praising it. Of this economy that the American Olavide in his *Evangelio en triunfo* ("Gospel in Triumph"), Volume 4[21] wanted so much that the Spanish should adopt, they had no idea, and under the pretext that it was necessary for brainwashing them, they tore them from their homes and piled the Indians into new towns set on infected sites, because the conquistadores reserved for themselves the best for their haciendas. This transplantation of thousands of families, that razed their homes left them reduced to misery, was executed with such rigor and cruelty that one cannot contain the tears to read its account by Torquemada.[22] The pain of the Indians came to such an extreme, that some killed themselves, something so unheard of among them it astonished the whole land. Never, says the historian, could one adopt a more disastrous and murderous measure. These are the deeds of the Peninsular Spaniards in America.

Their tyranny is that which has caused in the Indians the kind of stupidity with which they insulted them. But the wise men of Europe know that they have done nothing but formulate nonsensical theories, as if they were speaking of absolute savages without monuments nor writings, but the Indians in New Spain had magnificent libraries, of hieroglyphics it is true, except that they read very well from right to left, and if they heard a *Nahuatlato* or "Interpreter" explain them, they would see that they do not stop speaking like when we are reading. The Emperor Carlos V sent to Mexico as the first Bishop Fray Juan de Zumárraga,[23] *"for having had a good hand in the commission of casting out the witches of Vizcaya."* these are the words of Maestro Dávila, Royal Chronicler, in his *Historia Eclesiástica de las Indias.*[24] Such a Bishop continued to see his witches in the Mexican hieroglyphics that he made it his duty to exterminate as magic figures, searching them out with great diligence. His Franciscan missionaries served him in this with much zeal, staying the Saint, carrying it out on the same day in all the cities, in 1526 they burned the magnificent *Teocallis* or "Temples" of the Indians where their libraries were. That of the City of Texcoco where the University of Anáhuac was, lifted like a mountain, says Don Fernando de Alba,[25] when they took it out to burn. Fortunately, the Prince's librarian later gave us in Castilian a Catalog of what it contained, and in that he ought to be very accustomed by the obligation that he had to answer the inquiries of all the courts. Another Royal Prince Don Fernando Ixtlilxóchitl,[26] who inherited from his forefathers many of these Manuscripts, escapees from the flames, fashioning histories to explain them and he had the precaution of presenting before the 80 Justice Elders who swore to the conformity of that which he had written with the hieroglyphics that he exhibited, and the poems of the nation that were another fountain of the history. Many other Indian gentlemen such as Tezozómoc,[27] who found himself in Mexico at the time of its conquest, and Chipalmáin,[28] etc., etc., also wrote elegant histories in their Nahuatl language, and in Castilian. Boturini[29] cites them in his Museum which exists in Mexico, although much plundered, Clavijero,[30] Gama,[31] the Father Sahagún[32] (from whom there exists a 4 Volume *Historia Universal de Nueva España*,) and Torquemada, who preferred their accounts to those of the Spanish, for having found them more exact and truthful, since among the

Indians the historian that lied suffered the penalty of death. Carlos IV at the request of the Royal Academy of History ordered the Count of Revilla Gigedo being his Viceroy to bring to Spain some of these writings, and so they sent him 30 written volumes. If the Indians have not proceeded to write, it is because the Spaniards suppressed Santiago College,[33] where the Franciscan monks gave studies to the natives.

In these entire works one sees the excellence of their government and of their laws accommodated to the climate and consequent inclinations. I could not talk of them without doing so in volumes: it is enough to say that a wise man as accredited as Count Carli,[34] after having profoundly examined the government of the Incas, concludes that one considers possible a government so perfect only because it has existed. The goodness of the Mexican laws exists in the testimony of the Code of the Indies,[35] where the King of Spain orders they should keep and live according to them, because, having examined them, they have seemed very good. Wine or pulque, for example, was not allowed among them except with great precautions, and he who became drunk, if he was noble his hair was shaved, and his house was demolished, if a plebeian, he had the penalty of death. The Spanish to the contrary, in the interest of a sordid profit, opened everywhere free temples to Bacchus, and the Indians, filled with oppression and bitterness, gave themselves over without limit to drunkenness, to stun their pain. In vain the parish priests have opposed this with the liveliest zeal: The King's Administrators who take from that innumerable perennial criminal fountain, a substantial income, closed their mouths with the embezzlement passed on to the Royal Household. Thus, the demoralization of the Indians, as is their ignorance, was the work of the Spanish.

But that on which they are most insistent is in the lack of agriculture (that they also, as we already saw, destroyed), with the intention to make believe a depopulated New Spain and to refute Casas[36] when he assures, his countrymen that in 40 years they caused 12 to 15 million men to die. Certainly, an admirable thing, that the Spaniards want us to believe them, that the living Emperor Hadrian supported 50 million in the arid and dry little corner of Spain, and they do not care that New Spain might have even a few more, four times more than in Old Spain, New Spain where there is not sterility in the women and the land produces 400 for one. — Lord, they that had no oxen—. But by chance does the land there need immense fertilizers as in Europe? I have seen the sowing of the Indians done with their hoes, beside those of the Spanish worked with plows, and the Indians do not grow less than them in foliage and beauty, some such as Cortés says that all New Spain was made a fertile garden. The Indians support themselves with little, because the climate does not demand either much nor very heavy food, and for this they were frightened by the voraciousness of the Spaniards. — Alright: but the human sacrifices — . These are the voices of tyrants, responded Casas to Sepúlveda,[37] because there were only a few. In effect, only prisoners of war were sacrificed to the gods, as in almost all the nations of the world before the Gospel, and in Spain with horrible cruelty which one reads in Strabo's Geography.[38] In Spain they also sacrificed the children according to the rite of the Carthaginians, and it is known that they ate their parents when they became elderly. There were no sacrifices in New Spain until the Mexicans introduced them: nor do I believe they ever did them in the kingdom of Texcoco, and much less in Guatemala, where the death penalty was unknown. Anyway, from Acosta,[39] it appears that they already had many meetings in the Kingdom of Mexico, to abolish the bloody sacrifices. — But, and the wars they did? — I read the History of Spain, and I do not see, since the most remote times, anything but a web of civil and foreign wars, so bloody that it amazes me how men could have survived, and with all, they say that there were 50 million.

If I were to write a dissertation to propose, to prove the immense population of New Spain, I would pile up the historians' texts that they saw it and they were able to know it with certainty and by the census of the personal taxes that they paid to their Emperors, and later to the Spaniards. I would cite the registers of the Franciscan Monks whom it appeared, according to Torquemada,[40] that they alone had baptized six million by 1540. But here, I will infer with some calculations from the losses of the numerous ten plagues that fell upon the Indians, based upon the venerable Father, Fray Toribio Benavente or Motolinía.[41] How many Indians do they accept died in the conquest of Anáhuac that they defended inch by inch against the Spaniards, and the Mexicans who later helped them after the conquest? The historians say that in Mexico City alone a million and a half died, because in addition to the many who entered the city for its defense, the city had 120,000 houses of five to ten inhabitants, of which only a few 30,000 souls remained alive, the piles of the dead reaching to the roofs, when the Spaniards entered the streets. But I want to give them cheap that in all Anáhuac the war did not cost them only those million and a half men. We already previously counted 24,000 dead in the reconstruction of Mexico City from general fatigue and work without pay in all the cities, three-quarters of their population were employed in construction in 1540: and more than 30,000 died in the construction of the drainage system. There were another two great fatalities in the same century, when they absolutely prohibited the regional drink pulque and the sowing of white corn, according to the *Historia Civil de México*, in Latin as well as in Castilian, by Sir Andrés Cavo.[42] In *Estudio de Armas de México*, Becerra[43] deals with the 18 *matlazahuatl* or plagues[44] that they have suffered since then, and the scholarly astronomer Gama,[45] Official of the Viceroyalty Secretariat, in his erudite letters to Cavo refers to the number of the dead in each epidemic, evidenced by the Indians' tax archives.

In none did the dead fall below 140,000, not including, as one supposes, the women, the children up to 16 years, the old above 60, the Tlaxcaltecans,[46] and the nobles who do not pay taxes. We must add smallpox, this fatal gift that Spain now and again gives us, and that starting from Veracruz rapidly carries the most horrible desolation to the farthest corners of America inhabited by the savages, which causes entire nations to disappear in one blow. The first was carried by Pánfilo de Narváez's Negro,[47] in 1520, and Cortés tells the Emperor, that having taken exact information, in the Mexican Empire alone three million died, including their Emperor Coanacoátzin. The second did not take much longer, and Torquemada says that 800,000 Indians died. How many would measles take away, another gift from Spain? How much syphilis, also a gift from Spain? Yes, from Spain. I know well that the Spaniards and Italians call it *Gallic*, as if it came from the French, they call it *Neapolitan Malaise*, and the Germans call it *Spanish Scabies*, when all their armies, fighting in Naples, suffered its ravages, the year 1482. There were no Americans there, the time had not even come for Columbus's first voyage, but the tyrant Oviedo[48] later attributed it to America, because from there came the medicines lignum vitae and sarsaparilla, so from there ought to come the disease, as if mercury were not from here. Thus, they have always paid America its dues; but Brazil's Sánchez, Santa Fe's Valverde, Germany's Shuediau, Veracruz's Clavijero, and Langles, Director of France's National Library, have already demonstrated that in Europe this plague was very ancient, and far from receiving it, transmitted it to America.[49] If we add those buried in the mines, under the Indian porters' bundles, under the tyranny of the territorial partitions, under the cruelty of the holders of the encomiendas,[50] from the slavery and transport of slaves to the Spanish Peninsula, affliction that the missionaries so deplored as exterminators of their neophytes, and we see that there still remains in New Spain even more than two million, according to the calculations of Humboldt.[51] How many and how large must have been their previous population?

From what the *Breve Relación de la Destrucción de las Indias* reckons, which Casas directs to the Sovereign,[52] the Europeans knew that the Archbishop of Santo Domingo, Royal Chronologist, Dávila Padilla, in his *Historia de Santo Domingo de México,*[53] dedicated to Felipe II, affirms in the Life of Casas that said account of this, is nothing but a compendium of the summary which the conquistadors made in Sevilla, with the attestation of how many respectable people were then in America, and by the same processes that the conquistadors did to one another. They knew that Remesal,[54] a very truthful author, a contemporary of Casas and an eye witness, says in his Life, *Historia de Santo Domingo de Chiapa,* that in this account he cannot admire enough, the prudence and moderation of the Bishop how he chose to tell the King of the least cruel acts of the conquistadors. Least Cruel! Yes, when they print the three folio volumes which remain, and in which Casas wrote the true history of the Conquest, they will tremble. Could not all that he says be proved in an authentic way by the laws of the Indies? Each one has been passed to restrain a criminal excess of the Spaniards. I have read accounts by the King's Ministers, the same as those of Casas. Much of it was written by the historians, who are printed; but I am certain that almost all are on that part mutilated, because I have seen the originals of many. Don Juan Bautista Muñoz[55] alone, extracted from the archives and libraries more than 200 folio volumes of complete Histories of America, whose exactitude and truthfulness cannot be compared with the printed ones: and for this they have not permitted that they are. They knew, anyway, those alien Europeans, that there is an express law in the Code of the Indies that nothing is allowed to be printed over there regarding them: which is observed with such rigor that Don Ignacio Carrillo was not able in 1801 to print a thing so simple as the *Cronología de los Virreyes de México.*[56] If by chance, something ever is permitted to be printed, the Government will prohibit it, such as the *Escudo de Armas de México* by Cabrera,[57] if the Inquisition has not already advanced, as with Casas's *Relación*. Clavijero could not achieve a printing in Castilian, even in Spain, his *Historia Antigua de México*, so celebrated in Europe, however much; Muñoz consulted by the Council of the Indies, urged by his impression says that his accuser the ex-Spanish-Jesuit Diosdado, was in no way comparable to him.[58] Therefore, he was obligated to translate it into Italian, adding, in order to have it passed even so, notes against his own text, against Casas and against his intention, notes which have surprised with reason Florentino the editor of Carli's *Cartas Americanas.*[59]

When Liberty opens the curtain to these iniquitous mysteries, the conduct of the Spaniards in the Americas will appear in all their blackness, even though it would be enough to have seen that which they did to their Kings. Because did they not owe favors to the good Moteuhzoma?[60] With everything, they killed him by terrible blows. So, say it, Fathers Sahagún and Torquemada with all the Indian authors.[61] This was the personage that the Spaniards report the Indians found dead on the Sorrowful Night,[62] and they stopped to cry over him, the Spaniards in the meanwhile capturing a temple of the Goddess of the Waters, dedicated afterwards to the Virgin, they called it, for this, of the Relief, according to Acosta, and today they call it *de los Remedios.*[63] They burned in a slow fire the feet smeared in oil of the young Emperor Cuatemoczin,[64] a torment in which his Prime Minister died, and later Cortés hanged him from a tree, in the Hibueras,[65] with seven kings, only because it fancied him, says Bernal Díaz[66] and Cortés's chaplain Gomara,[67] on this crime, finds no excuse whereby he could absolve him. They killed Catzonzin, King of Michoacán, the second in power of Anáhuac, because after a kingdom so opulent was ceded to them without war, he did not have two thousand pesos of common gold to give them. Did the unfortunate Atahualpa[68] have any other luck, after having given them for his ransom the immensity of gold that they asked? But it is not necessary to go so far back: in 1780 Túpac Amaru,[69] legitimate heir of the Inca Empire, incited by the same Spaniards to oppose the robberies and demands on the Indians by the King's Administrators took the lead of those. They caught him anyway, and after taking him to a balcony, so that he could witness the death of a hundred and so Incas, his relatives, who were hanged, and they put as a scepter in his hands, a burning iron, and on the head an iron crown, also burning, and four horses tore at his limbs, which not being able to be torn apart, the soldiers cut saber wounds. The Spaniards have written the account. It they have done this with the kings and their heirs, when they already have laws, what might they have done with the rest when they had nothing more than their whim, and were they almost all criminals taken from Spain's jails?

We will leave the ancient Spaniards and look at how the current ones of Mexico continue informing the Courts in their Representation, of the current state of New Spain. I cannot imitate the cruelty of the scene they fashion with a feather tinged in the blood of cannibals, but in substance they say: "That the Indians are as stupid as at the beginning, drunkards by instinct, lascivious in all the variations of this vice, lazy, thieves, without instruction not even in Christian Doctrine. The Castes have the same vices as that of the Indians, and they are even worse, for the money that they spend to encourage them: nevertheless, naked, without knowing shame, they are weak up to laziness, and unworthy of compassion. The Creoles are irreligious, hypocrites, squanders of the paternal wealth, an exasperated and idle nation: without any sense whatever of community, since neither the priests nor the monks comply with the obligations of their institution, etc. While half can deem themselves lower class people, without character to direct the affairs of the city, the other half leans towards independence. At the most 500,000 men, including 74,000 Europeans, can be represented. Anyway, all three classes are no more than five million automatons, or at the most orangutan monkeys. It is true that 25,000 have been seen to fight in favor of the Peninsula, apparently with valor and perseverance, but it is nothing, but the apathy and insensibility of machines adapted to the climate. That the district councils ought to be electives and elect the Deputies, *, 70, 71 this is, Europeans to Europeans, to protect the Indians and Castes. The body of Europeans is that which ought to sustain itself, to uphold the Hearing, of the Viceroy Calleja y Cruz.[72] Hence, the deceived representatives have deceived the Courts, because the best government that is right for them is that, which they have by the laws of the Indies and the Council of the same."

Thus, they end as tyrants ought to end, since the Laws of the Indies, in 300 years, have not been able to correct the Indians, and have produced the Castes and Creoles, so sinful and useless, it is accurate that they be bad and execrable, since men are what the laws want them to be.

What can the tobacconists and thieving clerks pretend, but that the slavery of the Americans endures? The coup d'état test to be their Representatives in the Courts, is prodigious; the picture in which they portray them, could touch the hardest hearts of their clients: they would be the wolves advocating for the sheep, in a Congress of tigers. They were accustomed to what, the Government of Spain hearing them one believes is listening to the victims, whose sighs they were imitating. Even to still elude you, they published posters on September 16, 1808, saying that the Mexican people had seized control of the person of Iturrigaray[73] and imperiously asked for his removal from office, when the true people, a part was locked up in jails, because it intended to liberate the Viceroy, and a part wrote on the market of the European merchants, among whom not even one Creole was mixed, *hic est populus* ("These are they").[74] Venegas[75] proclaims in August of this year that finally he is going to do the justice that the people are asking him for, there is time, and while the true people of Mexico, that the 3rd day had attempted their fourth conspiracy to undo themselves from his most abhorrent tyranny, and he is raising hundreds to the scaffolds and going to the forts. For this the Europeans when they have read discussions in the Courts, of the true Americans, have torn and ground underfoot the newspapers, and in the drunkenness of their vengeance, they vomited, to refute the Deputies, this infamous torrent of calumnies and horrors, with which they have made evident the hatred that wants to conceal their hypocrisy.

What a pity that the troops don't know the favor these 74,000 gallants do to their bravery, that vilely quartered between Veracruz and Mexico City, they are encouraged against their countrymen, with the unworthy means of the excommunications, proclamations and lying gazettes, while they celebrate as much the victories as the defeats, saying that in the end all are less enemies! Vile rag-pickers! The Indians as Europeans like Mexicans are as valiant as the Spaniards in the histories. The Castes, mixed of one and another, clearly, they have bettered in valor, crossing with the ferocity of the Africans. The mild American climate, may have sweetened the character of the Creoles, as did the climate of Spain the toughness of the Northern Barbarians, your progenitors, but it did not extinguish the warrior germ. The despotism that has weakened the Lion of Spain has brought down the Eagle of Anáhuac; but liberty will restore elasticity to the soul, and ye, if ye do not abandon the field, thou shalt loose thy impulses of vengeance that deserve thy insults.[76]

What do they do there these 74,000 good men, put among six million rascals? Doth thou not pay attention to what one saithe: tell me with whom thou walketh I will tell thee who thou art? Get thee out: there are enough beautiful examples that are left for us to imitate, at the east and west entrances of the Cathedral of Mexico City, are the portraits of the many Saints who have gone from Spain beautified by the hands of the Inquisitors with flames and stigmas. What unfortunate spell detains thee even at the cost of thy life in this fatal climate which thou represent degraded?

Yes, this cursed zone flowing immense rivers of gold and silver has changed the face of Europe, and impoverished Spain, where previously one was called to mass with a bull's horn, they manufactured the receptacles for the Holy Sacrament with willow twigs [Calancha, *Historia de San Agustín del Perú*,][77] the Kings of Aragon and Castile waged a desolating war for 36 duros two reals, a King such as Don Enrique pawned his jacket for a shoulder of mutton to have dinner, a Queen such as Doña Juana was prosecuted by the Cortes because she daily threw a quarter of a chicken into her cooking pot, another such Grandee of Spain, Knight of Santiago and Marquis of the Oaxaca Valley, and they gave him in fiefdom many places and many thousands of vassals throughout Mexico, instead of the Kingdom of Michoacán which he did not want. (Gomara, *Historia de Indias*.)[78]

This cursed climate: that has produced maize (a term from the Haitian language) by which three-fourths of Spain's regions sustain themselves, eating flat-cakes or cornbread, and corn flour drink from ground corn, christened with the name of porridge and farina: that has produced coffee, codfish, turkeys, potatoes, of which all of Europe sustains itself, yams or sweet potatoes; that only caught on in Málaga, the prickly pear, peppers of all classes, devouring even the spiciest, many species of beans, squashes, tomatoes and chocolate (both Mexican terms), from which the Spaniards make their delights, and sugar not only in abundance, but it came from Brazil to the Canary and Balearic Islands, it was not from Granada as is already demonstrated in one of the Memorandum of the Royal Academy of Lisbon. Cursed climate: that produces elk and tapir hide, the otters, the bison, the furs from vicuna and beaver, and cotton, with which they cover and wrap themselves: the indigo, the scarlet grain, woods from Campeche and Brazil, that give the dyes for their cloths, etc., sarsaparilla, lignum-vitae, guayule, copaiba, quinine, a thousand balms, resins and drugs which heal them, mahogany, and a thousand exquisite woods which furnish their homes; the pearls, the topazes, the emeralds, the diamonds, etc., which adorn them. Even that which America received, such as cattle, it gives back with interest, in the immensity of hides from which all Europe gets its shoes.

And, the men? The depopulation which the Spaniards lament is owed to their, wars all over Europe, from the ambition of Carlos V and Felipe II, and to the revolt in their time of the communities of Castile, and with the Moors; to their Inquisition, which deprived them of Flanders and Holland; to the sudden expulsion of so many millions of agricultural Moors, and of Indian merchants, to their exclusive greed, as Estrada[79] has proven to their barbarism which depopulated America, from where people would have flowed back to the Peninsula, to their ignorance, to their abysmal Government, to 22 shared causes which Gándara (*Del bien y mal de España*) points out[80] all without any fault of America. Nothing but a handful of adventurers conquered America, paying the cost of the expeditions of Columbus, with the sale of slaves they brought to Spain. This is the way they desolated the Antilles, populated according to Herrera,[81] by three million, and Campeche, from where in only one trip, they brought 48 ship loads of slaves, a maiden sold there for a cheese, to choose among a hundred, and giving a hundred maidens for one horse (Remesal).[82] In 1612, what Torquemada ended up writing, there were not more than 8,000 Spaniards in Mexico, including the Creoles. If this was 130 years after the Conquest, where was this ponderous emigration?[83] What has happened afterwards, despite the Government's prohibitions, is the flight from misery that for every abuse for its remedy, and they should be grateful to have found it, for themselves and for Spain, since half of them only subsist from the aid that their relatives send them. To have someone in America is considered here like a letter of credit. These are the evils that the Spaniards have caused who both curse their climate and insult their subordinates.

Americans! Ye have heard the injuries: The Courts have not wanted to do us justice, therefore we have the right of taking by our hand. Your [sic] demons hasten to purge the Promised Land of monsters, in time these ungrateful Indians will return to eating their garlics and onions, in the pots of your exaggerated Spain,[84] and we shall stay singing in our Homeland with Father Vaniere,

Praedium rusticum.[85]

Fertilibus gens dives agris, aurique metallo,
Ditior ingeniis hominum est, animique benigna Indole.[86]

("Nation of rich fertile land, gold metal,
Rich in the character of men endowed of a kind spirit.")

CHAPTER 4 NOTES

1. Fray Servando Teresa de Mier, (1763-1827), "La Nota
Undécima de la Segunda Carta De un Americano"), sent via the
Consulate of Mexico to the Spanish Cortes, first printed in *El
Español*, by William Glindon Publisher, London, England, 1812.
"The Eleventh Note" is translated from the Spanish text found in,
Servando Teresa de Mier, Escritos y Memorias, Biblioteca del
Estudiante 56, Prologue and Selection by Edmundo O'Gorman,
Editions of the Universidad Nacional Autónoma, México City,
1945, pp. 1-25.

2. *Fundamentos de la Historia de América*, Edmundo O'Gorman,
Imprenta Universitaria, 1942.

3. Authors referenced are most likely: Corneille de Pauw;
Georges Louis Leclerc, Count of Buffon; Guillanume Thomas
Raynal, abbé de Raynal; William Robertson; Georg Wilhelm
Friedrich Hegel; Francisco Javier Clavijero; Benito Jerónimo
Feijóo; and Count Gian Rinaldo Carli.

4. Juan López de Cancelada was a member of the Consulate
of Mexico. Cancelada had the upper hand when seeking to smear
the Mexican Deputies assigned to the Courts, as the owner and
publisher of the newspaper *El Telégrafo Americano*, Cadiz, Spain.
Fray Mier refutes Cancelada and his political party in his *Historia
de la revolución de Nueva España*.

5. Corneille de Pauw (1739-1799) was author of a well-known
book of the time, *Rechérches philosophiques sur les Américains*, Berlin,
1768-1769. Fray Mier errs when he says Paw was Prussian. He was
Dutch.

6. Juan Bautista Muñoz (1745-1799), *Historia del Nuevo Mundo*,
Tomo 1 was published in Madrid by Ibarra's widow, 1793. English
translation 1797, *The History of the New World*, London: G. G. &
Robinson, Volume 1. Muñoz was a Spanish historian appointed

1770 to be Major Cosmographer of the Indies by Carlos III, King of Spain.

7. Francisco Iturri (1738-1822), *Carta crítica*, Madrid, 1797, second edition published in Buenos Aires, 1818, was a pamphlet attacking the originality of Muñoz's writing.

8. Pedro Estala (1757-1815), *El viajero universal o noticia del mundo antiguo y nuevo, obra recopilada de los mejores viajeros* was translated to Spanish and the original corrected and illustrated with notes, Madrid, 1795-1801, 43 Volumes.

9. Count Gian Rinalda Carli, (1720-95), wrote a criticism of de Pauw's *Delle Lettere Americane*, Cosmopoli, 1780, New Edition, with an addition in Cremona, Italy 1781-1783. This was translated to Spanish by Agustín Pomposo Fernández, Mexcio City, 1821-1822, 3 Volumes.

10. Louis-Mathier Langlés (1763-1824) famous Orientalist, Conservator of the oriental manuscripts of the Imperial Library of France. It is not known to which of Langlés's many published works Fray Mier refers.

11. Francisco Javier Clavijero (1731-1787) *Storia Antica del Messico* published in Cesena Italy 1780. The English version, *The History of Mexico* was 1st published in London, 1787, 2nd in Richmond, Virginia, 1806, 3rd in London, 1807, and 4th in Philadelphia, Pennsylvania 1817. Clavijero's was born and educated in Mexico; however, his *History of Mexico* was 1st published in Spanish in 1826 in London and it was 1st published in Mexico in 1844. Fray Mier most probably studied Clavijero's *History of Mexico* in Europe and in Italian. It is today a popular and classic work in Mexico on Mexico's ancient history.

12. Jefferson, Thomas (1743-1826), third President of the United States of America 1801-1809.

13. Antonio de Solís (1610-1686), *Historia de la conquista, población y progresos de la América septentrional, conocida con el nombre de Nueva España*, Madrid 1684. Fray Mier classified Solís's *Historia* as an "epic romance in eulogy of the conquistadors," Mier's *Historia*, Vol. 1, p. xiii, 2nd Edition. Fray Mier expressed his contrary views in *Historia de la Revolución de Nueva Expaña, antiguamente, Anáhuac o verdadero origen y causa de ella con la Relación de sus progresos hasta el presente año de 1813*, London, William Glindon Publisher, 1813, 2 volumes. Written under the pseudonym, José Guerra, a second edition was printed by Mexico's Congress, Chamber of Deputies, Mexico City, 1922.

Volume 2 has an Appendix which includes documents relating to the Guadalupe Issue.

14. Hernán Cortés (1485-1547), *Cartas de Relación de Hernán Cortés*, Edition annotated by Dr. Julio Le Riverend, Editorial Concepto, S.A., Mexico City, 1983. Cortés' letters written 1519 to 1526 to the Emperor Carlos V of Spain describing the conquest of Mexico. In his First Letter, July 10, 1519, Cortés describes making landfall on the island of Cozumel. The island lies 20 miles off the coast of the Yucatán Peninsula. Cortés's *Cartas*, page 38, has the following comment: "The said island is small, and there is no river whatever on it nor stream, all the water that the Indians drink is from wells, and on it is not another thing but stones and rocks and scrub lands and the profit which the Indians of it have is apiaries, and our procurators are taking to Your Highness the sample of the honey and earth of these said apiaries that they might be seen." Bees are not mentioned by Fray Mier, but bees serve as an example of the European centric folklore Father Mier rails against in his "Eleventh Note." Ignoring this witness of Cortés on Indian culture, modern biologist, agriculturalist, historians generally credit the English with the introduction of the honeybee to the Americas at Jamestown, Virginia, 1607. Eighty-eight years after the Spanish are impressed enough when finding beehives in America to charge procurators to carry honey and earth (honeycombs) to the Spanish Emperor Carlos V. Cortés and his Spanish companions are so unfamiliar with beekeeping that they describe the honeycomb crust as "earth." The bee error is perpetuated in the Mormon historical community by Dr. Hugh Nibley in *The Collected Works of Hugh Nibley: Volume 5, The Book of Mormon–Lehi in the Desert, The World of the Jaredites; There were Jaredites*, Deseret Book Co., Salt Lake City, Utah and Foundation for Ancient Research and Mormon Studies, Provo, Utah, Copyright 1988, pp 189-194. "Concerning Deseret–The word *deseret*, we are told (Ether 2:3), "by interpretation is honeybee." "The survival of the word "bee" in the New World after the bees themselves had been left behind is a phenomenon having many parallels in the history of language, but *The Book of Mormon* nowhere mentions bees or honey as existing in the Western Hemisphere." Fray Mier's angst of an adulterated American history goes beyond the facts he cites and did not end in his lifetime.

15. See Note 14 above.

16. Ancient Mexico City was divided into four districts: Moyotla (San Juan), Tlaquechiucan (Santa María), Atzacualco (San Sebastián), and Teopan (San Pablo).Santiago Tlaltelolco was not in the four districts from Joaquín García Icazbalceta, *La antigua ciudad de México. Obras.* Volume 1, p. 369, Colectivas Agüero, Mexico, 1898.

17. Fray Juan de Torquemada (1562-1629), Los veintiune libros rituales y monarquía *indiana*, Sevilla, Spain, 1615.

18. The Latin Vulgate Bible, Exodus 1:14: "Atque ad amaritudinem perducebant vitam eorum *operibus duris luti et lateris* omnique famulatu quo in terrae operibus premebantur." King James Bible, Exodus 1:14: "And they made their lives bitter with *hard bondage, in mortar, and in brick,* and in all manner of service in the field: all their service, wherein they made them serve, was with rigour." The words in italic are the words Fray Mier quotes in Latin. He judges Israel's bondage to Egypt to be equal to Mexico's bondage to Spain.

19. Bishop Bartolomé de Las Casas (1474-1566) while not referenced by Fray Mier, also wrote a gut-wrenching 16th Century account that reads like a 20th century genocide: *Brevísima relación de la destrucción de las indias,* First Edition, Imprenta de Sebastián Trujillo, Sevilla, Spain 1552. More current Edition Prologue by Olga Camps, Editorial Fontamara, S.A., Mexico City, 1984.

20. Luis Gonzáles Obregón, *Memoria histórica, téchnica y administrativa de las obras del desagüe del Valle de México*, Mexico, 1902; and, Francisco de la Maza, *Enrico Martínez, Cosmógrafo e impresor de Nueva España*, Mexico, 1943. O'Gorman, op. cit., references these works as validating Fray Mier's discussion of the ancient engineering of Mexico City.

21. Pablo de Olavide (1725-1803), born in Lima, Peru, died in Baeza, Spain, was the Count of Pilos and Mayor of Sevilla. The Pablo de Olavide University, a public university founded 1997 in Sevilla, is named after Olavide. He wrote: *Triunfos del Evangelio, o memorias de un filósofo convertido,* 4 Volumes, Imprenta de Joseph de Orga, Valencia, Spain, 1797.

22. See Note 17, Torquemada, op. cit.

23. Bishop Juan de Zumárraga (1468-1548) was a Basque Franciscan monk. A classic biography of Bishop Zumárraga was written by Joaquín García Icazbalceta (1824-1894) *Don fray Juan de Zumárraga, primer obispo y arzobispo de México*, Rafael Aguayo

Spencer y Antonio Castro Leal, editors. Mexico City: Editorial Porrúa, 1947, (originally published 1881).

24. Bishop Agustin Dávila Padilla, (1562-1604) *Historia de la fundación y discurso de la Provincia de Santiago de México*, Madrid, 1596, Brussels, 1625. Dávila was born in Mexico City became a Dominican Friar and died while Bishop of Santo Domingo.

25. O'Gorman, op. cit., Page 27, Footnote 17. O'Gorman believes Fray Mier erred in referring to Mexican historian, Fernando de Alba Cortés Ixtlilxóchitl (1577-1648). Fernando de Alba *Ixtlilxóchitl*, was a descendent of Aztec royalty, a source for early Spanish missionary writings. Fernando de Alba Ixtlilxóchitl wrote *Obras históricas*, between 1600-1608, and *Historia Chichimeca*, between 1610-1640. O'Gorman believes Fray Mier may be referring to Bartolomé de Alba Ixtlilxóchitl, a son, or in some sources referred to as a brother of Fernando de Alba Ixtlilxóchitl. Bartolomé Ixtlilxóchitl, wrote *Pláticas en lengua mexicana, contra las supersticiones que han quedado entre los indios*, Mexico City, 1634."

26. See Note 25. Mier's references two different individuals, Prince Fernando de Alba and Prince Fernando Ixtlilxóchitl, and two difference historical accounts.

27. Hernando de Alvarado Tezozómoc (1525-1610), *Crónica mexicana*, written about 1598; and *Crónica mexicáyotl* written about 1609. *Crónica mexicáyotl* in the Nahuatl language is mostly ancient genealogy.

28. Domingo Chimalpahin Quauhtlehuanitzin, (1579-1660) *Anales*, and *Diferentes historias Originales*.

29. Lorenzo Boturini Benaduci (1702-1753), *Idea de una nueva historia general de la América septentrional*, Madrid, 1746, Mexico City 1871. Benaduci born in Italy went to New Spain in 1736 where he lived for eight years. He studied and wrote on the Virgin of Guadalupe.

30. See Note 11, Clavijero, op. cit.

31. Antonio de Leon y Gama, (1735-1802), Mexican astronomer, his most cited work is *Descripción Histórica y cronológica de las dos piedras que se hallaron en la plaza principal de México en 1790*, Mexico City, 1792.

32. Fray Bernardino de Sahagún (1499-1590,) *Historia general de las cosas de Nueva España*, likely the same as Fray Mier's referenced *Historia Universal de Nueva España*. Born and educated in Spain, Fray Sahagún immigrated to New Spain in 1529 where he lived for the next 61 years. The most famous extant text of

Sahagún's Historia is known as the *Florentine Codex* with 2,400 pages and 2,000 illustrations. A more recent edition was published in 5 Volumes, Robredo, Mexico City, 1938.

33. The Colegio de la Santa Cruz de Santiago Tlatelolco, founded 1533, was the First European-founded college in America.

34. See Note 9, Carli, op. cit.

35. O'Gorman, op. cit., Page 28, Footnote 25. O'Gorman cites: *Recopilación de leyes of los Reinos de las Indias*, Second Edition, Madrid, 1756, 4 Volumes. The "Laws of the Indies" was a compilation of legislation promulgated by the Spanish monarchs to regulate their territories in America and the Philippines. The Laws were sanctioned by King Carlos II of Spain (1665-1700) by means of a legal code signed in Madrid, Spain, May 18, 1680. It is divided into 4 Volumes, a total of 9 Books, containing 6,385 laws, grouped into 218 Titles. Each Law indicated the year, the King, and place of issue of said rule.

36. See Note 19, Casas, op. cit. Modern authors cite Fray Mier as a great admirer of Bishop Casas. Additional Casas writings to which Fray Mier may be referencing are—*Historia de las Indias*, 1561; *Apologética Historia*, written as an extension of "*Historia de las Indias*," approximately 1561; and *Del único modo de atraer a todos los pueblos a la verdadera religión*, first published in Latin 1597 by the Dominican College of San Gregorio, Valladolid, Spain, again in Latin 1942, in Spanish 1942, Second Edition in Spanish, Colección Popular, Mexico City, 1975. "True Religion" is Casas's thesis on the principle of free agency in proselyting the Gospel of Jesus Christ. Casas's writings are available in modern Spanish editions.

37. Juan Ginés de Sepúlveda, (1489-1573), was an opponent of Bishop de las Casas in the controversy on the nature of the American Indians. Sepúlveda wrote on the controversy: *Sobre las justas causas de la guerra contra los indios*, Mexico City, 1941 edition.

38. Strabo or Strabon, (63? B.C.-24? A.D.), Greek geographer and historian, is most famous for his 17-volume work *Geographica*, which presented a descriptive history of people and places from different regions of the world known to his era. The first Latin version was 1469.

39. Fray Joseph de Acosta, (1539-1600), Spanish missionary to America author of a very important book, *Historia natural y moral de las Indias*, Sevilla, 1590. A more recent edition was printed in Mexico City, 1963, Universidad Nacional Autónoma de México,

Biblioteca del Estudiante Universitario, No. 83, Prologue and Selection by Edmundo O'Gorman, *Vida Religiosa y Civil de los Indios*. Clavijero, op. cit., Page 544 references Father Acosta as a scholar of Peruvian history.

40. See Note 17, Torquemada, op. cit.

41. Fray Toribio de Benavente, or Motolinía, (1482-1568), was one of the first twelve Franciscan missionaries to arrive in New Spain in 1524 where he took the Nahuatl name Motolinía, meaning "The Poor Little One." He wrote, *Historia de los indios de Nueva España*, first published in Mexico, 1858, current Spanish editions in Mexico.

42. Fray Andrés Cavo, (1739-1803), *Historia civil y politica de México*, later republished titled, *Los tres siglos de México, durante el gobierno español*, published 1836 by Carlos María de Bustamante, second edition published by Biblioteca Histórica Mexicana in Jalapa, Mexico, 1870. Fray Cavo was a Mexican Jesuit and historian born in Guadalajara, Mexico.

43. Luis Becerra Tanco (1603-1672) was a Mexican Catholic Priest. *Estudio de Armas de México*, O'Gorman op. cit. on page 29, Footnote 31, notes: "Father Mier suffers here a grave confusion. The book to which he refers ought to be *Escudo de Armas de México* by Cabrera. Mier intended to cite Becerra's, *La felicidad de México: Origen milagroso del Santuario de Ntra. Sra. de Guadalupe*, México, 1666. The confusion comes about because both books deal with the same subject."

44. The plagues and high mortality described by Fray Mier are well documented. However, there is ongoing controversy over the cause and source of the plagues. There were two different diseases which reoccurred multiple times from 1545 to 1576, an estimated 70 to 80 percent of the population died of these infections. Their Nahuatl names are *matlazahuatl* and *cocoliztli*. *Matlazahuatl*, smallpox, was of European origin; and, *cocoliztli*, hemorrhagic fever, may be of American origin caused by climate change.

45. Vasco da Gama (1469-1524), a Portuguese born explorer, studied astronomy as a youth and was honored with titles and callings by the Kings of Portugal.

46. Tlaxcaltecans are excluded from Fray Mier's death count because they were never a vassal state to the Aztecs. His reference to Indian death counts should be understood to be limited to dead among the conquered Mexican or Aztec people. Tlaxcaltecans

were the first and very important ally to Hernán Cortés in his conquest of Mexico. Fray Mier's exclusion of the Tlaxcaltecans evidences the Spaniards continued to honor this alliance by exempting Tlaxcaltecans from the payment of taxes to the Spanish Viceroy. They probably had the same mortality but there is no tax record to document the death-count.

47. Pánfilo de Narváez (1478-1528), a Spanish military officer, participated in the conquest of Cuba from 1511 to 1514. In 1520, Narváez was sent by Diego de Velázquez de Cuéllar, the Governor of Cuba, to Mexico to subdue Cortés. It was Velázquez who sent Cortés to Mexico, but Cortés mutinied upon reaching Mexico, refusing to follow instructions from Cuba. Narváez was defeated by Cortés at Cempoala, Mexico. This freed Cortés to take all honor for victory in the conquest of Mexico. Narváez had a Berber slave named Estebanico who is noted to have traveled through New Spain in 1537.

48. Gonzalo Fernández de Oviedo y Valdéz (1478-1557): *Historia general y natural de las Indias*, Madrid, 1851-55. Summary edition published in Toledo, Spain, 1526. Oviedo's fellow contemporary, chronicler of the Spanish colonization of America, Bishop de las Casas, denounced Oviedo and his *Historia* as one of the greatest tyrants, thieves, and destroyers of the Indies, whose *Historia* has a few more pages than lies. See Footnote 19 above, op. cit. page 586. Fray Mier's prejudice of Oviedo is probably founded on Casas's critique of Oviedo.

49. See Note 11, Clavijero, op. cit., Book X, Ninth Dissertation, Origin of the French Illness, Pp. 579-592, Footnote 1, references William Becket, (1684-1738) London surgeon, and Antonio Rivero Sánchez. Becket wrote three papers titled, *The Antiquity of the Venereal Disease*, 1718, arguing that the French Illness was known in England since the 16th century. Rivero wrote *Disertación sobre el origen del mal venéreo, en la cual se prueba que no ha sido llevado de América*, Paris, 1765. Rivero's dissertation is in the catalogue of the Spanish books and manuscripts, added to Volume IV of the *Historia de América*, by Dr. William Robertson. Clavijero's Footnote 1 states it is not known if Rivero is Spanish or Portuguese. Rivero Sánchez is probably Mier's Brazilian Sánchez. Becket, Robertson, and Rivero Sánchez writings are probably the sources Mier references as authors Sanchez, Valverde, and Shuediau. Clavijero concludes, the origin of venereal disease is unknown, but it was probably Africa, and the disease was

endemic in Europe before Columbus returned from his first voyage of discovery to America. See Footnote 10 above, which references Langlés.

50. "Encomienda" is an estate in Latin America granted to the Spanish during the colonial era. The Indians living on the land were put into the service of their *encomendero*, or holder, to whom they were enslaved. The *encomendero* was to look after the interests of the Indians in his territory and convert them to Christianity. The encomienda system is feudal slavery by another name.

51. Baron von Friedrich Heinrich Alexander Humboldt (1769-1859), *Essai politique sur le royaume de la Nouvelle Espagne*, Spanish translation, Mexico, Edición Robredo. Humboldt was a Prussian geographer, naturalist, and explorer.

52. *Brief Report of the Destruction of the Indies*, see Footnote 19, Casas, op. cit.

53. *History of Mexico's Santo Domingo*, see Footnote 24. Mier abbreviates the title.

54. Antonio de Remesal (1570-1619), Historia de la Provincia de San Vicente de *Chiapa, y Guatemala, de la Orden de Nuestro glorioso Padre Santo Domingo de Guzmán*, Madrid, 1619. Fray Mier abbreviates the title. Fray Remesal was a Spanish Dominican monk who served as a missionary in Guatemala. Fray Remesal follows the line of Bishop de las Casas.

55. See Note 6, Muñoz, op. cit.

56. *Chronology of the Viceroys of Mexico*, O'Gorman, op. cit., footnote 38, p. 29, believes Fray Mier refers to Ignacio Carrillo y Perez who is given extensive notice by José Mariano Beristáin de Souza in his *Biblioteca hispano-americana septentrional*, Mexico, 1816 & 1819.

57. Cayetano Cabrera y Quintero, (1705-1775) *Escudo de Armas de México: Celestial Protección de esta Nobilísima Ciudad, de la Nueva España, y de casi todo el Nuevo Mundo, María Santísima, en su portentosa imagen del Mexicano Guadalupe, etc.* Mexico City, Viuda de Hogal, 1746.

58. See Note 6, Muñoz; and Footnote 11, Clavijero op. cit., and Raimundo Diosdado Caballero (1740-1830), historical writings included works on America: *Observaciones americanas, y supplemento critico á la historia de México; Medios para estrechar más la union entre españoles americanos y europeos;* and *Consideraciones americanas.*

59. See Note 9, Carli, op. cit.; and Footnote 11, Clavijero, op. cit., p. 544 references Count Carli's "American Letters" in a section on the "Arts of Mexico" with specific reference to the production of paper in ancient Mexico for writing Mexican hieroglyphics. Clavijero was born, studied, and ordained a Jesuit Priest in New Spain. When the Jesuits were expelled from the Spanish-American colonies, he went to live in Bologna, Italy, where he wrote *"Ancient History of Mexico"* in Spanish. The "History" was translated into Italian and first printed 1780 in Italy. Translated from Italian to English it was published 1787 in London, 1806 in Richmond, USA, 1807 in London, and 1817 in Philadelphia, USA. Translated from Italian to Spanish it was published 1826 in London, various translations 1833, 1844, 1853, 1861-62, 1868, 1917, and 1944 in Mexico. Translated from Italian to German it was published 1789-1790 in Leipzig. Clavijero's original Spanish history text was first published in Mexico 1945 and 1968. First printed in Spanish 53 years after its printing in Italian and not printed in a Spanish language nation until 60 years after first publication, and printed in Italian, English, and German. The publishing history of Clavijero's writings on Mexico bears witness to Fray Mier's Inquisition and his conspiratorial theory on how Mexico's true Pre-Conquest history was shrouded in secrecy, and it still is.

60. Montezuma II, (1470-1520), the last Aztec Emperor of Mexico (1502-20), was Emperor in 1519 when Cortés arrived in Mexico.

61. See Note 32, Sahagún, op. cit., and Footnote 17, Torquemada, op. cit.

62. Noche Triste, "Sorrowful Night," June 20, 1520, was the night Hernán Cortés was badly defeated by the Mexicans in the Aztec metropolis of Tenochtitlán, now the eastern part of Mexico City. Clavijeo, op. cit. pp 362-363. *19. Death of Montezuma and of Other Lords.* "On one of these days, which was, on what appears to be, the 30 of June, the King Montezuma died within the Spaniards' quarters at the age of 53 years and at 17 years and almost 10 months of reign, after more than seven months of imprisonment. As to the cause and circumstance of his death there is such variety and contradiction among the historians that it is impossible to come up with the truth. The Mexican historians fault the Spaniards, and the Spaniards the Mexicans."

63. The church of Nuestra Señora or Virgen de los Remedios, ("Our Lady or Virgin of the Remedies") is built atop the great pyramid Tlachihuyaltepetl in Cholula, Puebla, Mexico. It is the largest pyramid temple site in the Americas.

64. Cuauhtémoc, (1495-1525) the last Aztec Emperor, ruled 1520-1521. O'Gorman, op. cit. p. 30, footnote 40, recommends, *Cuauhtémoc*, a biography by Héctor Pérez Martínez published in Mexico City, 1945.

65. Hibueras is a village in Veracruz State, Mexico, and was the ancient name for Honduras.

66. Bernal Díaz del Castillo, (1492-1580), *Historia verdadera de la conquista de la Nueva España*, 1632, modern editions in Spanish & English titled, *The Conquest of Spain*. Díaz was a Spanish soldier and chronicler who participated in the conquest of Mexico under the leadership of Cortés.

67. Francisco López de Gomara, (1511-1566), *Historia general de las Indias*, Volume I & II, 1553, published 1943 in Mexico titled *Historia de la conquista de México*. Gomara was a Spanish chronicler, secretary, and chaplain to Hernán Cortés, but never traveled to America. His history of the Conquest of Mexico included first-hand interviews with Cortés that were criticized by Diaz. See Chapter 4, Footnote 66 op. cit.

68. Atahualpa, (1502-1533) was the last Inca or emperor of Peru. He was imprisoned and executed in Cajamarca, Peru, by order of Francisco Pizarro (1478-1541).

69. Túpac Amaru, also known as José Gabriel Condorconqui, was a Peruvian Chieftain (1740-1781) descendent of the Incas who rose in rebellion against Spain's colonial authority in 1780. He was defeated by the Viceroy Járuregui and executed.

* [A note written by Fray Mier] "According to the command, they say, of the Central Assembly. Another deception: the Americas called for the Courts, but the mode of electing and the number of their Deputies is a birthing worthy of the past Regency, whose power, already convinces Señor Argüelles, it was illegitimate, in his discussions against Lardizábal."

70. Agustín Argüelles (1776-1844), was a prominent Spanish politician and orator, who played a key role in writing the 1812 Spanish Constitution at the 1812 session of the Cádiz Courts.

71. Miguel de Lardizábal y Uribe (1744-1824), born in Tlaxcala, Mexico, represented New Spain in the Central Assembly of Cádiz (1808), Regency Member (1810), was exiled for

publishing a manifesto against the Courts. Fernando VII named him Minister of the Indies, but he fell in disgrace and was jailed.

72. Félix María Calleja del Rey (1758-1828) was a Spanish General and Viceroy who led Spain fight against the liberating troops led by Father Miguel Hidalgo, Father of Mexican Independence. Calleja defeated Hidalgo's Mexican troops 1811. As Viceroy of New Spain, the total focus of his administration was to squash Mexico's liberation movement.

73. José de Iturrigaray, (1742-1815), served as Viceroy of New Spain January 4, 1803 to September 16, 1808. He was removed from office for being a partisan of the Courts in Cádiz, Spain.

74. Latin Vulgate Bible, Numbers 4:41: "*Hic est populus Gersonitarum quos numeraverunt Moses et Aaron iuxta verbum Domini.*" King James Bible, Numbers 4:41: "*These are they* that were numbered of the families of the sons of Gershon of all that might do service in the tabernacle of the congregation, whom Moses and Aaron did number according to the commandment of the LORD." The English translation out of its Biblical context is: *This is the people.* In its Biblical context, Fray Mier is saying: *hic est populus*; you Europeans play the role of a self-ordained chosen people of the Lord in the rule of America; a repeat of the theme of Chapter 5, Footnote 18.

75. Francisco Javier Venegas (1754-1838), Viceroy of New Spain from September 14 ,1810 to March 4, 1813, received the title of Marquis of the Reunion of New Spain in 1816.

76. Fray Mier for the first time addresses the reader in the familiar tense, which is lost in English. Two things are communicated by this shift: he expresses his oneness with and love for the Mexican peoples, and secondly, he is using the language he would use when giving a Priest's sermon from the Church pulpit, adding a sense of ecclesiastical authority to his diatribe.

77. Antonio de la Calancha, (1584-1654), *Coronica moralizada del Orden de San Agustín en el Perú*, Printed in Barcelona, Volume I, 1638, Volume II 1653. Fray Calancha born in Bolivia, studied and lived in Lima, Peru, was a monk of the Order of Saint Augustine.

78. Gomara, op. cit. See Note 67.

79. Alonso de Estrada, (1480-1533/37), born in Spain died in Mexico. Estrada was rumored to be the illegitimate son of King Ferdinand II of Aragon. He fought in Flanders, returned to Madrid where he fought in the Castilian War of the Communities,

opposing the rebels against Emperor Charles V. For this, Charles rewarded him with the position of Corregidor of Cáceres, and later named him Treasurer of New Spain.

80. Miguel Antonio de la Gándara, (1719-1786), *Apuntos sobre el bien y el mal de España,* written by the order of King Carlos III, first published 1811, Valencia, Spain. Father Gándara was a Catholic Priest, essayist, and economist.

81. Antonio de la Herrera y Tordesillas, (1559-1625), *Descripción de las Indias Occidentales,* Madrid, Spain Second Edition, 1730. O'Gorman, op. cit, page 30 footnote 43, writes the Second Edition is preferable to the First Edition, printed 1601.

82. See Note 54, Remesal, op. cit.

83. See Note 17, Torquemada, op. cit. Fray Mier probably refers to the 1492 conquest ofAmerica beginning with Columbus cited in Torquemada's 1612 writing.

84. Fray Mier writes [sic], to emphasize they are "your" demons not ours. See Footnote 18. Fray Mier uses "garlics and onions" as another allegory comparing Israel's enslavement by Egypt to Mexico's enslavement by Spain. The King James Bible, Numbers 11:4-5. "(A)nd the children of Israel also wept again and said, . . .We remember the fish, which we did eat in Egypt freely; the cucumbers, and the melons, and the leeks, and the onions, and the garlik:"

85. Jacques Vanière, or Jacobi Vanierii as the name is commonly written in Latin, (1664-1739), *Praedium rusticum,* First edition 1707, Paris, 10 Volumes. Vanière was a Jesuit Priest and French poet. *Praedium rusticum* is cited in Roman Civil Law as defining land adapted to and used for agricultural and pastoral purposes.

86. "Nation of rich fertile land, gold metal, Rich in the character of men endowed of a kind spirit." A verse by Fray Benito Jerónimo Feijóo Montenegro (1676-1764), who encouraged scientific and empirical thought to debunk myths and superstitions, the very theme of Fray Mier's "Eleventh Note of the Second Letter from an American.

CHAPTER 5

Farewell Letter to the Mexicans [1]

FOREWORD BY EDMUNDO O'GORMAN

Father Mier wrote his "Farewell Letter to the Mexicans" in 1820 when he was a prisoner in the Castle San Juan de Ulúa on the eve of being deported to Europe. He calls attention by saying goodbye to his fellow countrymen: Father Mier chose as a topic most suitable an exhortation with the end of pleading to them that they must conserve the use of the letter x in the writing of the name Mexican and they should not permit the substitution of the letter j. From here the author passes insensitively to the subject of the preaching of the Gospel in America by the Apostle Saint Thomas that, since the famous Guadalupe Sermon, was for him a permanent obsession. This justifies, in part, the inclusion of the Letter in this selection.

But, why did Father Mier choose these topics to say goodbye to the Mexicans? In another place, I had the occasion to explain this rarity, and for this I will limit myself to a brief statement. [2] It is about the following: the movement for Independence was founded, among other things, on a popular sentiment growing more each time that wanted forgetfulness of the Spanish Colonial past as if one was dealing with a nightmare. This sentiment is expressed in a romantic intent of restoring the Pre-Cortesian indigenous past. From there the great interest that there was in all things that tended to formalize this restoration, as is the case with Father Mier's Letter, in this way earns an unforseen importance.

The intimate connection with the previous is the topic of the American preaching by the Apostle Saint Thomas. The favor with which such an absurd thesis was received, because of the desire to make evident to the Spaniards that the True Religion was not due to them, nor even the notice. In this way, at the time that the debt to Spain depreciated, Mexican antiquity was gilded with the varnish of Christianity, worthy, yes now, of being restored without ugly reservations.

Given these explanations, the "Farewell Letter. . ." will be comprehensible and worthy of attentive consideration.

FAREWELL LETTER TO THE MEXICANS
BY FRAY SERVANDO TERESA DE MIER

To return from the other world, is worth almost as much as coming out of the Inquisition's dungeons, where the Government, *for it agrees,* had me archived three years, I find myself with a great variation in the spelling and the "x" excluded from the regular strong letters, however much the words' origin demands it. As the Spanish Academy had charged that this should not be completely ignored, even though it tries to conform the spelling to the pronunciation; on the other hand, it not only saw the system of reform incomplete, but in some printings the "j" was already the only guttural letter, in others the "g" alternated with the vowels "e"and "i", I believed that all this novelty must have come from the printers.[3] Finding itself charged to work with the freedom of the press and not knowing to distinguish the origin of words in order to allot the 3 guttural letters; they had sought a quick solution. But some have told me that this came from the same Spanish Academy in its last writing system, others no such thing, but that it only comes from the editors, of the Academy's dictionary, who have adopted the system promoted by a few modern grammarians who heed nothing but the pronunciation. Locked up in this Castle, I have not been able to verify the truth.

Asking a renowned Spanish literato at the end of the last century, why he was not abiding by the Academy's rules of grammar and spelling, he responded to me that when these works came to light, all the great men that were in it had already died. I do not wish to say, that now there could not be others, but in the Land of Letters we are not obliged to kiss a scepter other than that of reason, and I hope to see those that the innovators may have had on the subject. I taught the Spanish language in Paris and Lisbon, I have meditated much upon it, I have come to be fixated by its prosody, and have many reasons to oppose these useless novelties, and especially against the extension it wants to give to the "j", as ugly in its pronunciation as in its form, as unknown by the Latins as by the ancient Spaniards, which will hinder our learning of Latin and of its European dialects. As soon as I have a room, I will set forth my reasons.

Whatever you want it to be, this Letter is reduced to begging by farewell to my Anahuacan fellow countrymen:[4] reject the suppression of the "x" in the Mexican or Aztec names of the places that are left to us, and especially of Mexico, because it would be the end of ruining them. And it is a great shame, because all are significant, and in their topographical, statistical, or historical meanings.

The first missionaries, to write the *Náhuatl* language or sonorously what we call Mexican, agreed according to Torquemada,[5] with the most learned Indians found in the College de Santiago *Tlatilolco*,[6] and as it is pronunciation has two Hebrew letters, *Sadhe* and *Shin*, they substituted in their writing by approximation the first "tz" and the second soft "x". But as for softening this even though the circumflex accent over the following vowel was not adopted, and the conquistadors were mostly Extremadurans and Andalusians, or Arabs in their pronunciation, they pronounced hard all the "x's" written by the missionaries, and they filled with guttural letters the terms that they adopted from the Mexican language, which does not permit any [guttural sound].

For this the Spaniards pronounce México (Méjico),[7] even though the Indians only pronounce Méxîco (Mescico) with the Hebrew letter *Shin*. And it is a pain, Mexicans, that Italians, French, English, and Germans may pronounce better than we the name of our native land, since nobody, except us, pronounces Mexico with a guttural letter. In all cases, my countrymen, we must continue to write it with "x", or to keep up with the time, if the new spelling prevails, to pronounce this as one ought to and the rest of Mexican terms, or not to cast into entire forgetfulness one of our greatest glories. Yes, *Méxîco* with soft x as the Indians pronounce it means: *Where Christ is* or (where) *Christ is worshiped*,[8] and Mexicans is the same as *Christians*.

Certainly, one finds the complete word *Mescichô*, as the Indians pronounce it in Hebrew 2nd verse of Psalms 2, where the Vulgate translated *Christum eius*, his Christ.[9] Clavijero,[10] despite everything, believes that Mexico's particle *co* is the Mexican term for *where*, and taking charge of the different interpretations that have been given to the name of Mexico by the words *Metl*, maguey, or *Metzi*, moon or month, of which it may be composed, he resolves that the true meaning has to be deduced from Mexican history, and according to it what it ought to mean is: *Where Mexî or Méxîtl is worshiped.*[11]

And *Mexî*, I ask, what does it mean? Pronounced as the Indians pronounce it, it is a Hebrew word, which means, taking it from the

Latin *unctus*, we call anointed, taking it from the Greek *Chrestous*, we call *Christ*, and taking it from Hebrew *Mesci*, we call Messiah.

And in the understanding of the Mexicans what did *Mexî* mean? Again, it is history which must tell it to us with certainty. *Mexî* was a man God, called by other names the Lord of the Crown of Thorns, *Teohuitznáhuac*, Lord of Paradise *Teotlaloc* &. &.,[12] who a virgin called Saint Mary *Malintzin*, conceived by a work of heaven, and she gave birth to him, already a perfect male, without injury to her virginity. *Foemina circundabit virum*.[13] So Father Torquemada tells it.[14]

Saint Tomé[15] was who gave them news of son and mother, so they also called her for this *Cilma-cóhuatl* the Tomé Woman, and *Coatlantona*, Mother of the Tomés or disciples of Saint Tomé, who wearing the hair cut in the shape of a crown, *sénchon-huitznáhuac*, made three vows, of poverty, obedience, and chastity, and served in the Temple of the Lord of the Crown of Thorns: *huitznáhuac-teocalli*.

To this virgin the Mexicans celebrated two principal festivals. One, the 2nd day of February, Day of the Purification of Our Lady,[16] and they presented children to her as she presented hers at the temple, and they had to be precisely purchased: *omne primogenitum pretio redimes*.[17] And, they made sure that they must be blondes or fair little ones in memory of Saint Tomé having been the one who instituted the festivals.

The other they had on Tepeyácac the day of winter solstice another day of Apostle Saint Thomas, and they offered her [Our Lady] flowers and images that they had of her that they worshipped there with the name of *Tzenteotinantzin*, which is to say, Mother of the true God, or *Tonantzin*, Our Lady and Mother, because they said that this virgin Mother of their God was mother of all the people of *Anáhuac* which we now call New Spain. Her figure was that of a girl with an encircling white and resplendent tunic, to whom for this they also called her *Chalchihuitliche*, with a sea-green blue robe, *Matlalcneye*, star studded, *Citlacui*.

Her son *Mexî*, the Mexicans painted with the hieroglyphics corresponding to the attributes of Man-God, having in his right-hand a Cross formed with five feather globes, just as his Mother they also painted on her hair a tiny cross. They also painted *Mexî* as we do Christ hanging from the Cross, although not with nails but tied, and they believed this is the way he was crucified says Torquemada. A circumstance very noteworthy, thus Saint Tomé's

Christians in Oriental India faithfully paint the images of the Crucified Christ, because in those countries the torment of the cross is done with cords. In a word: the proof of what the Mexicans understood for *Mexî, Christ Anointed* or *Messiah*, is what they said, according to Torquemada in the Mexican journey; that thus they called themselves since this their God commanded them, to put on their faces a certain ointment. This means Chrism, and is to say, since they were confirmed, anointed, or Christians. And they celebrated, Torquemada also says, the festival of *Mexî* all anointed and besmeared.[18]

If I will surprise someone that they would call Jesus Christ with a Hebrew name, we also call him Messiah, and Jesus is a Hebrew name although specified, as Christ is Greek although Latinized. The Indians could not say Christ, because their language has no "r", nor Jesus, because neither does it have a "j", and they were more comfortable with *Mexî* in keeping with their language; and above all they always preferred the names that they could write depicting their meaning as that of *Mexî*; being that the Hebrew language is the liturgical language of Saint Tomé's Christians in the orient, from where it seems Christianity came to the Mexicans: The truth is, according to the Holy Bishop Casas in his *Apología de los Indios*,[19] they were baptized by the Tomé Priests with all our ceremonies in the name of the Trinity in Hebrew; since the three names which he refers to that they said in the baptism, are precisely the names of Father, Son, and Holy Ghost in Hebrew, although he did not know it. The fountain in which they were baptized in Mexico, (because it was a true fountain as in the primitive Church, from whence a fountain came to be called the baptismal font) it was called the fountain of Saint Tomé *Coápan*, which was discovered when they opened the foundations of the Cathedral,[20] and Torquemada complains that they superstitiously covered it up, since it was of good water.[21]

The Christians fugitives from the persecution of Huémac, King of Tula, against Saint Tomé, which is to say *Quetzal-cóhuatl*, he who fled to Cholula, took refuge in the Lagoon or Lake Anáhuac, a sandy isle that for this they called *Xâltelolco* and later *Tlatelolco* or Earth Island. Pursued there and with a thousand hardships, although always protected by their God, they founded *Tenochtitlán* on a small contiguous hill where they found a prickly pear, which is what *tenochtitlan* means, and it was the same small hill upon which the Cathedral is situated.[22] And, they called the combination of both places or districts *México*, where Christ is or is worshiped.[23] Demanding of his leaders, who in the beginning were perhaps his Bishops, they were named and were Saint Tomé's acknowledged vicars and deputies, when they had them, as they were effectively called according to Torquemada by even the emperors of Mexico, because first it was a republic, later it had kings, and finally emperors.

Hernán Cortés knew of this anecdote and he pretended to be Saint Tomé's ambassador. "My boldness," he writes to Carlos V "was to make Moteuhzoma believe that Your Majesty was the same Saint Tomé, whom the people awaited."[24] "If in this thou do not bring some trick," Moteuhzoma told him, "and it is certain that this great Lord who sent thee is our lord Saint Tomé (*toteotl-quetzalcóhuatl*),[25] this empire is yours, and, I will do what you command. As to the religion that you have proposed to me, I see that it is the same that He had taught us, and we agree. We with the course of time, have forgotten or confused it; thou who now comes from His court, will have it more current; thou must do no more than to go saying that which we ought to be and to believe, and we will go practicing it." From what Acosta says,[26] that had there been no other purpose than the religion, it would have been established without a drop of blood. The preaching and prophecies of Saint Tomé about the coming of people of their same religion and of coming from the East, who would rule the country for some time, is the true key to the conquest in both Americas. I have studied it well: and while this foundation is not agreed to, nothing but absurdities and foolishness will be written.

Mexico's main temple or *teo-cal-li* (a word entirely Greek and with the same significance) was built, says Torquemada, in the district of the *Lord of the Crown of Thorns* upon the sepulcher of Saint Bartomé, martyr in Tula, disciple of Saint Tomé, who was very venerated says Acosta and Torquemada, until the conquest. This is the famous *Cópil*, of course, it means son of Tomé, and this signifies in Hebrew Bartomé, whose head was ordered cut off by Huémac, it was tossed into the Lagoon at the site that since then was called *Cópilco*, where Cópil or Bartomé is.[27]

In the building and services of the temple the Mexicans wanted to imitate Solomon's temple.[28] From there came the famous pillar of Mexico City, which dominated the lake's seven cities or lagoon as they incorrectly say. Thus, was the pillar of Solomon's temple, which according to the Second Book of Paralipomenon, had a height of 130 cubits beyond the roof's 40 cubits.[29]

When they say that in the dedication of Mexico's Temple 22 thousand human victims were sacrificed, it is an equivocation with the 22 thousand oxen that Solomon immolated according to the Scripture in the dedication of Jerusalem's Temple. And it is to be admired, that to put the Indians in disfavor someone believes to the letter, an absurdity as large as the peaceful beheading of a city or army of 22 thousand men in order to dedicate a temple, when nobody believes to the letter the Mexicans' famous journey via the wilderness with the same mansions and wonders, which lasted 40 years, and which is no more than a literal copy of that of the Israelites.[30] The Indians had in their power (as the missionaries in Veracruz gave in written testimony to the celebrated Fray Gregorio García) the entire Bible in images and hieroglyphic figures, they confused them with the passage of time, they put into practice the Scripture's histories, and confused their own history and their religion.[31]

What was the Mexican religion, but Christianity confused by time, and the mixed-up nature of the hieroglyphics? I have made a great study of their mythology and in its depth, it comes down to God, Jesus Christ, his Mother, Saint Tomé, his seven disciples called the seven Tomés *chicome-cohuatl* and the martyrs that died in the persecution of Huémac. The Spaniards, because they did not recognize it in another language and liturgy and had introduced enormous abuses, destroyed the same religion that they were professing and replaced the same images that they burned, because they were under different symbols. What an immensity of things I have to say about this!

If these were the errors, blasphemies, impieties that the Dark-Brown Horse in Señor Haro's noisy edict was said to have found in my Guadalupe Sermon, I am not astonished, because the fools blaspheme everything that they ignore.[32] But the Royal Academy of History did not believe such things in the detailed examination it did of my sermon by order of the Council of the Indies.[33] And far from condemning it, they requested, that the Archbishop's edict, unworthy of a prelate, was withdrawn as an inflammatory and fanatical libel. It stood by me in all that was said: I was currently writing upon this when I left the Inquisition, and enough has already been printed of it in a short dissertation at the end of the 2nd Volume of the *Historia de la revolución de Nueva España*, which I brought to light in London in two volumes, 4th.[34]

For if my persecutors should give an end to my life in the prisons, or as well as not letting it run its course, because the truths embitter them, they said Historia de la Revolución; will bury in the Inquisition all that I wrote upon these most glorious antiquities of our Country, I will here raise two curious notices, in order that in such investigations they may serve as a guide to other antiquarians.

Among the Memoirs in a folio volume published by the National Institute of France, they will find one on the existence of an unknown island between our America and China, whose author I do not remember. I carried notes on this, that with many other documents, and my same worked writings, I threw into the Soto la Marina River that Arredondo might not take from them a pretext to satisfy his desire to dispatch me from this world.[35] But certainly the author of the cited Memoir had studied in Beijing the same geography in the books and maps of the Chinese and in them saw how in the first centuries of Christianity they had commerce with both Americas. It recounts the names that they gave them, demarcates the course they sailed, and tells how in 1450 a monk returned from among those who had crossed over to our America, telling of the great progresses that the de Foe religion had made there.[36] As it is very similar to Christianity it can be mistaken for it. The Mexican Calendar is almost identical to that of the Chinese Tartars; the Mexican language is full of Chinese words, and in Campeche they called Saint Tomé *Chilan-cambal*, which in the Chinese language means Saint Thomas.

My fellow countrymen will also find in Maltebrun's most erudite Geography, that was printed in Paris the year 1814,[37] unambiguous evidence, that since the 10th Century there were in our America colonies (and they know their names) Danes or Norsemen, Irish and Scots. Read Mitrídates about this, a very curious German work.[38] Torquemada says that it is apparent, that four generations before the conquest there was already in our America clear knowledge of the Christian Religion and of the future arrival of the Spaniards.[39] To this epoch it appears, belong the four renowned prophets of Yucatán, whose remarkable prophecies Montemayor relates.[40]

Veytia[41] says, it is evident from the Mexican Manuscripts gathered by Boturini,[42] that there were two Preachers of the Gospel in Anáhuac: one very ancient who came twelve years after a great eclipse, that he and Boturini calculated to be the one at the death of Christ, and another about the 6th Century.[43] And, he believes that the first Apostle Saint Thomas may be that same celebrated Quetzalcóhuatl of the Indians. Of this same opinion, were Don Carlos de Sigüenza in his *Fénix del Occidente, el Apóstol Santo Tomé;*[44] a Mexican Jesuit who wrote in Manila the *Historia del verdadero Quetzal-cóhuatl, el Apóstol Santo Tomé,*[45] and other serious foreign authors, Spanish and American.

In my lengthy Apologia[46] that starting after my Guadalupe Sermon in 1794, I wrote in the Inquisition, I developed the serious fundamentals that there are for believing that the preacher of around the 6th century was the Holy Bishop Abad from Saint Brendan, Ireland, commonly called San Borondón.[47] His famous journey in the 6th Century to an unknown island where with his seven disciples ordained bishops, he founded seven churches, it can be mythical in the circumstances, in the remote and rare marvelous things are always added; but this does not prove at the bottom that the journey itself is not true. Precisely in the 6th century, Torquemada puts the landing of *Quetzal-cóhuatl* in Pánuco[48] with seven disciples later venerated in Mexico as saints, and he believes they were all Irish, because they were blond, white, blue eyed, and the faces striped with blue, as in those centuries the Irish did theirs. However, it is necessary, that one of the two preachers may have been oriental, because I find among the Mexicans the entire liturgy, clothes, customs, and discipline of the Oriental Churches. I wrote much on this in the Inquisition and even much more remains for me to say.

Already one supposes that the enemies of the glories of our native land must call all these fables, deliriums and even blasphemies and impieties: and if they should take me in hand, helped by the adulators' cloak *ex omni gente et populo* ("Out of every people and nation "), they would recommence the persecution that for this same the Archbishop Haro aroused me since the year 1794. But my fellow countrymen should know that I forced him to an argument before the Council of the Indies, I won it, it ordered him scolded, fined, his edict withdraw, to return me to the native land with all honors at the expense of the Exchequer, to reinstate all my honors and goods, and to indemnify me at the expense of my persecutors for all my persecutions and sufferings. Now I will tell at length in my *Manifiesto Apologético* [49] that I am concluding for the press.

My fellow countrymen stop howling and instruct yourselves. Sigüenza's *El Fénix de Occidente* was lost, but the *Historia del verdadero Quetzal-cohuatl* which I cited, exists in Mexico. I see from the gazettes that they are printing Veytia's antiquities. It brings forth the good about Saint Tomé, although it is a shame, says Gama,[50] the explanation of the Mexican Calendar may be mistaken, and it is all full of gross misconceptions. Gama, according to his letter that I saw in Rome, had applied to write the ancient Mexican history. And this Gentleman brought to the judgement and the criticism all the knowledge necessary for a complete work. Anyway, read Fray Gregorio García, *Predicación del Evangelio en el Nuevo Mundo viviendo los Apóstoles*, printed in Baeza.[51] And, Fray Antonio Calancha, *Crónica de San Agustín del Perú*,[52] that takes all the 2nd book in proving the preaching of Saint Thomas in America. There you will see cited many other authors: The Deists themselves today confess that the ancient preaching of the Gospel in America is beyond doubt.

Printed in Puebla, Mexico, in the *Imprenta Liberal of Don Pedro Garmendia,*
The Year 1821

CHAPTER 5 NOTES

1. O'Gorman op. cit., p. XXII, Footnote 2 writes: "The Guadalupe Sermon.—The documents relative to this sermon and to the ecclesiastical cause that with this motive was taken against him, they can be seen in *Colec. de Docs*, de Hernández de Hernández y Dávalos. Vol. III.—Mier argued that the tradition of the Guadalupe apparition was not true: instead he defended the thesis of the evangelic preaching in America by the Apostle Saint Thomas, and at that time went back to the miracle of Tepeyac image. His "Farewell Letter to the Mexicans" in this selection deals withthis matter. It was first published by Imprenta Liberal of D. Pedro Garmendia, Mexico City, 1822. This translation of the "Letter. . ." is from: *Servando Teresa de Mier, Escritos y Memorias*, Biblioteca del Estudiante 56, Prólogue and Selection by Edmundo O'Gorman, Editions of the National Autonomous University of Mexico, México, D.F. 1945, pp. 31-50. O'Gorman's source for the letter is a draft copy of *Manifiesto apologético en Escritos inéditos de Fr. Servando Teresa de Mier*, notes and organization by J. M. Miquel, I. Vergés, and Hugo Díaz-Thomé, El Colegio de México, Centro de Estudios Históricos, México City, 1944, Footnote 1. pp. 137-143. Fray Mier's "Farewell Letter. . ." is the shortest and most focused writing on the Gospel in America before the Conquest, as a

compendium of his forty years of researching, writing, and persecutions for his preaching on Christianity in Ancient America. He wrote in the despair of prison with every expectation of further persecutions and sufferings in the belief that this was his last will and testament of the truths he spent his lifetime advocating.

2. Edmundo O'Gorman, (1906-1995), *El pensamiento político del Padre Mier*, Mexico, 1945, Prologue, is cited by O'Gorman as "another place" from which he extracts his "brief statement." See Chapter 5, Note 1., O'Gorman op. cit., p. 33, Footnote 1. Fray Mier's "Farewell Letter to the Mexicans" is translated from O'Gorman op. cit pp. 35-48.

3. The pronunciation of the Spanish "g" and "j" when written before "e" or "i" has no English pronunciation equivalent. In Spanish, the sounds "g" and "j" are from the throat as with the guttural "ch" in Scottish loch or German Bach.

4. See Chapter 4, Note 11, Clavijero, op. cit., p. 1. Anáhuac or Anahuacans, the people of Anáhuac, according to its etymology, in the beginning the name was given only to the Valley of what is today Mexico City. The title, Anáhuac, was later extended to include almost all the land that became known as New Spain. Chapter 4, Note 11, Clavijero, op. cit., p. 1: "Anahuac means–Next to the Water," and from this appears to have originated the name Anahualtacas, the name which was given to the cultured nations that populated the shores of the Mexican Lake."

5. See Chapter 4, Note 17, Torquemada, op. cit. Clavijero, op. cit., page XXX, 1968 edition, Torquemada, Fray Juan de. (1557-1664). *Monarquía indiana*, Madrid 1614, Mexico City 1943. ". .(I)t is without a doubt the most complete history with respect to Mexican antiquity, of the many that to date have been published (1780). The author (Torquemada) resided in Mexico from his youth to his death, he knew very well the Mexican language, he dealt with the Mexicans more than 50 years. He collected a vast number of ancient paintings and excellent manuscripts, and he worked on his book more than twenty years."

6. Fray Torquemada served as guardian to the Colegio de Santa Cruz de Santiago Tlatelolco, the more common spelling. The College, founded by Franciscans in 1535, located in the center of Mexico City gained a reputation for educating the children of the Aztec nobility. According to Fray Clavijero, the island of Tlatelolco lying to the north of the island city of Tenochtitlan was

settled by a group of dissenting Mexicans, whose bitter anger dated from the earliest pilgrimages. The jealousy between the two parties, passed from parents to children, broke into open fighting in 1338 forcing the migration of one of the groups to a sandy island. The earliest painted image of the new city was of an earthen hill, Xaltilolco, from which the island took its name. The hilltop was leveled and made into a marketplace, which led the historian and grammarian, Augustín de Betancourt, to believe that Tlatelolco derived from the numerous *tlatelli*, hearths or ovens found in that marketplace. Father Clavijero believed that the accepted spelling, Tlatelolco, ignored the earlier history of the place; Clavijero, op. cit., 72-73. Fray Mier writes *Tlatilolco* without elaboration, most likely, so as not to detract from his admonition to revere the spelling, pronunciation, and history of the word Mexico. Later in his "Farewell Letter. . ." he uses the accepted spelling, Tlatelolco. This discrepancy in spelling illustrates why Fray Mier so vehemently denounces the careless evolution of Mexican words with the resulting loss of ancient traditions. A minor change in spelling alters the original Tlatilolco, an earthen hill on an island refuge, to a later Tlatelolco, a busy, smoky, marketplace. And, the change is done at the hand of a grammarian.

7. Spanish spelling is an exact reflection of the pronunciation of the language. The pronunciation of a Spanish letter is subject to strict rules with no variations. The Spanish letter "x" (equis) is pronounced like the "ks" in thin<u>ks</u>. The "k" sound is veryweak. Example, Spanish *éxito*, English success is pronounced (éksito). By strict Spanish rules with no variations, the Spanish/English pronunciations of Mexico would be the virtually the same (Meksico). See Note 3 above; the Spanish pronunciation of Mexico is "Méjico" with a guttural "j" for the x sound like "ch" in Bach or Loch. The English pronunciation of Mexico is as the Indians pronounced it with the Shin, (Mecsico). Today the name Mexico is rarely written as Méjico, but this rare variant spelling is the universal Spanish pronunciation of the name. Fray Mier's legacy is that he preserved the "x" in the common spelling of Mexico but lost to the universal Spanish guttural pronunciation Méjico (Mechico), leaving lost in total forgetfulness the origin and meaning of the name Mexico.

8. The Farewell Letter. . ." in Spanish reads "*donde está o (donde) es adorado Cristo.*" Both "está" and "es" are the third-

person singular forms of the Spanish verbs *"estar"* and *"ser;"* the English verb *"to be,"* and both translate in English to *"is."* There is a nuance of meaning in Spanish which is lost in an English translation. *"Está,"* places Christ in a spatial position, temporary, or transitory state. While, *"es"* indicates Christ is an essential belief or permanent quality. *"Donde está adorado Cristo,"* translated to English confers the sense of, *"the place where Christ is worshiped."* While, *"Donde es adorado Cristo"* expresses more a sense of belonging, which in English might read, *"Where Christ in fact or truth is worshiped".* Using both Spanish verbs in his *"*Farewell Letter. . . "*,* Fray Mier suggests that the Mexican/Nahuatl language also gave *Méxîco* two subtle meanings.

9. Psalms 2:2, King James Bible: "The kings of the earth set themselves, and the rulers take counsel together, against the LORD and against *his anointed, . ."* Italics added as Fray Mier has written *Christum eius,* his Christ. "Anointed" in modern Hebrew is pronounced "Mashiah." In English the word is Messiah or the more common Greek origin word, Christ.

10. Chapter 4, Note 11, Clavijero, op. cit., p. 72, Footnote 35, ". . .(B)ut then I Disillusioned myself with the study of the history, and today I have no doubt that México is the same as the place of the God Mexitli or Huitzilopochtli. . . ."

11. Fray Mier writes in Spanish: *"dónde está o es adorado Mexî, o Méxîtl."* See Note 8.

12. Chapter 4, Note 11, Clavijero, op. cit., p. 147, "The Mexicans had an idea although imperfect of a Supreme Being, absolute and independent, to whom they confessed to owe adoration, respect and fear. They did not depict him in any figure because they believed him to be invisible, nor did they call him with other than the common name of God, that in their language is *teotl,* even more like the *theos* of the Greeks in its significance than in its articulation; but they gave Him various epithets highly expressive of the grandeur and power which they conceived in him. . . ."

13. Jeremiah 31:22, Latin Vulgate Bible: *"Quousque vagaberis (aut, cir cuibis) filia rebellis (immorigera)? quia creavit Jehova rem novam in terra, Foemina circundabit virum."* Jeremiah 31:22, King James Bible: "How long wilt thou go about, O thou backsliding daughter? for the Lord hath created a new thing in the earth, A woman shall compass a man."

14. See Notes 5 and 6, Torquemada, op. cit.

15. In Spanish texts the name is Santo Tomás, Saint Thomas. Fray Mier vacillates between Santo Tomás and Santo Tomé, Saint Tomé. English historical writings credit Fray Mier with originating the theory that Saint Thomas, one of original Apostles of Jesus Christ was the first Christian Missionary to the Americas. Mier believed passionately in the preaching of the Gospel by Saint Tomé in the Americas before the arrival of the Spaniards. Fray Mier says the Indians called him Tomé not the Spanish Tomás, "Thomas." Bishop de las Casas, Chapter 4, Footnote 19, writes on the Apostle Saint Thomas, as did many of his contemporaries. Such as, Bishop Juan de Zumárraga (1468-1548), who dates one of his letters "Eve of the Indian Apostle Saint Thomas," Joaquín García Icazbalceta, *Don fray Juan de Zumárraga, primer obispo y arzobispo de México*, Mexico City: Editorial Porrúa, 1947 (originally published 1881). The legend of Saint Thomas was found throughout America by Catholic missionaries from the beginning of the discovery.

16. February 2 is forty days after Christmas. The Law of Moses requires that when a woman bears a male, she shall be unclean as at the time of menstrual infirmity and shall remain in a state of blood purification for forty days. On the completion of her purification she shall bring to the priest a yearling lamb for a burnt offering, and a pigeon or a turtledove for a sin offering. If, however, her means do not suffice for a lamb, she shall take two turtle doves or two pigeons, one for a burnt offering and the other for a sin offering. The priest shall make expiation on her tenet, and she shall be clean, [Leviticus 12:2-8]. Mary, the Mother of Jesus, scrupulously followed this Law as portrayed in Luke 2:21-39. Early Spanish missionaries found the Law of Moses being practiced by the Mexicans. See: Chapter 4, Note 39, de Acosta, op. cit. Chapter 27, p. 70, "The Indians had other innumerable ceremonies and rites, and in many of them there is resemblance to the ancient law of Moses; in others they appear as those that the Moors use, and some resemble those of the Evangelical Law, such as washings or what they call *opacuna*. That was to bathe in pure water to stay clean of their sins. The Mexicans also had their baptisms with this ceremony, and it is that the recently born children sacrificed their ears and the virile member, that somehow mimics the circumcision of the Jew."

17. Exodus 13:13, Latin Vulgate Bible: "*Primogenitum asini mutabis ove quod si non redemeris interficies omne autem primogenitum*

hominis de filiis tuis pretio redimes." ("The firstborn of an ass thou shalt change for a sheep: and if thou do not redeem it, thou kill it. And every firstborn of men thou shalt redeem with a price." Translation from the Latin Vulgate Bible.) Fray Mier extracted "*omne primogenitum. . . . pretio redimes,*" which translates to: "every firstborn shalt (thou) redeem."

18. For anointing references see: [Exodus 29:7; Leviticus 8:12; I Samuel 10:1, 17:13; II King 9:3,6; Psalms 23:5, 133:2; Matthew 26:7; Mark 14:3; and Luke 7:46]. Also, *The New Standard Jewish Encyclopedia, Fifth Edition* Geoffrey Wigoder ed. Garden City, NY, 1977, p. 112, ANOINTING: "(W)as common in Palestine in biblical and post-biblical times. . . in religious rites and to consecrate kings, priests, and the sacred vessels of the Tabernacle. Thus, David was anointed by Samuel; and the descendent of David who would redeem Israel at the End of Days was called the Messiah (Heb. *Mashiah*, i.e. "The Anointed One")."

19. Bishop Bartolomé de las Casas (1474-1566) was known for his untiring work in favor of the natives of the New World as "Apostle of the Indies," "Prophet of the Americas," and "Protectorate of the Indies." He arrived in the Americas 1502 and became Bishop of Chiapas, Mexico, 1545. Casas was a Dominican Priest as was Fray Mier. Fray Mier is probably referring to Bishop de Las Casas's *Apologética Historica Sumaria*, written 1555-1559.

20. The Metropolitan Cathedral of Mexico City constructed 1563 stands on the southwest corner of an ancient Aztec temple.

21. Chapter 4, Note 11, Clavijero, op. cit. 159-163. "The Mexicans and other peoples of Anáhuac had, as with all the cultured nations of the world, temples and places assigned to the exercise of religion, wherein the people congregated to pay respect to their deities and to implore their protection. They called the temple *teocalli*, House of God, a name which after receipt of the Gospel they have given more correctly to the temples erected in honor of the true God." ". . .(A)mong the notable buildings which were among those temples, beside the four arsenals over the gates of the wall were another joined to the temple Tezcacalli (house of mirrors) the sanctuary so, called for being all covered with mirrors. There was also a house with its chapel annex called Teccizcalli, all adorned with shells, wherein the king withdrew himself at certain times to exercise prayer and fasting, and other austerities. Besides this was another place of retreat for the high

priests, which they called Poyauhtlan, and another for private matters." "They also had a good hospice to shelter strangers of distinction, who for devotion came to visit the temple, or to see for curiosity the greatness of the court. There were several pools in which the priests bathed themselves, and several fountains from which waters they drank. In one pool called Tezcupan (crystalline waters) many bathed themselves by personal vow which they made to their gods. Among the fountains was one which they said was Toxpalatl, whose water was thought of as holy; they drank it only on the most solemn festivals and aside from those it was not permitted to touch it." The editor of Clavijero's book, R. P. Mariano Cuevas, adds this footnote: "The fountain of Texpalatl, which was of very good water, was blocked up when the Spaniards laid waste to the temple, and it was again rediscovered 1582, as Torquemada testified in the small plaza of Marqués, which is now the Empedradillo; but I don't know for what motive they again blocked it up, depriving the public of the benefit of the water and increasing with it those of the lagoon."

22. The origin of Mexico is preserved on the Republic's national seal and flag, an eagle in profile, wings raised ready for flight, a serpent held in beak and right claw, left claw clinging to a prickly pear cactus. The site was memorialized by an ancient Mexican Temple and then a Catholic Cathedral. See Note 6 regarding *Tlatelolco*.

23. Fray Mier writes in Spanish: "*dónde está o es adorado Cristo.*" See Note 8.

24. Chapter 4, Note 14, Cortés, op. cit. Fray Mier gained wide acclaim in Mexico for his November 8, 1794 memorial service sermon honoring Hernán Cortés. His "Farewell Letter. . .," written in prison, without notes or printed texts, misstates Cortés' account and mixes historical sources. Cortés did not write about Saint Tomé in his Letter to the Emperor of Spain Carlos V telling of his first meeting with Montezuma. Cortés did play on Montezuma's perception of the November 8, 1519 meeting as a fulfillment of ancient Mexican scriptural prophecy. Cortés, op. cit. pp 108-109: (Montezuma): "(S)at, and proposed in this way: Many days ago, which by our, scriptures we have notice from our ancestors that I nor all those who live in this land are not natives of it, but foreigners and come to it from very strange parts; and we have by like manner that to these parts a lord brought our generation, whose vassals they all were, he who returned to his nature and

afterwards he came back coming after a long time, and so long, that they were already married those that had stayed with the native women of the land, and they had many generations and made villages where they lived; and wishing to take them with him, they did not wish to go, nor less to receive him for Lord; and so, he returned. And we have always had from those who from him might be descended they had to come to subjugate this land and we, as his vassals. And according to the part which thou saith that thou cometh, which is to where the sun rises, and the things which thou saith of this great Lord or King who sent thee here, we believe, and we know for certainty Him to be our natural Lord; and especially that thou saith to us that He many days ago has notice of us. And so be thou certain that we will obey and will have thee for Lord in place of this great Lord who thou saith, and who in Him there was not any fault nor deceit; and well thou can in all the land, I say that in that which I in my dominion possess, command to thy will, because it will be obeyed and done, and all that which we have is as thy might wish to order of it."

"I responded to him to all that which he told me, satisfying that which appeared to me advisable, especially in having him believe thy Majesty was who they awaited, and with this he took his leave; and went, we were very well provided with many hens and bread and fruits and other necessary things, especially for the lodging service. And in this manner, I was six days, very well provided of all the necessities and visited by many of those Lords."

25. Toteotl-quetzalcóhuatl means "God of the Serpent Armed by Feathers." Chapter 4, Note 11, Clavijero, op. cit., page 240 writes: "the *Teotl* of the Mexicans means the same as Theos to the Greeks and the God to the Spanish." Clavijero, op. cit. 151-153 writes: "*Quetzalcoatl* ("Serpent Armed by Feathers"). This was among the Mexicans and other nations of Anáhuac the God of the Air. They said of him that he had been high priest of Tolan; that he was white, tall and corpulent, of wide forehead, large eyes, of long black hair, and thick beard, that because of his modesty he wore full-length clothing."

"After having been twenty years in that city, he resolved to continue his journey to the imaginary kingdom of Tlapalan, taking with him four noble and virtuous youths. From the maritime province of Coatzacoalco he bid them farewell charging them that they should tell the Cholultecans that they could be certain that he would return some day to console them and govern them. To these youths, the Cholultecans later charged the government of that city out of respect for their venerated Quetzalcoatl, of which some say that he disappeared and others that he died in the same coast."

"Dr. Sigüenza y Góngora believed that the Quetzalcoatl that those nations consecrated was none other than the Apostle Saint Thomas, who announced the Gospel to them. He encouraged this thought with great profusion of erudition in a work that, as others of his learned pen, had the disgrace of perishing by the negligence of those who possessed them. In this work he made a parallel of the names of Didymus and Quezalcoatl, of his dress, his doctrine, and his prophecies, and he examined places where he walked, the traces he left and the wonders that his four noble disciples published. For lack of said manuscripts we will abstain ourselves from an opinion of censure, the author is safe in the respect that we owe to his enlightenment, but we cannot agree. Various writers of that kingdom have had for certain that some centuries before the arrival of the Spanish the Gospel had already been preached in America. The reasons that they had for this belief were various crosses that in diverse times and places were found, they appear carved before the Spanish. The 40-day fast that various peoples of that New World observed, the prophecies that they had of the future arrival of foreign and bearded people and the human footprints stamped in some stones that they believe are of the Apostle Saint Thomas. I have never agreed with these authors; but the examination of their fundamentals, especially in that which has to do with the crosses, demands another work very different from that which we are now writing."

Carlos de Sigüenza y Góngora (1645-1700) was a Jesuit Priest and celebrated Mexican Professor of Mathematics at the Universidad de México. Clavijero op. cit. xxxi: "This great man is one of the most distinguished in the history of Mexico, because he formed at great expense a copious and select collection of ancient manuscripts and paintings and he used them with the greatest diligence and perseverance illuminating the antiquities of that kingdom." "One large and very erudite dissertation on the diffusion of the Gospel in Anáhuac, which he attributes to the Apostle Saint Thomas, sustaining the tradition of the Indians, in the crosses found and venerated in Mexico and in other monuments."

In 1668, Fray Sigüenza began the study of Aztec history and Toltec writings. Fray Sigüenza is one of Fray Mier's sources for his Santo Tomé (Saint Thomas) writings on Christianity in ancient America. Fray Sigüenza had access to the documents of the historian Fernando de Alva Cortés Ixtlilxochitl and the kings of Texcoco. On the death of Ixtlilxochitl, Fray Sigüenza inherited Ixtlilxochitl's collection of documents, and devoted the later years of his life to the continuous study of Mexican history. Fernando de Alva Cortés Ixlitxochitl was a direct descendent of the Emperors of Texcoco and Tenochtitlan, Mexico. Roman Catholic and ancient Mexican Christianity were so similar that early Catholic Fathers sought an explanation. The most common theory was, that one of the original Twelve Apostles, Saint Thomas, had found his way to America, emigrating from east Asia, and in the period 1492 to mid-1500's the Spanish thought America was India and China, witness their calling the native people Indians.

26. Chapter 4, Note 39, Acosta, op. cit. p. 72. "In these other nations of the Indians, as in the province of Guatemala, and in the Islands and New Kingdom, and provinces of Chile and others that were as colonies, even though they had a great multitude of superstitions and sacrifices, none could compare with what was to be seen in Cuzco and Mexico, where Satan was as in his Rome or Jerusalem, until he was overthrown, and in his place was hung the Holy Cross, and the Kingdom of Christ, Our God, occupied that which the tyrant had usurped." The Law of Moses and Evangelical Christianity practices of Cuzco and Mexico were so like the practices of Rome and Jerusalem that Fray Acosta believes Satan was in America before the arrival of the Spanish Catholic missionaries. Over time, Fray Clavijero, Fray Sigüenza, Fray Mier, and others embraced the theory that not Satan but rather an Apostle of Christ Saint Thomas had preceded the Catholic Fathers to America.

27. Fray Mier strongly asserts that Christianity was practiced by the ancient Mexicans, before the arrival of the Catholic Church in America, a belief common among early Catholic missionaries. How did Mexican Christianity get here? Fray Acosta speculates it was the work of Satan. Early Catholic missionaries believed it was one of Christ's disciples. Tomé is a Spanish/Portuguese variation of Tomás, Thomas in English. Fray Mier believed Tomé was a Nahuatl name. He writes that there is evidence of Hebrew in the Mexican native language. The idea of Apostle Saint Thomas as the

135

source preacher originated 250 plus years before Fray Mier. His legacy is that he was the messenger who revived the history and culture discovered by the earliest Catholic missionaries. The legendary preaching of the Gospel of Jesus Christ to the Mexicans by the Apostle Saint Thomas may simply be the linking by early Spanish missionaries of the phonetics of the Nahuatl Tomé to the Spanish Tomás. Fray Mier writes of Saint Tomé and his son, Saint Bartomé, as preachers of the Gospel of Jesus Christ. Bartomé is a variant spelling of Bartolomé in Spanish, Bartholomew in English. *Random House Dictionary of the English Language, Second Edition–Unabridged* defines "Bartholomew: one of the 12 apostles: sometimes called Nathanael. Mark 3:18, 2. a male given name: from a Hebrew word meaning "son of Talmai." Talmai, Hebrew for furrowed, appears in the *Bible*, Numbers 13:22 and elsewhere in the *Bible*.

28. Chapter 4, Note 14, Cortés, op. cit. p. 95: Cortés described the city of Cholula, Mexico, in his Second Letter to King Carlos V of Spain, "This city is very fertile farmland, because it has much land and the more part of it is watered, and outside it is even a more beautiful city than there is in Spain, because it is much adorned with towers and fine masonry. And I certify to Your Highness that I counted from one mosque over four hundred towers in said city, and all are of mosques."

29. Second Book of Paralipomenon, is Second Chronicles in the Bible. For references to the pillars of Solomon's temple see II Chronicles 3 and I Kings 6.

30. King James Bible, 1 Kings 8:63: "And Solomon offered a sacrifice of peace offerings, which he offered unto the Lord, two and twenty thousand oxen." King James Bible, Deuteronomy 8:2: "And thou shalt remember all the way which the Lord thy God led thee these forty years in the wilderness, to humble thee, and to prove thee, to know what was in thine heart whether thou wouldest keep his commandments, or no."

31. Fray Gregorio García (1554-1627), *Origen de los Indios de el Nuevo Mundo eIndias Occidentales*, also *Tratado sobre el origen de los americanos*, Valencia, 1607. *Predicación del Evangelio En el Nuevo Mundo, viviendo los Apóstoles*. Baeza, Spain, 1625. Fray Garcia, a Dominican Priest preached in Peru and Mexico.

32. Archbishop Alonzo Núñez de Haro y Peralta (1729-1800), Archbishop of Mexico 1772 to 1800, and Viceroy of New Spain May 8 to August 16, 1787, incited the Inquisition of Fray Mier and

his December 12, 1794 Guadalupe Sermon. Fray Mier's first public delivery of the theme of this, his "Farewell Letter. . ." The sermon gave cause, from 1794 to 1821, for the Catholic Church in Mexico to imprison, exile, and to again imprison Fray Mier upon returning to Mexico. "Caballo Bruno," ("Dark-Brown Horse"), and Señor, are insults Fray Mier heaped upon Archbishop Haro.

33. Chapter 5, Note 1 O'Gorman, op. cit., p. 49, Note 8, for the opinion of the Royal Academy of History on Father Mier's Guadalupe Sermon see Hernández y Dávalos, Juan E. (1827-1893), *Colección de Documentos, Tomo III*, The Report of the Real Academia de la Historia on Fray Mier's 1794 Guadalupe Sermon has 13 documents.

34. Note 1 above, O'Gorman, op. cit., p. 49, Note 9: "History of the Revolution of New Spain" references an "Illustrative Note" added as an appendix to his History, which discusses the preaching of the gospel in America before the conquest. Published 1986, by Instituto Cultural Helénico, Fondo de Cultura Económica México (México) under the title *Historia de la revolución de Nueva España*, was first published in London under Fray Mier's pseudonym José Guerra as, *Historia de la revolución de Nueva España, antiguamente Anáhuac o verdadero origen y causa de ella con la Relación de su progresos hasta el presente año de 1813*, by William Glindon, 1813, in 2 Volumes. A 2nd edition was published in Mexico, 1922, by the Chamber of Deputies, Mexico's Congress. Fray Mier's dissertation brought to light in London and republished by the Mexico's Congress remains in the dark mist of Fray Mier's ostracism. The thesis of his "Farewell Letter. . ." is known by Mexican scholars and Catholic clergy, but largely unknown by the people of Mexico and the rest of the World.

35. Note 1, O'Gorman, op. cit., p. 49, Note 10, references Alamán Y Escalada, Lucas, *Historia de México* published, Mexico, 1849-52 (Volume VII, Chapter VI. Fray Mier sets ashore at Soto la Marina River, Tamaulipas, Mexico, April 1817, with a revolutionary expedition led by General Francisco Javier Mina. Mina surrenders to Spanish troops commanded by Royal Brigadier Joaquín Arredondo. The notes and writings that Fray Mier threw into Soto la Marina River were his collection from 22 years of research while an exile in Europe.

36. Fray Mier references a Memoir by an author whose name he does not remember; who reported commerce between China and the Americas before 1492; whose identity remains unknown.

Nonetheless, *1421 The Year China Discovered America* by Gavin Menzies, originally published in Great Britain, 2002, cites mapmakers and authors who might have been Mier's source. The "de Foe religion" is probably a paradigm to Daniel Defoe (1659-1731), author of *Robinson Crusoe.* Defoe, a Presbyterian dissenter who refused to conform to the traditions of the Church of England, wrote well-read Dissenter pamphlets on religious and political topics, which lead to his incarceration. Living an exile life in London,1811-1813, where his *Historia* was first published, Fray Mier would have learned and may have embraced Defoe's Dissenter ideals and their parallel lives in religious dissent.

37. Conrad Malte-Brun, (1755-1826) born in Thistel, Denmark died in Paris, France. A Danish author, his real name was Malthe Konrad Bruun. He wrote, among other works, *Geographie Matématique, physique et politique de toutes les parties de monde* in collaboration with Mentelle Edme, another celebrated geographer, which was published 1803 to 1807 in Paris. Note 1, O'Gorman, op. cit. 49, Note 12, the date of printing mentioned by Fray Mier ought to be 1804, not 1814.

38. Johann Christoph Adelung, (1732-1806), a German grammarian and philologist is the author of *Mithridates, oder allgemeine Sprachenkunde*, published 1806 in Berlin. Mithrídates's subjects are grammar, languages, ethnology, and the Basquelanguage. Adelung believed strongly that the orthography of the written languages hould match that of the spoken language. He declared: "Write as you speak and read as it is written."

39. Chapter 4, Notes 17, 5, and 6, Torquemada, op. cit.

40. Juan Francisco de Montemayor y Córdoba de Cuenca, (1618-1685), colonial Governor of Santo Domingo (1660-1662). Author of *Discurso político histórico jurídico del derecho y repartimiento de presas y despojos aprehendidos en justa Guerra* ("Legal Historical Political Discourse of the Prey and Loot Apprehended in a Just War "), Mexico, 1658. O'Gorman cites this title, but states he is not certain if this is the work to which Fray Mier refers, Note 1, O'Gorman, op. cit., p.49, footnote 13.

41. Mariano Fernández de Echeverría y Veytia (1718-1779), born in Puebla, Mexico, wrote among other works, *Historia antigua de México*, a continuation of the unfinished work of Lorenzo Boturini published 1836 in Mexico. The first English translation of Veytia's *Historia* is, *Ancient American Rediscovered, A Historical Look at This Ancient Land According to the Man Who Experienced It,*

Donald W. Hemingway and W. David Hemingway, copyright 2000, Bonneville Books, Springville, Utah.

42. Lorenzo Boturini Benaducci, (1702-1753) wrote *Idea de una nueva historia general de la America Septentrional. Fundada sobre material copioso de figuras, symbolos, caractères, y geroglificos, cantares, y manuscritos de autores indios, ultimamente descubiertos.* Madrid: Juan de Zuniga, 1746, published 1887 in Mexico. Italian historian, father of Mexican ethnology, Boturini lived in Mexico 1736 to 1743. He collected valuable Pre-Columbian documents, which are archived in the National Library of Paris and the National Museum of Anthropology in Mexico City.

43. Chapter 4, Note 11, Clavijero, op. cit. references Boturini numerous times in his History, op. cit., p. 50. Clavijero affirms Boturini as a reliable source.

"The Gentleman Boturini, on the faith of the histories of the same Toltecs, says that these having acknowledged in their ancient country, Huehuetlapallan, the excess of almost six hours of the solar over the civil year that they used, they arranged by means of a day inserted each four-years which they executed, he says, a hundred and some years before the Christian Era. The same author recounts the year 660 of Christ, when Ixtlilcuechahuac reigned in Tula, Huematzin, celebrated astronomer, summoned with the king's agreement the nation's wise men and described that grand book they drew which they called Teoamoxtli (Divine Book) in which with distinct figures was given the message of the Indians origins, of their dispersion after the confusion of the tongues in Babel, of their pilgrimages in Asia, and the first cities which they had in the continent of America, of the foundation of the Tula Empire, and of their progresses until that time; of the heavens, signs, and planets; of their calendar, cycles, and characters, of the mythological transformations in which they included their moral philosophy, and lastly, of the arcane of the common wisdom hidden among the hieroglyphics of their gods, with all pertinent to the religion, rites and customs. The cited Gentleman adds that the Toltecs had noted in the pictures the solar eclipse which occurred upon the death of our Redeemer, in the year *7 Tochtli*; [7] and that having some erudite and instructed Spaniards in the histories and pictures of the Toltecs, confronting their chronology with ours, they found that, that nation was numbered from the creation of the world until the time in which Jesus Christ was born, 5,199 years, which is punctually the Chronology of the Roman Church, following the computation of the Seventy." [Clavijero op. cit., p. 50, Footnote 7]:

"All those who have studied the history of the cultured nations of Anáhuac, know that those nations were accustomed to noting in their pictures the eclipses, comets, and other phenomena of the heavens. I, having read that which Boturini says, had the curiosity to compare the Mexican years with ours, and I found that the year 34 from Christ or 30 of the Common Era, was 7 *Tochtili*. Whoever may wish to certify should follow the chronological table at the end of the second volume, using the same method that is observed there, until the time of Christ. This I executed for mere curiosity, and not with the end of confirming such anecdotes."

"Make whatever you may of these anecdotes of the Gentleman Botruini, that he left to the free judgement of the prudent and instructed readers, it is certain that the Toltecs had clear and unambiguous notice of the Universal Flood, of the confusion of tongues and of the dispersion of the peoples, and they even named the first primogenitors of their nation who separated from the other families of that dispersion. It is equally certain, as we will see in another place (even though incredible to the European critics, accustomed to measuring by a harrow all the American nations) that the Mexicans and other cultured nations had aligned the civil year to the solar (year) by the means of inserted days, as the Romans from the ordination of Julius Caesar, and that this exactness is owed to the enlightenments of the Toltecs."

44. Fray Sigüenza spent the last years of his life in the completion of his writings on Aztec history and the deciphering of the hieroglyphs and symbolical writings of the Toltecs. Chapter 4, Note 3, O'Gorman, op. cit. p. 50, Footnote 16. *Fénix del Occidente, el Apóstol Santo Tomé*, known today only by reference, is lost. O'Gorman, further, says: "the best biography of Sigüenza to date is Irving A. Leonard's book, *Don Carlos de Sigüenza y Góngora, A Mexican Savant of the Seventeenth Century*, Berkeley, 1929."

45. The author and text of *Historia del verdadero Quetzalcóhuatl, el Apóstol Santo Tomé*, is unknown.

46. Dr. Mier's "Apologia," translated by Gary Bowen, published in *Fray Servando Teresa De Mier: Writing on Ancient Christianity and Spain's Evangelism of Mexico*.

47. Note 1, O'Gorman, op. cit., p. 50, Footnote 18. "St. Brendan of Clonfert, legendary figure, it is said that he was born 484 A.D. and that he crossed the Atlantic in search of the Promised Land. The Medieval geographers believed in the existence of the Isle of San Borondón that they sited near the Antilles Isles. The oldest version of the legend, "*Navigatio Brendani,*" dates from the 11th Century." There are numerous Internet sites that corroborate the legend Fray Mier references on Irish immigration to America.

48. The Pánuco River flows into the Gulf of Mexico at Tampico, Tamaulipas, Mexico.

49. Fray Mier began writing his *Apologia,* 1794. Prepared for publication in 1821, it was never published in his lifetime.

50. Antonio de León y Gama, (1735-1802), was a Mexican archeologist, geographer, astronomer, and author. In 1790, an Aztec calendar-stone was discovered in the Plaza of Mexico. Fray Mier is likely referencing Gama's most cited work, *Descripción de las Dos Piedras,* Mexico City, 1792, which was an early writing on the stones identified as the Mexican Calendar.

51. Baeza, Spain.

52. Fray Antonio de la Calancha, (1584-1654), *Corónica moralizada de Orden de San Agustín en el Peru,* Barcelona, Spain, 1638. Born in Bolivia, Fray Calancha was an Augustinian monk and pioneering anthropologist studying the South American natives.

CHAPTER 6

Alexander Von Humboldt's Contribution To Mexican Anthropology

In 1797, Fray Mier escaped from detention by the Inquisition in Burgos, Spain, fleeing north to France. He arrived in Paris, France June or July 1801 where he lived for one year. He later wrote a memoir, *Desde que llegué a Paris hasta mi salida de alli*, ("Since I Arrived in Paris until My Departure from There"), written when he was imprisoned by the Inquisition in the year 1817.[1] In Paris, he came to know Simon Rodriguez, a tutor to Simon Bolivar. Rodriguez and Mier partnered, opening a Spanish language academy, but Fray Mier's focus continued to be his studies of Mexico's ancient religion and culture. In Paris, he learned that there were noted European scholars who also believed that Christianity existed in ancient America before Columbus. The year he was in Paris a National Council of France convened over formally restoring the Catholic religion in France. He attended Council discussions sharing his Mexican religious beliefs with the Council. Fray Mier's Paris memoir, "Since I Arrived in Paris until My Departure from There," tells of his attendance at the National Council of France.

The celebrated Gregoire, Bishop of Blois, was the soul of this Council, as the first and main support of religion in France. In the name of the Bishops gathered in Paris as agents of the Clergy, he gave an account to the Council of all that happened since the first Council, within and outside of France, and the article regarding Spain is mine. He has written many works, among them the history of the religious sects in the XVIII century that is very curious. A very esteemed work, *Los Anales de la Religión* ("The Annals of Religion"), are almost all his, and he is under the anonymous title of "a Bishop of France" when it is advertised. He told me that the preaching of the Apostle Saint Thomas in America was very probable, after he saw the Latin letter that I wrote about this to Langles, celebrated orientalist, from whom I believed came the notes to Carli's American letters, in which their author, even though a deist, says that the ancient Christianity of America is evident. Carli's notes, as others of Ulloa, are from Mr. Wite-Brune. Gregoire, after having read the short dissertation that on the same I put at the end of the history of the Revolution of New Spain, exhorted me to verify the subject more completely when returning to America, for the glory of religion and the refutation of the incredulous. Also, Baron von Humboldt told me in Paris: "I believed that it was an invention of the friars, and thus I said in my statistical essay; but after I have seen your curious dissertation, I see that it is not so.[2]

The Prussian explorer, geographer, naturalist, and historian, Baron Alexander von Humboldt, extensively explored Latin America from 1799 to 1804. He is honored in history and geography by the "Humboldt Current," plus numerous natural and man-made monuments throughout the Americas. He lived in Paris where he may have first met Fray Mier in 1801. Humboldt dedicated the years 1805 to 1834 writing and publishing his thirty volume *Voyage aux régions équinoxiales du Nouveau Continent* ("Voyage to the Equinoctial Regions of the New Continent"). Humboldt's Latin America travels included a year's residency in Mexico, March 1803 to March 1804. One volume, *Vues des Cordillères et monumens des peuple indigènes de l'Amérique* ("Views of the Cordilleras and Monuments of the Indigenous Peoples of America") published 1810-1813, has been edited and translated into Spanish by Dr. Jaime Labastida, a professor at the Autonomous University of Mexico. It was published in Mexico with the title *Alejandro de Humboldt Aportaciones a la antropología mexicana* ("Alexander von Humboldt, Contributions to Mexican Anthropology").[3]

Dr. Labastida writes in his book foreword how it came to be published in Mexico.

In 1974 the Secretary of the Treasury and Public Credit of Mexico gave to the printers the complete version of *Vues des*

Cordillères et monumens des peuple indigènes de l'Amérique. Of this edition, Katún now publishes that which refers exclusively to our Country, forty-one plates of a total of sixty-nine, or it could be, almost two-thirds of the referenced total graphics, and appreciably the larger part of the work of what touches on this written text.[4]

Fray Mier's Paris meetings with Humboldt led to his memoir of Humboldt's disbelief in ancient American Christianity as an "invention of the friars," and then Humboldt's change of opinion after reading Fray Mier's "curious dissertation" that gives cause to believe that Humboldt's 1803 to 1804 residency in Mexico was sparked by his encounter with Fray Mier and the consequential result of Humboldt's "statistical essay," which very likely is his anthropological work on the indigenous people of Mexico.

Humboldt was well known and respected in New Spain. While living in New Spain, he was offered a cabinet position in the national government, which he declined. The building where Humboldt lived, 80 República de Uruguay Street, Mexico City, is memorialized by a plaque. He lived near the central plaza in the heart of the historic center of Mexico City. He is also memorialized at the corner of 69 República de Uruguay and Isabel la Católica, the site of the National Library of Mexico with a bronze statue on the Library's street corner. The Library was founded 1833 but the building is a remodel of the San Agustín Church that would have existed at the time of Humboldt's stay in Mexico City. A block away is the Porta Coaeli College where Fray Mier studied. These historical markers exhibit Mexico's admiration of Humboldt. The proximity of Humboldt's living quarters, near a National Library, close to where Fray Mier lived and studied further evidence that Humboldt's year in Mexico City to study Mexico's history and anthropology was very probably planned in consultation with Fray Mier.

Labastida's "Contributions to Mexican Anthropology," applies the scientific method of a questioning, doubting, anthropologist. Humboldt lacks the believing faith of a "French Bishop" or a "Mexican Dominican Friar." Nevertheless, the doubting Prussian anthropologist puts forth scientific and historical evidence backing the findings of the Mexican Friar. "Contributions to Mexican Anthropology" is Humboldt's analysis of forty-one plates touching on ancient Mexican culture, which were survivors of the Spanish conquest. The following are selected quotes extracted from Humboldt's analysis of the plates and their anthropological history witnessing the history and culture of the indigenous people of Mexico. Humboldt's extracted quotes are summary notes explaining how Humboldt's research bears witness to Fray Mier's thesis that "the ancient Christianity of America is evident."

"PLATE VIII"

"GENEALOGY OF THE PRINCES OF ATZACAPOTZALCO"

Alexander von Humboldt wrote:

The paper that has served for the hieroglyphic paintings of the Aztec peoples show much similarity with the ancient Egyptian papyrus, made with the fiber of the papyrus reed (*Cyperus papyrus*). The plant that was used in Mexico for the fabrication of paper is what in our gardens is commonly known under the name aloe: it is the agave (*Agave americana*), called *metl* or *maguey* by the peoples of the Aztec race. The procedures used in the fabrication of this paper are very similar to those used in the islands of the South Seas, for making papers with the bark of the white mulberry tree (*Broussonetia pauyrifera*). I have seen pieces of three meters long by two meters wide. They currently cultivate agave not to make paper but to prepare its juice, in the moment in which the plant unfolds it thorns and flowers, the intoxicating drink known as *octli* or *pulque*, as the pita or *metl* can at once replace the hemp cloth of Asia, the papyrus reed of Egypt, and the grapevine of Europe.[5]

I visited Teotihuacán, Mexico, 30 miles to the northeast of Mexico City in 2013. Teotihuacán is believed to have been the largest city of pre-Columbian America with an archeological history beginning 100 B.C. Taken to a curio shop near the ancient pyramids, I was shown the many usages of the maguey by the ancient Aztec culture. The curio shop proprietor used an obsidian blade to cut the thorn from the tip of the agave leaf withdrawing it with attached hemp threads ready for sewing cloth. He then sliced into the leaf extracting membrane from the leaf's interior about 4 inches by 10 inches that looked like a sheet of wet parchment paper. Taking a ballpoint pen from his pocket, the shop owner wrote a note on the wet paper to pass around for us to read. The Aztecs did not have ball point pens, but a quill pen and ink could have been readily made for an Aztec scribe. The proprietor then explained how pulque, a fermented drink, is made from maguey juice. Today pulque is most commonly distilled into mezcal and tequila, popular Mexican alcoholic beverages.

Dr. Jared Diamond is an American geographer, anthropologist, historian, author, and Professor of Geography at University of California, Los Angeles. His best-known popular science book, *Guns, Germs, and Steel; The Fates of Human Societies*, was published 1997. *Guns, Germs, and Steel. . ."* was an international best-seller, and received several prizes including the 1998 *Pulitzer Prize, Aventis Prize for Science Books*. In *Guns, Germs, and Steel. . .,"* Dr. Diamond. on the invention and origins of writing. reports:

> The two indisputable independent inventions of writing were achieved by the Sumerians of Mesopotamia somewhat before 3000 B.C. and by Mexican Indians before 600 B.C.; Egyptian writing of 3000 B.C. and Chinese writing (by 1300 B.C.) may also have arisen independently. Probably all other peoples, who have developed writing since then have borrowed, adapted, or at least been inspired by existing systems.[6]

Dr. Diamond identifies "Mexican Indians" as the inventors of writing in the Americas. These "Mexican Indians" were the probable writers of *The Book of Mormon*[7], an abridgement of ancient records in America. Humboldt tells how paper was made from agave by the people of Mexico. *The Book of Mormon* tells of records burned and epistles exchanged between enemy forces. To read Humboldt and Diamond, and to witness a wet paper sheet pulled from an agave leaf and then written upon are evidences that agave paper sheets were the source of papyrus like scrolls for the keeping of records, and for epistles written and exchanged in the wilderness between enemies locked in ferocious warfare as described in *The Book of Mormon*.

Fray Mier writes in his "Farewell Letter to the Mexicans:"

The Indians had in their power (as the missionaries in Veracruz gave in written testimony to the celebrated Fray Gregorio García) the entire Bible in images and hieroglyphic figures, they confused them with the passage of time, they put into practice the Scriptures' histories, and confused their own history and their religion.

Humboldt provides evidence that Mexican maguey paper writings would be the source for these Scriptures that ancient Mexicans wrote in hieroglyphic to record and spread the religious message of ancient Christianity .

"P L A T E   I X "

"A Z T E C A   H I E R O G L Y P H I C   M A N U S C R I P T, C O N S E R V E D   I N   T H E   V A T I C A N   L I B R A R Y " [8]

Alexander von Humboldt wrote:

We see that the practice of hieroglyphic paintings was common to the Toltecas, the Tlaxcaltecas, and the Aztecas and to another multitude of tribes that since the VII Century of our era appeared in succession on the plateau of Anáhuac. But nowhere do we find alphabetic characters: you could even believe that the perfection of the symbolic signs and the facility with which they painted the objects, have impeded the introduction of letters.[9]

Valadez [sic] and Acosta, the first monks who visited America, already spoke of the Aztec paintings as "writing similar to that of the Egyptians." [10]

According to the investigations that I have done, it appears that at the present time there exist no more than six collections of Mexican paintings in all Europe: those of Escorial [Spain], Bologna [Italy], Velletri [Italy], Rome [Italy], Vienna [Austria], and Berlin [German].[11]

In spite of the enormous quantity of paintings considered as monuments of Mexican idolatry that were burned in the beginning of the conquest by order of the Bishops and the first missionaries, the Gentleman Boturini, from whom we remember the misfortunes further back, even had good

148

success, toward the middle of the past century, in gathering close to five hundred of these hieroglyphic paintings. This collection, the most beautiful and rich of all, has been scattered; and the same has happened to that of Sigüenza, of which only scarce remains survived in the Library of San Pedro and San Pablo in Mexico until the expulsion of the Jesuits. Some few of the paintings collected by Botoruni were sent to Europe on a Spanish ship that was the prey of an English pirate. Never has it been known if these paintings got to England of if they were thrown to the sea as if they were a coarse woven canvas and badly painted.[12]

The cosmogony of the Mexicans, their traditions about the mother of mankind, fallen from her estate of primitive happiness and innocence; the idea of a great inundation from which only one family escaped upon a raft: the history of a pyramid-shaped building raised by the pride of mankind and destroyed by the anger of the gods; the ceremonies of ablutions practiced at the birth of the children, those idols made with kneaded corn flour and distributed in small portions to the people meeting in the confines of the temples; those confessions of sins made by the penitents, those religious congregations that are like our monasteries of men and women; this belief, universally spread, that white men and of long beards, practitioners of a great quantity of customs, had transformed the political and religious system of the people: all these circumstances had made the monks, who accompanied the Spanish army at the moment of the conquest, believe that in a very remote age Christianity had been preached in the new continent. Some learned, Mexicans believed they recognized in this mysterious personage the Apostle Saint Thomas, the great priest of Tula, who the Cholutecas knew as under the name of Quetzalcóatl. There is no doubt that Nestorianism, mixed the dogmas of the Buddhists and the Shamans, it may have spread by the Tartarian of the Manchurians, in the northeast of Asia; in consequence, one could suppose, with certain semblances of reason, that some Christian ideas were communicated, by the same way, to the Mexican people, above all to the inhabitants of this boreal region from which the Toltecs came and which we ought to consider as the great manufactory of men (*officina virorum*) in the New World.

This supposition would be, actually, much more

admissible than the hypothesis according to which the ancient traditions of the Hebrews and Christians had come over to America through Scandinavian colonies, established from the Century XII, on the coasts of Greenland, Labrador, and possibly, even on the Island of Newfoundland. Without doubt, these European colonists visited a part of the continent to which they gave the name of *Drogeo*; they knew countries situated to the southeast, inhabited by cannibalistic people gathered in populous cities; but, without going to examine here if these cities were those of the province of Ichiac and Confachiqui, visited by Hernando de Soto, the conquistador of Florida, it will suffice to observe that the religious ceremonies, the dogmas, and traditions, which astonished the first Spanish missionaries were found, without any doubt in Mexico, ever since the arrival of the Toltecs, and by consequence three or four centuries before the navigations of the Scandinavians to the eastern coasts of the New Continent.[13]

By the time Humboldt found and examined Plate IX, "Azteca Hieroglyphic Manuscript," it had been hidden in the Vatican Library for nearly 300 years. Chapter 3, "The Mier Paradox," sets forth the politics of slavery in the New World, which is the probable cause for the suppression of this manuscript. In his essay on the manuscript, Humboldt, a famous anthropologist, authenticates Fray Mier's writings on Saint Thomas and Hebrew-Christian religious ceremonies, dogmas, and traditions that the first Spanish missionaries found, beyond any doubt, in Mexico.

Humboldt writes of Mexican hieroglyphic paintings and manuscripts in "writing like that of the Egyptians." Fray Mier writes that the Mexicans wrote in hieroglyphics and read the hieroglyphic folios as we would read a book written in Spanish or Latin. Humboldt and Fray Mier provide evidence of *Book of Mormon* Christianity in The Americas, and evidence that the writing of Mexican records was in "the language of the Egyptians."[14] Note also, Plate IX pictures two men fighting or embracing one another one brown and the other white; evidence of the racial diversity in the ancient Americas described in *The Book of Mormon*.

Humboldt credits "Valadez [sic] and Acosta" as "the first monks who visited America." They were early, but they were not the first missionaries in the Americas. Fray Diego de Valadés, author of *Rethorica Christiana*, published 1579, was born in Tlaxcala, New Spain, the mestizo son of a Mexican woman and Spanish conquistador Diego de Valadés from Extremadua, Spain. Fray Joseph de Acosta, born in Medina del Campo, Spain, lived and traveled throughout Central America, Peru and Mexico. His best-known work is *Historia natural y moral de las Indias* ("Natural and Moral History of the Indies"), published 1590.[15] In the 1963 Spanish edition prologue, Dr. Edmundo O'Gorman writes "that not all in the *History* was an original of the Father (Acosta)." O'Gorman says Fray Acosta plagiarized the writings of those first monks. That said, O'Gorman does not deny the authenticity of Fray Acosta's *History*, in which Acosta writes Chapter 27, "Other Ceremonies and Rites of the Indians Similar to Ours," and cites Indian practices like the Law of Moses and Gospel Laws, such as ritual bathing and the cleansing of sins, baptismal ceremonies, and circumcision.[16]

Humboldt's anthropological synopsis of ancient Mexican traditions on the origin and development of earth is a replica of Old Testament Judaic accounts of Eve, Noah, the Tower of Babel, and the Law of Moses; also add, New Testament Christian practices of sacrament, confessions, and church worship. Who were those white men of long beards, practitioners of customs that transformed the political and religious system of the ancient people of Mexico to Christian ceremonies, dogmas, and traditions in a very remote age? Humboldt speculates they may have been any of the following: the Apostle Saint Thomas, a mix of Orientals, or Scandinavians. Like Fray Mier, Humboldt finds evidence of ancient Christianity, but how Christianity came to America before Spanish missionaries arrived was pure speculation by anthropologist Baron Alexander von Humboldt and theologian Fray Servando Teresa de Mier.

"PLATE XI"

"AZTEC HIEROGLYPHICS FROM THE MANUSCRIPTS OF VELLETRI [ITALY]"[17]

Alexander von Humboldt wrote:

Of all the Mexican manuscripts that survive in Italy, the Velletri *Codex Borgianus* is the largest and most notable, because of the splendor and extreme variety of its colors. It has between forty-four or fifty-five *palms* (close to eleven meters) long and thirty-eight folds or sixty-six pages. It is a ritual and astrological almanac that by the distribution of the simple hieroglyphics of the days and by the groups of mythological figures, it appears very much like the *Codex Vaticanus*.

One is unable to fix eyes upon these paintings without a swarm of interesting spiritual questions appearing. Did hieroglyphic paintings made in the time of the Toltec dynasty, and by consequence from the VII Century of our era, still exist during the lifetime of Cortés? In this period, were there no copies of the famous *Divine Book*, called *Teoamoxtli*, redacted in Tula the year 660 by the astrologer *Huematzin*, and in which one found the history of heaven and earth, the cosmogony, the description of the constellations, the division of time, the migrations of the people, the mythology, and the morality? This Mexican *Purana*, the *Teoamoxtli*, whose memory has been conserved through the passage of so many centuries of Aztec traditions. Was this one of the books the fanaticism of the monks set fire to in Yucatán, of which Father Acosta, more learned and cultured than his contemporaries, deplores the loss?[18]

Then, whatever may be the relative antiquity of the different human races established in the mountains of Mexico, which constitute the American Caucasus, it appears certain that none of these people knew since a long time ago the barbarous practice of sacrificing human victims. The principal deity of the Toltecans was called Tlaloctecuhtli and was, at the time, the god of the water, the mountains, and the storms. To the eyes of this mountainous people, on the high peaks always covered by clouds that mysteriously made the thunderclap and lightening: is there where the mansion of the Great Spirit Teotl is found, this invisible being who is called *Ipalnemoani* and *Tloque-Nahuaque* because *he does not exist but for himself*, and because *he holds everything within himself*. The Aztecs followed this same cult until the year 1317 in which the war with the inhabitants of the city of Xochimilco gave them the first idea of human sacrifice. The Mexican historians who, immediately after the capture of Tenochtitlan, wrote in their own language, but made use of the Spanish alphabet, have conveyed to us the details of this repulsive event.[19]

Everywhere in the ancient continent, we find traces of

human sacrifices, the origin of these is lost in the darkness of time. The Mexicans' history, on the contrary, has conserved for us the story of the events that have given a ferocious and bloodthirsty character to the religion of a people that, primitively, did not offer to the deity anything other than animals or the first fruits of the earth.[20]

Humboldt's portrayal and dimensions of the Velletri manuscripts tell us these were not mere painted sheets of paper. They were in fact encyclopedic Mexican folios. He identifies the content of the Velletri manuscript as a Mexican *Teoamoxtli*, or *Divine Book*, with the kind of historical and moral values we call Holy Scriptures. Humboldt writes that the Velletri manuscripts were among the few survivors of ancient books burned en masse by early Spanish monks, an act deplored by Father Acosta. He also writes that the manuscripts evidence when religious sacrifices like the Law of Moses morphed to human sacrifice in the year 1317 A.D. In his "Apologia", Fray Mier states human sacrifices were practiced at times and then prohibited. In his "Eleventh Note of the Second Letter from an American," Fray Mier writes that human sacrifices were no more common in Mexico than they were in Europe. Europe's human sacrifices, which Fray Mier references are the Inquisition's torture and burning at the stake of heretics of Christian dogma.

"PLATE XII"

"AZTEC BAS-RELIEF FOUND IN THE GREAT PLAZA OF MEXICO CITY"[21]

Alexander von Humboldt wrote:

Señor Dupé, who I had the opportunity of citing at the beginning of this work, copied all the relief; in the same place, I have compared the exactitude of his drawing, a small part of which I have engraved in this plate. I have chosen the notable group in which is found a bearded man. In general, it can be observed that the Indians of Mexico have a little more beard than the rest of indigenous Americans and it is not even unusual to see mustaches on them. Could there have been an ancient province whose inhabitants had long beards? Or what is seen on the relief, is it false? Did it form part of those fantastic adornments by means of which the warriors sought to inspire terror to the enemy?[22]

Male facial hair is not a genetic trait of the indigenous people of America, but Humboldt notes bearded men were carved on the Mexican bas-relief. Beards were so rare that Humboldt sets forth the conundrum: could beards have simply been an adornment on the bas-relief to inspire terror? *The Book of Mormon* accounts of the migration of two groups of people to ancient America: "One came from Jerusalem in 600 B.C. . ." "The other came much earlier when the Lord confounded the tongues at the Tower of Babel."[23] Both migrant groups had the genes of bearded men. Humboldt's noting of the beards and mustaches seen on the ancient Aztec bas-relief found in Mexico City is evidence that the indigenous people of Mexico had a set of genes different from most indigenous people of America.

"PLATE XIV"

"RELIEF IN BASALT WHICH REPRESENTS THE MEXICAN CALENDAR"[24]

Alexander von Humboldt wrote:

The monks and other Spanish writers who visited Mexico a little after the conquest gave us vague and frequently contradictory notions of the different calendars used by the peoples of the Toltec and Aztec races. These notions are found in the works of Gomara, Valadés, Acosta, and Torquemada. The latter, despite his superstitious credulity, has passed on to us in his *Monarquia indiana* a collection of precious facts that prove an exact knowledge of the places: he lived for fifty years among the Mexicans; he arrived at the city of Tenochtitlan [Mexico City] at a time in which the natives still preserved a great quantity of historical paintings, and in front of the house of the Marques del Valle [Hernán Cortés] on the *Plaza Mayor* [Great Plaza of Mexico City] were still seen the remains of the Great *Teocalli* [Temple] dedicated to the God Huitzilopochtli. Torquemada poured over the manuscripts of three religious Franciscans: Bernardino de Sahagún, Andrés de Olmos, and Toribio de Benavente, all profoundly instructed in American languages and who had arrived in New Spain at the time of Cortés, before the year 1528. Despite these advantages, this historian of Mexico has not provided us all the clarification, about the Mexican chronology and calendar that would have been expected and hoped from his zeal and education. He even states with so little exactitude, that in his work one reads that the Aztec year ends in December and begins in February. For a long time, there existed in Mexico, in the convents and in the public libraries, materials more instructive than the accounts of the first Spanish historians. Indigenous authors, such as Cristóbal del Castillo (native of Texcoco and deceased in 1606, at the age of eighty years), Fernando de Alvarado Tezozomoc, and Domingo Chimalpain, left manuscripts in Aztec language on the history and chronology of their ancestors. These manuscripts include an enormous quantity of dates, signs of the time according to the Christian era, and the civil and ritual calendar of the indigenous people that have been studied with benefit by the wise Carlos de Sigüenza, Professor of Mathematics in the University of Mexico; the Milan traveler Boturini Benaducci; the Abbot Clavijero, and in later times, by Señor Gama, of whom I have had the occasion in another work of citing very favorably his astronomical works. Anyway, the year 1790 a stone of enormous volume was discovered in the foundations of the ancient *teocalli* loaded with characters evidently relative to the Mexican calendar, the religious holidays, and days in which the sun passed by the zenith of Mexico City. This stone served, at the time, to clarify doubtful points and to call the attention of some indigenous people well-informed on the Mexican calendar.[25]

This Aztec Calendar Stone, discovered December 17, 1790 buried in Mexico City's Zócalo, is on exhibit in Mexico City's National Museum of Anthropology. Fray Mier refers to the Aztec Calendar stone, as well as most of the authors cited by Humboldt in his Mexican calendar essay. This heightens speculation that Humboldt's one-year residency in Mexico was instigated by his Paris meeting with Fray Mier, which drove Humboldt to his anthropological investigation of Fray Mier's dissertation on Christianity in ancient America.

"PLATE XIX"

"HIEROGLYPHIC HISTORY OF THE AZTECS, FROM THE FLOOD UNTIL THE FOUNDATION OF MEXICO CITY"[26]

Alexander von Humboldt wrote:

The drawing of the migration of the Aztecs formed part anciently of Doctor Sigüenza's famous collection, the hieroglyphic paintings that he had received in inheritance from an Indian nobleman, Juan de Alva Ixtlilxochitl. This collection, as Abbot Clavijero affirms it, was conserved until 1759 in the College of the Jesuits in Mexico. It is not known what may have happened to it after the dissolution of the Order. In vain I have leafed through the Aztec paintings conserved in the University library: I could not find the original of the drawing that appears on the plate; but in Mexico various ancient copies exist that, certainly, were not made from the Gemelli Carreri engraving. If one compares the hieroglyphic content on the Rome and Velletri manuscripts and in the collections of Mendoza and Gama, with all those that the painting of the migrations offer of symbolic and chronology, one certainly could not testify to the hypothesis according to which the drawing of Gemelli is the fiction of some Spanish monk who had intended to prove, by means of apocryphal source materials, that the traditions of the Hebrews come to be found among the indigenous peoples of America. Everything we know of the history, of the worship and cosmogony fables of the Mexicans, forms a system whose parts are closely linked among themselves. The paintings, the bas-reliefs, the idols ornaments, and of the divine stones (*teótetl* among the Aztecs, ζεον πέτρα among the Greeks) everything accuses the same character, the same physiognomy. The cataclysm from the beginning of the Aztecs history, and of how Coxcox saved himself in a small boat, is shown under the same circumstances in the drawing that represents the destructions and regenerations of the world. The four indications (*tlalpilli*) that relate to these catastrophes or with the divisions of the *Great Year* are found sculptured on a stone discovered in the foundations of the *teocalli* of Mexico City.[27]

Juan de Alva Ixtlilxochitl was the son of Fernando de Alba

Cortés Ixtlilxochitl (circa 1568 to 1648). Fernando de Alba Ixtlilxochitl was a direct descendant of the kings of Acolhuacan and Tenochtitlan, an author of Aztec history, and collector of inherited Aztec manuscripts and codices. Fernando de Alba Ixtlilxochitl's collection was passed on by his son to Father Carlos de Sigüenza y Gongora (1645-1700), who was dismissed from the Jesuit Order after six years to then become a secular priest. The writings of Fernando de Alba Ixtlilxochitl have survived. His best-known complete work is *Historia de la nación chichimeca* ("History of the Chichimea Nation").[28] Other diverse historical works and fragments have also survived and been published like, *Obras históricas de don Fernando de Alva Ixtlilxóchitl* ("Don Fernando de Alva Ixtlixóchitl Historical Works").[29]

Truth or a fiction of the monks, Humboldt leaves unanswered the question of the origin of Hebrew traditions he finds in the hieroglyphic history of the Aztecs. He records how Coxcox survived a cataclysmic flood. In some Aztec legends Coxcox is in the image of the biblical Noah. From Humboldt's anthropological study, no longer should it be said that there are no signs of Hebrew-Christian influence among the pre-Columbian indigenous tribes of America. How Hebrew-Christian influence came to America still requires further study of the surviving native hieroglyphic histories and the writings of the Catholic priests.

"PLATE XXVI"

"FRAGMENT OF A HIEROGLYPHIC MANUSCRIPT CONSERVED IN THE ROYAL LIBRARY OF DRESDEN"[30]

Alexander von Humboldt wrote:

In accordance with this principle of which the monuments explain one another, and to better study the complexity of a people's history; it is necessary to have before one's eyes the collection of the works in which this people have marked their impression and their character. I [Humboldt] decided to have engraved extracted fragments of the Mexican manuscripts from Dresden and Vienna. The first of these manuscripts was for me a complete unknown when I initiated the printing of these pages. It is not easy to give a complete report of the hieroglyphic paintings that escaped the destruction that threatened them, at the time of the discovery of America, by the monastic fanaticism and the stupid indifference of the conquistadors.[31]

According to the reports that the gentleman Böttiger had the kindness of communicating to me, this Aztec manuscript appears to have been bought in Vienna by the librarian Götze, during the literary journey that he took through Italy in 1739. It is of *metl* (*American agave*) paper or cardboard, like those that I have brought from New Spain: it makes up a *tabella plicatilis* of almost six meters long that contains forty sheets, covered on both sides. Each page is 0.295 meters [7 inches and three lines] long, by 0.085 meters [3 inches and two lines] wide. This format, like the ancient *Díptychs*, distinguishes the Dresden manuscript from those of Vienna, Velletri, and the Vatican; but what above all makes it extremely notable is the disposition of the simple hieroglyphics, many of which are put in order by lines, like in a true symbolic scripture.[32]

Despite his criticism of the "monastic fanaticism and the stupid indifference of the conquistadors," Humboldt found ancient Mexican manuscripts written in hieroglyphics on agave paper conserved in European libraries after he returned from his year in Mexico. The Dresden Codex is a calendar of ritual dates, as Labastida defines it, written in hieroglyphics, which evidence a written language by the Maya as well as Aztec civilizations of Mexico. Chapter 3, "The Mier Paradox," sets forth a hypothesis on why Mexican manuscripts were destroyed by the conquistadors.

Karl August Böttiger (1760-1835) was for 31 years the Director of the Dresden Museum of Antiquities. Humboldt adds a footnote on a work by Böttiger, *Ideen zur Archailogie der Malerei*, ("Ideas for Archaeology of Painting"). Johann Christian Götze (1692-1749) was, from 1734 to his death in 1749, Director of the Royal Library of Dresden. Humboldt has a footnote on a work by Götze, *Denkwüdirgkeiten der Dresdner Bibliothek, erst Sammlung*, ("The Curiosities of the Royal Library of Dresden, First Collection"). Plate XXVI is known as the Dresden Codex, and is believed to be the oldest surviving manuscript written in America. Tradition is that it was sent in 1519 by Hernán Cortés to Spain's King Charles I as a tribute. Humboldt describes the Dresden Codex as an "Aztec manuscript," Jaime Labastida, the translator of Humboldt's work published in Mexico 1974, 1986, under the title, *Aportaciones a la antropología Mexicana* ("Contributions to Mexican Anthropology"), adds the following footnote to Plate XXVI. "As is known, the Dresden Codex is not Aztec but Maya; and in it one finds phrases, like those they have put forth in relief of a multitude of investigations, there are numerous quantities that have a direct relation with the calendar and the ritual dates." *Tabella plicatilis* is a "fan plate." The pages of Plate XXVI are folded like a hand-held fan or accordion. The page size: 0.295 meters (11.62 inches) by 0.085 (3.35 inches) is the size of the sheets Bowen saw cut from a maguey leaf at Teotihuacán. Humboldt's parenthetic description of the pages as (7 inches and three lines long) by (3 inches and two lines wide) may be his defining the writing margins of a page.

"PLATES XXX AND XXXI"

"RUINS OF MIGUITLAN OR MITLA IN THE PROVINCE OF OAXACA; PLAN AND HEIGHT"[3]

Alexander von Humboldt wrote:

After having described in this work so many barbarous monuments that only offer a purely historical interest, I experience a certain satisfaction in letting you know of a building built by the Zapotecs, ancient inhabitants of Oaxaca, covered with elegant and extremely remarkable ornaments. This building is known in the country by the name of *Mitla Palace*. It is situated to the southeast of the city of Oaxaca or Guaxaca, ten leagues distance, on the road to Tehuantepec, in a granite region. *Mitla* is no more than a contraction of the word *Miguitlan*, that in Mexican means: "Place of Desolation, Place of Sadness." This designation appears well chosen, for a site of such a savage and mournful mode, that according to the story of travelers, one almost never hears the chirping of birds there. Zapotec Indians call these ruins *Leoba* or *Luiva, Tomb*, this alluding to the excavations below the walls loaded with arabesques.[34]

Mitla is within the modern municipality of San Pablo Villa de Mitla, Oaxaca, Mexico. An ancient religious center of the Zapotec people, Mitla was inhabited since 100-650 A.D. and perhaps as early as 900 B.C. Humboldt's translation of Mitla as "Place of Desolation" matches the term found in *The Book of Mormon* "Land of Desolation" and "City of Desolation."[35]

"PLATE XXXVI"

"FRAGMENT OF A CHRISTIAN CALENDAR, EXTRACTED FROM AZTEC MANUSCRIPTS, CONSERVED IN THE ROYAL LIBRARY OF BERLIN. [36]

Alexander von Humboldt wrote:

> This is about the hieroglyphic calendar made after the arrival of the Spaniards, of which we spoke at the beginning of this work. The paper is of *metl*; the figures are only profiles and lack colors, as in some strips of Egyptian mummy: it is writing, rather than a painting. The holidays are indicated by circles that designate units. The Holy Ghost is found represented in the figure of the Mexican eagle, *coxcaquauhtli*.
>
> By the time, in which the calendar was composed, Christianity was confused with Mexican mythology; the missionaries not only tolerated they even assisted, up to a certain point, the mix of ideas, symbols, and worship. They persuaded the indigenous people that the Gospel, in the most remote times, had already been preached in America; they sought its signs in the Aztec ritual with the same ardor that the learned suppose, in our days, in devoting themselves to the study of the Sanskrit, or in discussing the extensive analogy between Greek mythology and that which originated on the borders of the Ganges and the Bourampouter.[37]

Fray Mier ends his "Farewell Letter to the Mexicans" declaring: "The Deists themselves today confess that the ancient preaching of the Gospel in America is beyond doubt." A Deist holds the religious belief that God created the universe and established rational comprehensive moral and natural laws but does not intervene in human affairs through miracles or supernatural revelation. Baron Alexander von Humboldt is on a list of famous "Deists" and people who have in some way expressed beliefs which can be classified as "Deistic."[38]

Fray Mier's first acquaintance with Humboldt was probably during the 1801 Nation Council of France in Paris, which provoked Humboldt's year in Mexico to study Mexican anthropology and Fray Mier's proposition on ancient Christianity in The Americas. Humboldt's extracted essay quote, on "Plate XXXVI, Fragment of a

Christian Calendar," puts forth an anthropological and deistic response: "Christianity was confused with Mexican mythology; the missionaries not only tolerated they even assisted, up to a certain point, the mix of ideas, symbols, and worship. They persuaded the indigenous people that the Gospel, in the most remote times, had already been preached in America. A counter argument can be found in Fray Mier's "Apologia," where he writes:

> And, who does not know of the blasphemies of the incredulous against the Christian religion, whose divinity, they say, for sixteen centuries was put to the test, up to crushing their bones, with its expansion into all the world by only twelve men, and with the universality of the Church; and in the end a New World was discovered where nothing was known of it? It is false. All throughout America, monuments and vestige evidences of Christianity were found, according to the unanimous testimony of the missionaries.

Humboldt found vestige evidences of Christianity, disclosed in "Contributions to Mexican Anthropology;" nevertheless, he declares those vestige evidences to be a theological invention of the missionaries. Fray Mier and Christian missionaries would call an allegation of an invented theocracy a "blasphemy of the incredulous against the Christian religion". Which theory is correct Humboldt's "an invented theocracy created by missionaries;" or Fray Mier's, "it is false to declare a New World was discovered where nothing was known of Christianity?"

Briefly, there are two arguments in contradiction to Humboldt's theory that the ideas, symbols, and worship of ancient Christianity in The Americas were inventions of the missionaries.

The First is outlined in Chapter 7, Subsection XIV "Ethnicity" quotes from *Los Indios de México y Nueva España* ("The Indians of Mexico and New Spain") by Fray Bartolomé de las Casas (1474-1566), Bishop of Chiapas, Mexico, 1545 to 1547. Bishop de las Casas writes that the indigenous people of Yucatan, Nicaragua, and nowhere else in America practiced circumcision. Humboldt identifies Father Joseph de Acosta (1539-1600), one of the earliest monks to visit America, as more learned and cultured than his contemporaries. Father Acosta in *Historia natural y moral de las Indias) Vida Religiosa y Civil de los Indios* ("Natural and Moral

History of the Indies) Religious and Civil Life of the Indians ")
writes "Of Other Ceremonies and Rituals of the Indians Similar to
Ours." He parallels the similarity of "their" and "our" ceremonies
and rituals with the statement: "The Indians had other innumerable
ceremonies and rituals, and in many of them there is a similarity to
the ancient law of Moses."[39] The Law of Moses and circumcision
were controversial issues in the early Christian Church recorded in
the New Testament. It is incredible to believe that the Law of Moses
and circumcision were ideas, symbols, and worship tolerated and
taught by 16th Century missionaries to the indigenous people of
America.

The Second is slavery, a subject discussed in Chapter 3, "The
Mier Paradox." Rarely mentioned in histories of the conquest of
America is the encomienda system, which granted a Spanish
emigrant property rights to a plot of land and to the indigenous
Americans living on the land. The outcome was the native
inhabitants of a deeded plot became slaves. These Spanish
landlords became most unhappy, when informed by a few vocal
missionaries that that their encomienda ownership of native slaves
was a flagrant violation of Catholic dogma decreed by Papal Bulls
issued between the years 1434 to 1526, if the native bonded slaves
were Christians. This created a political and religious scandal in
America and Spain. The bad luck of the Spanish encomenderos was
that "throughout America, monuments and vestige evidences of
Christianity were found" by the missionaries, quoting Fray Mier.
In summary, if Spain accepted Christianity was practiced in
America before 1492, encomienda rights were void. One solution,
described by Humboldt in his Plate XXVI section, was the
destruction of the records of the native people at the time of the
discovery of America, "by the monastic fanaticism and the stupid
indifference of the conquistadors." The destruction of those Native
American records was a knowing and willful decision to erase any
evidence of ancient Christianity. A few surviving records were the
basis of Humboldt's anthropological study. Beyond that, all that
was left were traces of oral history, mythology, the diaries of the
missionaries, and confusion. Humboldt wrote: "Christianity was
confused with Mexican mythology; the missionaries not only
tolerated, they even assisted, up to a certain point, the mix of ideas,
symbols, and worship. They persuaded the indigenous people that
the Gospel, in the most remote times, had already been preached in
America; they sought signs of it in the Aztec ritual." An example of

the mix of ideas, symbols, and worship tolerated by the missionaries is Fray Mier's Inquisition for his Virgin of Guadalupe sermon. He refused to admit that he had denied the sacred Virgin of Guadalupe. His defense was that the Mexican Virgin of Guadalupe was a mix of ideas, symbols, and worship of the Mexican Tonantzin, Mother of the true God, with the Spanish Virgin of Guadalupe. The purpose of the mix was to hasten the evangelization of the Mexican people. The evangelism theme is pervasive in Spanish writings on the conquest of Mexico. Converted to the Catholic faith the native people were exempt from slavery, but as converts they were made docile, subservient, subjects of the King and Church of Spain.

Baron Alexander von Humboldt verified Fray Mier's historical account of the existence of ancient Christianity in Mexico, then came to a Deist conclusion that it was theocracy invented by the missionaries. Fray Mier, who had not one year but decades of study as a Doctor of Theology, came to a Christian conclusion.

CHAPTER 6 NOTES

1. *Escritos y memorias Servando Teresa de Mier*, Biblioteca del Estudiante Universitario 56. Prologue and Selection by Edmundo O'Gorman, Ediciones de la Universidad Nacional Autonoma, Mexico, D.F., 1945, pp. 53-90.

2. Ibid., 75-76.

3. de Humboldt, Alejandro; Spanish translation from French, and comments by Jaime Labastida; *Aportaciones a la antropología mexicana*. Mexico, D. F.: Editorial Katún, S. A., 1974.

4. Ibid., VIII-IX.

5. Ibid PLATE VIII, 63-68. Ibid., 63-64.

6. Diamond, Jared. *Guns germs, and Steel; The Fates of Human Societies*. New York: W. W. Norton & Company, 1997, p. 218.

7. The Church of Jesus Christ of Latter-day Saints. *The Book of Mormon, Another Testament of Jesus Christ*. Salt Lake City, Utah, U.S.A. 1992, First published 1830.

8. Humboldt, op. cit., PLATE IX, 71-100.

9. Humboldt, op. cit., 73.

10. Humboldt, op. cit. ,77-78. Fray Diego Valadés (1533-1582) author of *Rhetorica Christiana*, and Fray Joseph de Acosta (1539-

1600) author of *Historia natural y moral de las Indias) Vida Religiosa y civil de los Indios.*

11. Humboldt op. cit., 88.

12. Humboldt, op. cit., 93. Boturini and Sigüenza are sources reference by Fray Mier in his writings.

13. Humboldt, op. cit., 98-99.

14. *The Book of Mormon.* 1 Nephi 1:2; Mormon 9:32.

15. de Acosta, Joseph. Prologue and selections by Edmundo O'Gorman. *(Historia natural y moral de las Indias) Vida Religiosa y civil de los Indios.* Biblioteca del Estudiante Universitario No. 83. Mexico, D. F.: Universidad Nacional Autónomoa de México, 1963, published in Spain in 1590.

16. Ibid., 70-72.

17. Humboldt, op. cit., PLATE XI, 109-121.

18. Humboldt, op. cit., 109-110.

19. Humboldt, op. cit., 114.

20. Humboldt, op. cit., 116.

21. Humboldt, op. cit., PLATE XII, 123-128.

22. Humboldt. 126.

23. *The Book of Mormon,* op. cit., Introduction.

24. Humboldt, op. cit., PLATE XIV, 135-206.

25. Humboldt, op. cit., 137-138.

26. Humboldt, op. cit., PLATE XIX, 239-248.

27. Humboldt, op. cit., 242-243.

28. de Alva Cortés Ixtlilxóchitl, Fernando; *Historia de la nación chichimeca;* Linkgua ediciones S.L., Barcelona, 2008, originally written circa 1611.

29. de Alva Ixtlilxóchitl, Fernando; *Obras históricas de don Fernando de Alva Ixtlilxóchitl,* Volume 1 and 2, Reprint from the collection of the University of Michigan Library, originally written circa 1608-1611.

30. Humboldt, op. cit., PLATE XXVI, 276-278.

31. Humboldt, op. cit., 277.

32. Humboldt, op. cit., 277-278.

33. Humboldt, op. cit., PLATE XXX and XXXI, 289-296.

34. Humboldt, op. cit., 293.

35. *The Book of Mormon.* op. cit., Mormon 4:1-3.

36. Humboldt, op. cit., PLATE XXXVI, 311-313.

37. Humboldt, op. cit., 313. Paragraph in italics is from an 1811 Humboldt essay, *Essai politique sur le royaume de la Nouvelle-Espagne,* Volume I, p. 95.

38. www.adherents.com/largecom/fam_deist.html
39. Acosta, op. cit., 70-72.

SECTION III

After Darkness I Hope For Light

Post tenebras spero lucem. ("After darkness I hope for light."), Latin Vulgate Bible, Job 17:12; quoted by Miguel de Cervantes Saavedra in Don Quixote, Chapter LXVIII; printed on the title pages, Parts I and II of the 1605 and 1615 editions of Don Quixote became the defining motto in early editions of Don Quixote. Fray Mier uses Don Quixote as a parable when writing on the trials of his own life. Biographies often picture Mier as a negative quixotic character, traveling Europe, tilting with Mexican history, creating Christian myth. In truth, Fray Mier is the Ingenious Gentleman, Don Quixote, who brings Light to the history of Christianity in the Americas before Columbus while a veil of Darkness still hangs over Fray Mier and his writings. AFTER DARKNESS I HOPE FOR LIGHT.

MAP OF MEXICO - REFERENCE CHAPTER 7,
SUBSECTIONS III, IV, V, VI, VIII, IX, XII

AGAVE PLANT- REFERENCE CHAPTER 7,
SUBSECTIONS I, VII, XIII, XIV

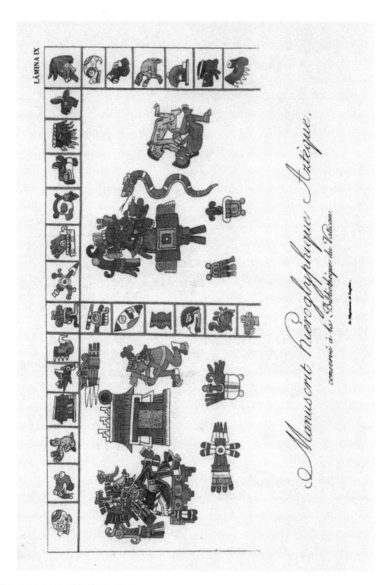

"MANUSCRIT HIEROGLYPHIQUE ANTEQUE" -
REFERENCE CHAPTER 6 PLATE IX, AND
CHAPTER 7, SUBSECTIONS I, VII, XIV

VIRGIN OF GUADALUPE - REFERENCE
CHAPTER 7, SUBSECTIONS XI

CHAPTER 7

Fray Mier and Mexican Anthropology's Contribution to the Historicity of *The Book of Mormon*

INTRODUCTION

It is one thing to write like a poet, and another like a historian: the poet can count, or chant things not like they were, but like they should be; and the historian has to write them not like they should be, but like they were, without removing or adding anything to the truth. [1]
—Miguel de Cervantes Saavedra, El Ingenioso Hidalgo Don Quijote de la Mancha—

The scriptural writings of the Bible, in many different versions, are accepted by Christians as the core doctrinal source of their beliefs. The Bible's religious message is corroborated by thousands of years of parallel secular history, passed down through time with a patina blurring the division between history and religious belief. This secular history helps sustain our faith in the Bible as Holy Scripture. World history confirms biblical history. Just within the past 100 years, parchment and papyrus scrolls of biblical texts have been discovered such as the Dead Sea Scrolls in Qumran, Israel, Coptic Codices papyruses, and the Nag Hammadi Library in Egypt. These modern discoveries further evidence the Bible's historicity and religious teachings.

Chapter 6 is an abridgement of anthropologist Baron Alexander von Humboldt's *Aportaciones a la antropología mexicana*, ("Contributions to Mexican Anthropology"), which evidences that Mexico's ancient literary culture wrote their language in hieroglyphics on paper made from the agave plant. They called it the Divine Book of religious scriptural writings. Chapter 6 also references Dr. Jared Diamond's *Guns, Germs, and Steel, The Fates of Human Societies*, which he writes in 1997. "The two indisputable independent inventions of writing were achieved by the Sumerians of Mesopotamia somewhat before 3000 B.C. and by Mexican Indians before 600 B.C." The few surviving Mexican hieroglyphic folios Humboldt found in libraries around the world gave him the chance to study ancient Mexican writings in the 19th century. Humboldt confirmed that Catholic clergy were instrumental in destroying Mexican records, nevertheless, they preserved ancient Mexican history in their own writings. Humboldt's findings and conclusions are not a blanket endorsement of Fray Mier's theological findings, but they do confirm historical and anthropological sources used by Fray Mier setting forth his religious propositions.

Mier and Humboldt are two of many writers of Mexican history who give historicity to *The Book of Mormon*. Just as we accept writings that give historicity to the Bible, the surviving hieroglyphic folios examined by Humboldt are of the type described in *The Book of Mormon*, Mormon 9:32: "And now, behold, we have written this record according to our knowledge, in the characters which are called among us the reformed Egyptian, being handed down and altered by us, according to our manner of speech." Fray Mier described Mexican folios that, "(W)ith the additional fables introduced with the lapse of time, it confuses and turns everything upside down, and by the nature of the same hieroglyphics causes fables since the code is forgotten in antiquity." *The Book of Mormon* records as collaborated by the writings of Fray Mier that with the lapse of time, the people of Mexico lost the Hebrew-Christian culture of their ancestors.

The Book of Mormon ancient record was written on plates of brass and gold with many references to written documents, for example: synagogues as places of worship, a synagogue does not exist without a written scroll of the Torah; government ruled by judges who had to have a written code of law; and epistles exchanged between hostile forces. The variety of written documents described were paper folios not engraved plates of gold or brass. *The Book of Mormon*, Alma 14: 8, cites: ". . .and they also brought forth their records which contained the holy scriptures, and cast them into the fire also, that they might be burned and destroyed by fire." Burned records were not plates of gold or brass, but paper folios, a harbinger of the Spanish burning of records 1600 years later. Hieroglyphic paper folios were indigenous to only one place in ancient America, Mexico, in the opinion of anthropologists and early missionaries. The few surviving agave folios from the repositories of Mexico reviewed by Humboldt validate Mesoamerica as the probable site in the Americas where the ancient writers of *The Book of Mormon* lived.

Chapter 4, Fray Mier's "Eleventh Note of The Second Letter from an American," tells of the devastation of Mexican civilization contributing to the loss of its religious history. He compares the conquest and rule of Mexico by Spain to the biblical account of the enslavement of Israel in ancient Egypt. He quotes the Latin phrase *operibus duris luti et lateris*, "hard-work in mortar and brick," Exodus 1:14, to describe the collapse and enslavement of Mexico. This collapse left tiny bits and pieces of the history from the time of the Prophet Moroni to the Emperor Montezuma. Fray Mier gathered shattered bits and pieces of "mortar and brick," the indigenous folios of Mexico's ancient history and the written witness of the Catholic missionaries. Mier fixed the bricks with hard work in the mortar of his research and writings to abridge Mexican history into what is a credible and fascinating link of Mexico to *The Book of Mormon*. Fray Mier wrote in his "Apologia": "All throughout America, monuments and vestige evidences of Christianity were found, according to the unanimous testimony of the missionaries."

What was not unanimous was the question: How did this come to be? Was Christianity brought to ancient America by the Irish, the Danes, the Vikings, the Scots, the Chinese, or most likely by the Apostle Saint Thomas? These were Fray Mier's hypotheses. To postulate and test a hypothesis in the search of truth does not make the hypothesis a fraud or raise it to a myth. The application of the scientific method may prove a hypothesis to be wrong, but it does not make the observed truths false. The truth is: The people of Mexico lived a Hebrew-Christian religion before Catholic missionaries arrived in America.

The biblical Saint Thomas in America theory did not originate with Fray Mier. Bishop Bartolome de las Casas (1474-1566) in 1527 began to write his *Historia de las Indias* ("*History of the Indies*")first published in Seville, Spain, 1555, which notes traces of Christianity and the Apostle Saint Thomas in the New World. Another writer on Saint Thomas as the first preacher of Christianity in America is Carlos de Sigüenza (1645-1700), a professor of mathematics and a

Jesuit Priest born in Mexico. Fray Sigüenza had as his source Fernando de Alva Cortés Ixtlilxochitl, a descendent of the Kings of Texcoco, a major city-state in the Valley of Mexico. Fernando Ixtlilxochitl inherited the records of his royal ancestors. Records likely handed down and altered, according to the manner of speech, confused and turned upside down, by the nature of the hieroglyphics caused fables since the code had been forgotten in antiquity.

In his "Apologia, Antecedents and Consequences of the Sermon up to the Opening of the Process " Fray Mier writes:

> This preaching has been defended by many and very serious Spanish Authors, foreign and American, even in works concerning not only manuscripts but printed in Spain, such as Diego Duran, Gregorio García, Alonso Ramas, Antonio Calancha, Nobrega, Mendieta, Remesal, Torquemada, Betancourt, Rivadeneira, Abraham, Justo Lipsio, the Spanish author of the Excellence of the Cross, Sigüenza in his *Fenix del Occidente, El Apóstol Santo Tomé* (*"Phoenix of the West, The Apostle Saint Thomas"*), the Jesuit author of the *Historia del verdadero Quetzacohuatl el Apóstol Santo Tomé* (*"History of the True Quetzacohuatle, the Apostle Saint Thomas"*), Becerra Tanco, Boturini, Veytia, and many others. Without having missed holy and wise Archbishops and Bishops of America, for example Dávila Padilla, Casas and Zárate; nor Cardinals of the Holy Roman Church, such as Gotti.

Fray Mier cites twenty-one authors by name and "many others" cited in modern writings of early American histories. Dr. Mier is a major source of Chapter 7, Mexican anthropology, geography, culture, and history—written in the style as Miguel de Cervantes Saavedra assets in Don Quixote ". . .not like they should be, but like they were, without removing or adding anything to the truth. . ."; that gives authenticity to The Book of Mormon.

I. WRITTEN LANGUAGE

In Chapter 5, Fray Mier's "Farewell Letter to the Mexicans," he writes: The Indians had in their power (as the missionaries in Veracruz gave in written testimony to the celebrated Fray Gregorio García) the entire Bible in images and hieroglyphic figures, they confused them with the passage of time, they put into practice the Scripture's histories, and confused their own history and their religion. What was the Mexican's religion, but Christianity confused by time, and the mixed-up nature of the hieroglyphics?

Alexander von Humboldt writes in "Contributions to Mexican Anthropology:"

> The paper that has served for the hieroglyphic paintings of the Aztec people observes much similarity with the ancient Egyptian papyrus, made with the fiber of the papyrus reed (*Cyperus papyrus*). The plant that was used in Mexico for the fabrication of paper is what in our gardens is commonly known under the name aloe: it is the agave (*Agave americana*), called *metl* or *maguey* by the peoples of the Aztec race.[2]

Fray Mier writes that many of those "magnificent libraries of hieroglyphics," were burned by Hernán Cortés in 1519. Chapter 4 "Eleventh Note of the Second Letter from an American:"

> But the wise men of Europe know, that they have done nothing but formulate nonsensical theories, as if they were speaking of absolute savages without monuments nor writings, but the Indians in New Spain had magnificent libraries, of hieroglyphics it is true, except that they read very well from right to left, and if they heard a *Nahuatlato* or "Interpreter" explain them, they would see that they do not stop speaking like when we are reading. The Emperor Carlos V sent to Mexico as the first Bishop Fray Juan de Zumárraga, for having had a good hand in the commission of casting out the witches of Vizcaya:" These are the words of Maestro Dávila, Royal Chronicler, in his *Historia Eclesiástica de las Indias* (*"Ecclesiastical History of the Indies"*) Bishop Zumárraga continued to see his witches in the Mexican hieroglyphics, so he made it his duty to exterminate such magic figures, searching them out with great diligence. His Franciscan

missionaries served him in this with much zeal, staying the Saint, carrying it out on the same day in all the cities, in 1526 they burned the magnificent *Teocallis* or "Temples" of the Indians where their libraries were.

When Alexander von Humboldt began his Mexican anthropological study in 1805, there were very few surviving paper folios. *The Book of Mormon* makes numerous references to writings and epistles which were likely written on the agave papyrus described by Baron Humboldt. *The Book of Mormon* records epistles written in fields of battle then sent to an enemy. These epistles were very unlikely to have been written on plates of brass or gold. *The Book of Mormon* history verifies the use of papyri, paper, records.

Therefore, I have written this epistle, sealing it with mine own hand, feeling for your welfare, because of your firmness in that which ye believe to be right, and your noble spirit in the field of battle. (*Book of Mormon*, 3 Nephi 3:5) (A)nd they also brought forth their records which contained the holy scriptures, and cast them into the fire also, that they might be burned and destroyed by fire. (*Book of Mormon*, Alma 14:8)

Alexander von Humboldt in "Contributions to Mexican Anthropology" writes of an incident at the Pyramid of Cholula which testifies that plates of gold were stolen out of greed and in compliance with orders to destroy anything connected with indigenous antiquities. The Spanish conquistadores raped, robbed, pillaged, and killed the native people for any asset made of gold and brass, often before the Catholic missionaries arrived at the scene so the theft was not recorded:

On top of the great Mexican pyramids were found two colossal statutes of the Sun and the Moon; they were of stone, garnished with gold plates: these plates were stolen by Cortés's soldiers since the religious Franciscan Bishop Zumárrage undertook the task of destroying everything that had a connection with the worship, the history, and the antiquities of the indigenous people of America, he also had destroyed the idols on the Road of the Dead. [3]

Dr. Jared Diamond, author of *Guns, Germs, and Steel–The Fates of Human Societies,* published in 1997, writes:

Nineteenth-Century authors tended to interpret history as

a progression from savagery to civilization. Key hallmarks of this transition included the development of agriculture, metallurgy, complex technology, centralized government, and writing. Of these writings was traditionally the one most restricted geographically: until the expansions of Islam and of colonial Europeans, it was absent from Australia, Pacific islands, subequatorial Africa, and the whole New World except for a small part of Mesoamerica. The two indisputable independent inventions of writing were achieved by the Sumerians of Mesopotamia somewhat before 3000 B.C. and by Mexican Indians before 600 B.C.; Egyptian writing of 3000 B.C. and Chinese writing (by 1300 B.C.) may also have arisen independently. Probably all other peoples who have developed writing since then have borrowed, adapted, or at least been inspired by existing systems. [4]

Dr. Diamond restricts the geographic origin of writing in the whole New World to a small part of Mesoamerica by Mexican Indians before 600 B.C. establishing a place, a people, and a time for any credible ancient written history of America. *The Book of Mormon* historical timeline concurs with Diamond's time for the invention of writing in America. And, Diamond's history of writing in the New World gives validity to Fray Mier's thesis of the existence of ancient Mexican hieroglyphic writings.

Fray Mier's historical sources covered over 275 years of Mexican historical research by Catholic missionaries from the Spanish conquest of 1519, to the date of his Guadalupe Sermon, December 12, 1794. Fray Mier did not learn the native languages, but some of the missionary authors he studied learned to speak the native languages and read the surviving hieroglyphic folios. Fray Mier describes how with the passage of time, even the native Indians lost the learning skills necessary to read hieroglyphic folios, which led with the passage of time to errors of interpreting the writings. The missionaries' historical folios that he studied did not go back far enough to tell how Christianity came to America, but his studied sources evidenced to him the Gospel of Christ was preached in America before the arrival of Catholic missionaries.

Before the Spanish conquest, petroglyphs, string symbols, carvings, and signs were found throughout the Americas; but a readable language written in hieroglyphics on agave papyrus and plates of ore was known only by the native Aztec (Nahuatl), Maya,

Zapotec, Epi-Omec, and preceding civilizations. These cultures inhabited what is now Mexico and Guatemala.

The Book of Mormon references ancient records written in the "language of the Egyptians," which is to say a language written in hieroglyphic figures. Nephi, Mosiah, and Mormon testified of this:

> (Nephi—), Yea, I make a record in the language of my father, which consisted of the learning of the Jews and the language of the Egyptians. (*Book of Mormon*, 1 Nephi 1:2)

> (Mosiah continues—), For it were not possible that our father, Lehi, could have remembered all these things, to have taught them to his children, except it were for the help of these plates; for he having been taught in the language of the Egyptians therefore he could read these engravings, and teach them to his children, that thereby they could teach them to their children, and so fulfilling the commandments of God, even down to this present time. (*Book of Mormon*, Mosiah 1:4)

> (Mormon also testifies—): And now, behold we have written this record according to our knowledge, in the characters which are called among us the reformed Egyptian, being handed down and altered by us according to their manner of speech. (*Book of Mormon*, Mormon 9:32)

II. MEXICO MEANS —"WHERE CHRIST IS WORSHIPPED,"AND MEXICAN MEANS—" CHRISTIAN."

In his "Farewell Letter to the Mexicans," Fray Mier writes:

> Whatever you want it to be, this Letter is reduced to begging by farewell to my Anahuacan fellow countrymen: reject the suppression of the x in the Mexican or Aztec names of the places that are left to us, and especially of Mexico, because it would be the end of ruining them. And it is a great shame, because they are significant, and in their topographical, statistical, or historical meanings.

> The first missionaries, to write the *Náhuatl* language or sonorously what we call Mexican, agreed according to Torquemada, with the most learned Indian found in the College de Santiago *Tlatilolco,* and as its pronunciation has two Hebrew letters, *Sadhe* and *Shin,* they substituted in their writing by approximation the first tz and the second soft x. But

as for softening this even though the circumflex accent over the following vowel was not adopted, and the conquistadors were mostly Extremadurans and Andalusians, or Arabs in their pronunciation, they pronounced hard all the x's written by the missionaries, and they filled with guttural letters the terms that they adopted from the Mexican language, which does not permit any. For this the Spaniards pronounce México (Méjico), even though the Indians only pronounce Méxîco (Mescico) with the Hebrew letter *Shin*. And it is a pain, Mexicans that Italians, French, English, and Germans may pronounce better than we the name of our native land, since nobody, except us, pronounces Mexico with a guttural letter. In all cases, my countrymen, we must continue to write it with x, or to keep up with the time, if the new spelling prevails, to pronounce this as one ought to and the rest of Mexican terms, or to not cast into entire forgetfulness one of our greatest glories. Yes, *Méxîco* with soft x as the Indians pronounce it means: *Where Christ is* or (where) *Christ is worshiped*, and Mexicans is the same as *Christians*. Certainly, one finds the complete word *Mescichô*, as the Indians pronounce it in Hebrew 2nd verse of Psalms 2, where the Vulgate translated *Christum eius*, his Christ. Clavijero, despite everything, believes that Mexico's particle *co* is the Mexican term for *where*, and taking charge of the different interpretations that have been given to the name of Mexico by the words *Metl*, maguey, or *Metzi*, moon or month, of which it may be composed, he resolves that the true meaning has to be deduced from Mexican history, and according to it what it ought to mean is: *Where Mexî* or *Méxîtl is worshiped*. And *Mexî*, I ask, what does it mean? Pronounced as the Indians pronounce it, it is a Hebrew word, which means, taking it from the Latin *unctus*, we call anointed, taking it from the Greek *Chrestous*, we call *Christ*, and taking it from Hebrew *Mesci*, we call Messiah.

And in the understanding of the Mexicans what did *Mexî* mean? Again, it is history, which has to tell it to us with certainty. *Mexî* was a man God, called by other names the Lord of the Crown of Thorns, *Teohuitznáhuac*, Lord of Paradise *Teotlaloc* &. &., who a virgin called Saint Mary *Malintzin*, conceived by a work of heaven, and she gave birth to him, already a perfect male, without injury to her virginity. *Foemina circundabit virum*. So, Father Torquemada tells it.

The Wikipedia Website "Toponimia de México" ("Toponymy of Mexico"), references Fray Mier on the Hebrew origin of Mexico. Fray Mier writes of Fray Gregorio García in his "Farewell Letter to the Mexicans," as does "Toponimia de México." The García books was published 1607/2005 titled *Origen de los indios del Nuevo Mundo e Indias Occidentales,* ("Origen of the Indians of the New World and West Indies"). García and other clergy argued that Mexitli, the legendary leader who led the Mexicas in his pilgrimage from Aztlán from which the name of Mexico is derived, was but a reflection of the Messiah. "Toponimia de México" also cites a book authored by Agustín de Vetancurt, (1698/1971 ed. facsimilar. The following is a quote from Vetancurt's work:

> With reason we should appreciate more this name Mexico, where it came to the redemption of many souls, where so much has extolled the name of Christ, our Redeemer and Messiah, because, as Fray Martin del Castillo says in explaining the Capitulate Act held in Toledo, printed the year 1657, Mexico in Hebrew, Chaldean and Syrian, is the same as Messiah and if the Messiah gave it the name of his lineage, Mexico is honored with the name of his real person, Messiahship was for happy prognosis that he had to link the true religion of the Messiah, and so, it becomes its most honorable title.

Fray Castillo was a recognized Hebrew grammarian and could have been another source for Fray Mier's research. These early Catholic Fathers' study of the origin and meaning of the word, Mexico, evidence that Fray Mier's writing on Messiah as the root meaning of Mexico was not his invention. The ancient land of Anáhuac, encircled by four seas, upon independence from Spain in 1821 embraced a much larger territory; and abandoned the name New Spain to adopt the name "Republic of Mexico" with little knowledge of its authentic original meaning. Fray Mier was an audacious advocate for preserving the heritage of Mexico by maintaining Mexico's correct pronunciation and spelling, and a trace of the history of the Messiah in America.

The Book of Mormon records King Benjamin giving his people a name:

> And moreover, I shall give this people a name, that

thereby they may be distinguished above all the people which the Lord God hath brought out of the land of Jerusalem; and this I do because they have been a diligent people in keeping the commandments of the Lord. And I give unto them a name that never shall be blotted out, except it be through transgression. (*Book of Mormon*, Mosiah 1:11-12)

And now, because of the covenant which ye have made ye shall be called the children of Christ, his sons, and his daughters; for behold, this day he hath spiritually begotten you; for ye say that your hearts are changed through faith on his name; therefore, ye are born of him and have become his sons and his daughters. And under this head ye are made free, and there is no other head whereby ye can be made free. There is no other name given whereby salvation cometh; therefore, I would that ye should take upon you the name of Christ, all you that have entered into the covenant with God that ye should be obedient unto the end of your lives. (*Book of Mormon*, Mosiah 5:7-8)

King Benjamin's "Children of Christ," became known by the name Mexican.

The name of Christ was not blotted out. However, "through transgression" with the passage of time the true origin and meaning of Mexico became lost. Fray Mier's definition of "Mexico," as derived from the Hebrew word Messiah, is a witness to *The Book of Mormon*'s language of origin. "Yea, I make a record in the language of my father, which consists of the learning of the Jews and the language of the Egyptians." (*Book of Mormon*, 1 Nephi 1:2)

III. A LAND AMONG MANY WATERS, THE LAND NORTHWARD COVERED WITH LARGE BODIES OF WATER.

Fray Mier refers to his homeland as Anáhuac, and to his countrymen as Anáhuacans. He taught that the Gospel of Jesus Christ was preached in Anáhuac before the Catholic missionaries arrived in America. Anáhuac is the Nahuatl name for the ancient Aztec empire. In 1519, the Spaniards discovered the valley of Anáhuac with its five interlocking lakes Zumpango, Xaltocan, Texcoco, Xochimilco, and Chalco. The Aztec city Tenochtitlán was built amid these lakes. The lakes are now dry and filled by metropolitan Mexico City with 21.2 million people in 2018.

Translations of Anáhuac are: Land next to the water, on the edge of the water, or between the waters.

Bishop Bartolomé de las Casas wrote:

All that has been said of the sacrifices and ceremonies in them, of the people of New Spain and of the provinces contained in it, that the Indians commonly call in their language Anávac, that means, large land enclosed and surrounded by water, due it is said for being between the two seas, that of the North, and that which we call of the South, the name comes from *atl*, which is water, and *navac*, that means within or around. [5]

Father Francisco Javier Clavijero wrote:

The name Anáhuac according to its etymology was initially given only to the valley of Mexico for its principal populations being located on the shores of two lakes, later it was extended to almost all the space of land that today is known with the name of New Spain. This very vast country is divided into the kingdoms of Mexico, Acolhuacán, Tlacopan and Michoacán; and the republics of Tlaxcala, Cholollan and Huexotzingo, and in many other private dominions.[6]

The Aztec kingdom of Anáhuac, translated as "next to the water," was a land northward covered with large bodies of water, a large civilized population, and a written language discovered by Hernan Cortés in 1519. *The Book of Mormon* records the emigration of remnants of Israel and Babylon refugees upon the many waters to the New World that Christopher Columbus would discover in 1492. Anáhuac, now Mexico, as described by Bishop de las Casas and Father Clavijero is a credible geographic location for history recorded in *The Book of Mormon* writings of Mosiah and Alma who describe their homeland as "a land among many waters."

And they were lost in the wilderness for the space of many days, yet they were diligent, and found not the land of Zarahemla but returned to this land, having traveled in a land among many waters, having discovered a land which was covered with bones of men, and of beasts, and was also covered with ruins of buildings of every kind, having discovered a land which had been peopled with a people who were as numerous as the hosts of Israel. (*Book of Mormon*, Mosiah 8:8)

Therefore, Morianton put it into their hearts that they should flee to the land, which was northward, which was covered with large bodies of water, and take possession of the land which was northward. (*Book of Mormon*, Alma 50:29)

IV. NORTH SEA AND SOUTH SEA, AND THE NARROW NECK OF LAND.

The Aztec Anáhuac became New Spain, the present southern states of Mexico. The four seas give oceanic boundaries to the land, which The Book of Mormon records. A map of Mexico shows its oceanic boundaries on the west, the Pacific Ocean and the Gulf of California; and, its oceanic boundaries on the east, the Gulf of Mexico and the Caribbean Sea. A Mexican history written by Fernando de Alva Cortés Ixtlilxóchitl, a direct descendant of the Aztec kings, Historia de la nación chichimeca ("History of the Chichimeca Nation"), written about 1640 makes numerous references to a North Sea and South Sea. Ixtlilxóchitl writes that the territory of Anáhuac had north-south latitude from the North Sea to the South Sea, and a four hundred league east- west longitude from the east coast provinces of Panuco and Yucatan on the Gulf of Mexico to the western Sea of Cortés, the Gulf of California. [7] Bishop Bartolomé de las Casas referred to his travel in southern Mexico between the North Sea and South Sea, quoted under the preceding Topic III. "A land among many waters, the land northward covered with large bodies of water." Bishop de las Casas describes the land of Anáhuac as, "being between the two seas, that of the North, and that which we call of the South."

The historian Marcel Bataillon writes on the naming of Fray de las Casas as Bishop of Chiapas that: "The same day, another royal order unites the Bishopric of Chiapas to the Province of Soconusco, on the Pacific coast, on the border of New Spain and Guatemala. Thus, Las Casas prepares to build a spiritual principality that goes from Yucatán to Soconusco, from the North Sea to the South Sea."[8]

Soconusco is a narrow strip of land wedged between the Sierra Madre Mountains of Chiapas and the Pacific Ocean on the border of Mexico and Guatemala. These geographic details by Ixtlilxóchitl, Bishop de las Casas, and Bataillon fit the geography of Mexico to Book of Mormon geography. Mexico's Gulf of Campeche is the

North Sea; the Gulf of Tehuantepec is the South Sea; and Soconusco is the "narrow neck" on the Gulf of Tehuantepec, which connects the "land southward" and the "land northward." The Chiapas Bishopric of Bishop de las Casas went from Chiapas on the Gulf of Tehuantepec and Soconusco, northeast to the Yucatán Peninsula and the Gulf of Campeche. Travel from the Gulf of Tehuantepec and Soconusco to the Gulf of Campeche is a journey north. Nowhere else in all the Americas, is there so clearly cited a "sea north,"and a "sea south;" as is recorded in Mexican history. Modern names, location, and historicity apply to each of the four seas cited in *The Book of Mormon*, which furthermore records that many Nephites migrated to the land northward where they came to large bodies of water about the year 46 B.C., which would be Mexico's Anáhuac; and furthermore, describes this land northward with large bodies of water as encircled by seas:

> And it came to pass that they did multiply and spread and did go forth from the land southward to the land northward and did spread insomuch that they began to cover the face of the whole earth, from the sea south to the sea north, from the sea west to the sea east. (*Book of Mormon*, Helaman 3:8)
>
> And it came to pass that Hagoth, he being an exceedingly curious man, therefore he went forth and built him an exceedingly large ship, on the borders of the land Bountiful, by the land Desolation, and launched it forth into the west sea, by the narrow neck which led into the land northward. (*Book of Mormon*, Alma 63:5)

V. THE CITY AND LAND OF DESOLATION

Chapter 6, "Alexander von Humboldt's Contribution to Mexican Anthropology," PLATES XXX and XXXI, is titled "Ruins of Miguitlan or Mitla in the Province of Oaxaca; Design and Height," Baron von Humboldt writes: "*Mitla* is no more than a contraction of the word *Miguitlan*, that in Mexican means: 'Place of Desolation, Place of Sadness'." The ancient Zapotecan inhabitants were highly cultured with a written language. The Spanish conquerors changed the Nahuatl word Miguitlan to the Arabic word Mitla to bring it in line with Spanish pronunciation, after all, the Arabs had ruled southern Spain for over 700 years until 1492. There is a Mitla Pass in the Sinai desert translated as "The place of the dead," which evidences Spain's transposition of word usage and pronunciation from the Old World to the New World at the time of the Spanish conquest of America. This is an issue that Fray Mier asserts in his "Farewell Letter. . ." explaining how Spanish spelling and pronunciation of the word Mexico corrupted its root heritage. Mitla, now known as San Pablo Villa de Mitla has 11,000 inhabitants. It is the site of on-going archeological studies located 132 miles inland from the south sea Gulf and town of Tehuantepec. When the Spanish discovered Tehuantepec, it was a commercial hub by land and sea between the lands of the north and the south. San Pablo Villa de Mitla is just to the north of the narrow neck Soconusco, in the southwest state of Oaxaca, Mexico. Tehuantepec, Mexico, fits the location of the seashore town Teancum cited in *The Book of Mormon.*

Critics state there is no geographic site in *The Book of Mormon* with a verifiable location. However, the city and land of Desolation is a beginning to connecting the history of Mexican cities to *The Book of Mormon:*

> And it came to pass that the armies of the Nephites were driven back again to the land of Desolation. And while they were yet weary, a fresh army of the Lamanites did come upon them; and they had a sore battle, insomuch that the Lamanites did take possession of the city Desolation, and did slay many of the Nephites, and did take many prisoners. And the remainder did flee and join the inhabitants of the city Teancum. Now the city Teancum lay in the borders by the seashore; and it was also near the city Desolation. (*Book of Mormon*, Mormon 4:2-3)

VI. ZARAHEMLA

Hernán Cortés, in his letter to Spain's King Carlos V, reports entering the city of Churultecal, now Cholula, Mexico. He notes that fifty thousand men were killed in the battle for this city. Cortés writes of Cholula: "This city is very fertile farmland, because it has much land and the more part of it is watered, and outside it is even a more beautiful city than there is in Spain, because it is much adorned with towers and fine masonry. And I certify to Your Highness that I counted from one mosque over four hundred towers in said city, and all are of mosques."[9] Born and raised in

Extremadura, Spain, Cortés was familiar with Muslim mosques and Catholic cathedrals. His choice of the word mosque to describe Cholula's religious buildings with their towers fits *The Book of Mormon* references to synagogues, which are like the architectural style and artwork of a mosque, not like the style and images of a Catholic cathedral. Over four hundred mosques identify Cholula as a religious center of the native people. Cortés further describes Cholula as a city of 20,000 houses with many others in the surrounding area. The demography of his quick census would have been 50 houses for each place of worship; making Cholula's citizens very dedicated to their religious faith.

In the Aztec land of Anáhuac, Cholula had a population second only to Tenochtitlán, now Mexico City. There are numerous archeological sites around Cholula, dating to its earliest settlement date of 500 B.C. to 200 B.C. Modern Cholula is the site of the Great Pyramid of Cholula. It is the largest pyramid in the Americas and Egypt. It is surrounded by a populated city, not in an isolated forest. Cortés discovered a Temple to Quetzalcóatl at the top of the Great Pyramid of Cholula. Quetzalcóatl in the Nahuatl language means "Feathered Serpent." Fray Bartolomé de las Casas writes on the "Religious Festivals of Quetzalcóatl in Cholula":

> The city of Cholula, that we said to be the largest and above all the most devout and frequent of all New Spain, for vows and pilgrimages, a sanctuary, among many and diverse fiestas that were held and celebrated, it was once each year the first day of May, offering Quetzalcóatl many roses and flowers, and the priests were dressed in some long clothes to the feet, white, strewn with black flowers, and they left with diadems on the heads, and this was a very delicate and not expensive fiesta; but they did other things similar to those mentioned, among those that they held one every four years, that they named the year of their God Quetzalcóatl; for reverence and devotion of this festival a terrible fast was held. In this fiesta there were very few who they sacrificed, and I believe it was because Quetzalcóatl when living prohibited them that they should sacrifice no man. According to the above, if I well remember, we declare. The day of the fiesta, in the morning, those fasting went with much joy each one to his house, where they had prepared new blankets for them highly painted with which they returned to Quetzalcóatl's temple to give him

thanks, and they rejoiced like on Easter. [10]

Chapter 4 , "Eleventh Note of the Second Letter from an American," includes Fray Mier's summary of the temple's destruction and replacement with the Church of our Lady de los Remedios by the Spaniards, which exists to the present time. Alexander von Humboldt in his work, "Contributions to Mexican Anthropology," Plate IV, "Cholula's Pyramid," offers the following opinion. "In the time of Cortés, Cholula was considered as a sacred city: nowhere could one find a greater number of *teocallis*, priest and religious orders, (*tlamacazque*); nowhere a greater magnificence in the culture nor more austerity in the fasts and penances." [11]

Hernán Cortés led a brutal attack, burning, and devastating Cholula, a city that had been inhabited for two thousand years. Cholula survived and is today a vibrant Mexican city with 118,000 residents, and a large archeological pyramid within its city boundaries. The following are extracts from Fray Mier's "Farewell Letter to the Mexicans," and *Fray Servando Teresa de Mier: Writings on Ancient Christianity and Spain's Evangelism of Mexico*, his "Apologia", reference Cholula and ties Cholula to Saint Tomé.

The Christian fugitives from the persecution of Huemac, King of Tula, against Saint Tomé, which is to say *Quetzal-cóhuatl*, he who fled to Cholula, took refuge in the Lagoon or Lake Anáhuac, a sandy isle that for this they called *Xâltelolco* and later *Tlatelolco* or Earth Island (Mier's "Farewell Letter").

From the belief of said prophesy, the magnificent gifts emanated that Mocteuhzoma sent to Cortés after he disembarked; and if we give credit to Torquemada, Cortés still being on the ship, the envoys believing that he was the same Saint Tomé put on him the episcopal garments which had been conserved in Cholula, (Mier's "Apologia").

Mier further wrote in his "Apologia, Antecedents and Consequences of the Sermon up to the Opening of the Process:"

> Huemac King of Tula, having raised a cruel persecution against the religion from which some apostatized and others suffered martyrdom, came to settle in Cholula. And Huemac going even there with an army to persecute him, after having been here exactly twenty years, he embarked to where the sun rises in Cuatzacoalco, since then it was called thus, that is, where Tomé hid himself. He sent from there four disciples to

govern Cholula, which they divided into wards or parishes, a division that lasted until the conquest; and as he left foretold the year in which people of his same religion would come from the east to dominate these countries. Of the future fulfillment of this remote prophesy he gave them, in the style of the prophets, a sign of a nearer event, and it was that the immense pyramid of Cholula would break into pieces; that having it verified, as also the persecution of Christianity in Tula followed by four years of famine and epidemic so horrific they almost ended the Tolteca nation, they had him from then as a Saint, and they believed the prophecy. For this as in significance of him who they were awaiting, they had his image laid down in his Cholula Temple, where for having been this father or apostle's cathedral in the community of the Aztecas, it was his Rome, and it had as many temples as days of the year.

Without so sinister an intention, what motive was there to have excited such an exorbitant scandal? Is the image of the Mother of God on the cape of an Indian more worthy, than the cape of an Apostle of Jesus Christ? If they left in America, according to the same Spanish authors printed in Spain, the Sacred Scriptures in images, images of Christ and of the Virgin and of the selfsame Saint Tomé, vestiges of his feet and his hands, and inscriptions engraved on stones; if in Peru they think to have one of his shoes, if here in Cholula his cape or episcopal pallium is conserved and all his clothes, that the Indians looked over Cortés believing that he was the selfsame Saint Tomé, why did it have to be a scandal that we have his cape in the linen of Our Lady of Guadalupe? The cape of the Apostles was a Jewish cape like that of the Indians. What Saint Tomé wore in America, according to Father Calancha, was of two cloths like that of Our Lady of Guadalupe; and to this, if it is the image of the *Mother of the true God* that the Indians worshiped in Tepeyácac, also called *Coatliene*, that means to say, 'her garment is from the Tomé.'

I have here enough for a very weak conjecture, as I warned that it was what I preached. If these things appear deliriums, they do not appear so much to those that have studied our antiquities.

The Book of Mormon references the city and land of

Zarahemla 139 times. A great temple and *Book of Mormon* prophet Alma are linked to Zarahemla:

> And now it came to pass that Alma returned from the land of Gideon, after having taught the people of Gideon many things which cannot be written, having established the order of the church, according as he had before done in the land of Zarahemla, yea, he returned to his own house at Zarahemla to rest himself from the labors which he had performed. (*Book of Mormon*, Alma 8:1)
>
> And now, it came to pass that Mosiah went and did as his father had commanded him and proclaimed unto all the people who were in the land of Zarahemla that thereby they might gather themselves together, to go up to the temple to hear the words which his father should speak unto them. (*Book of Mormon*, Mosiah 1:18)
>
> (And as recorded—") And Alma and Amulek went forth preaching repentance to the people in their temples, and in their sanctuaries, and also in their synagogues, which were built after the manner of the Jews. (*Book of Mormon*, Alma 16:13)

Cholula's Quetzalcóatl is found recorded in *The Book of Mormon*.

> But, behold, ye not only deny my words, but ye also deny all the words which have been spoken by our fathers, and also the words which were spoken by this man, Moses, who had such great power given unto him, yea, the words which he hath spoken concerning the coming of the Messiah. Yea, did he not bear record that the Son of God should come? And as he lifted up the brazen serpent in the wilderness, even so shall he be lifted up who should come. And as many as should look upon that serpent should live, even so as many as should look upon the Son of God with faith, having a contrite spirit, might live, even unto that life which is eternal." (*Book of Mormon*, Helaman 8:13-15)

This is Fray Mier's history of Cholula. Tula, Mexico, like Cholula is an important archeological site north of Mexico City, still inhabited today with the name "Tula de Allende." King Huemac was the last of the Toltec kings, circa 11th Century. Any information about him was written by the Aztecs centuries later. The history of Huemac was lost with the Spaniard's destruction of the Aztec archives and the loss over time, before and after the arrival of the Spaniards, of the ability to read ancient hieroglyphic writings. King Huemac, circa 11th Century, does not match the time of St. Thomas, circa 52 A.D., or Santo Tomé and Bartomé, or Alma and son of Alma, circa 148 B.C to 52 B.C. Nevertheless, the Huemac history cited by Fray Mier is like *The Book of Mormon* record of King Noah. Accounts of four disciples sent by Tomé to govern the church in Cholula is like the four sons of Mosiah in *The Book of Mormon*. And, the ancient religious status of Cholula duplicates *The Book of Mormon* profile of Zarahemla. Archeological studies of *Book of Mormon* history focus on abandoned sites in the forests, and deserts of America. Ancient cities recorded in Biblical history like Nazareth, Bethlehem, and Jerusalem, are still inhabited. Why then, is it not possible that inhabited cities of Mexico like Mitla, Tula, Cholula, and Mexico City are sites of ancient history recorded in *The Book of Mormon*? Cholula was the religious center of ancient Mexico, as was Jerusalem the center of Biblical history. Bishop Bartolomé de las Casas's writing of the Spanish conquest of Mexico in his *Very Brief Account of the Destruction of the Indies,* [12] reads like a holocaust of the native people, their culture, and their history. So much was lost, but there are surviving fragments of historical evidence. Fray Mier wrote: "If these things appear deliriums, they do not appear so much to those who have studied our antiquities." Could the ancient sacred city of Cholula be the site of the land and city of Zarahemla oft quoted in *The Book of Mormon*? It very probably is.

The cover of *Christianity in The Americas Before Columbus* is a photograph of Cholula, Mexico, surrounding the pyramid of Cholula with the Church of our Lady de los Remedios a top the pyramid. In the background is the volcano mountain, Popocatepetl. The pyramid is not the tallest, but the volume of space it occupies makes it the largest pyramid. Walking to the top of the pyramid and looking down into the city and surrounding country feels like a visit to the site of King Benjamin's sermon recorded by Mosiah in *The Book of Mormon*.

VII. THE BIBLE IN ANCIENT AMERICA

Quoting from: *Fray Servando Teresa de Mier: Writings on Ancient Christianity and Spain's Evangelism of Mexico,* Chapter 2,

"Antecedents and Consequences of the Sermon up to the Opening of the Process:"

> The first missionaries found in the hands of the Indians, the Bible in images and figures, and the wise Father Gregorio García says that fearing it would not be believed in Spain, he asked the missionaries in Veracruz for their written testimony, and they gave it to him. Torquemada tells of a book that the Otomi had with the doctrine and image of Jesus Christ, and they buried it to hide it upon the arrival of the Spaniards. Equally accountable that the Dominican missionaries also found described in the paintings of the Indians various articles of our faith such as the Annunciation to our Lady or the Incarnation, and the Resurrection of Our Lord.

Chapter 5, "Farewell Letter to the Mexicans," Fray Mier writes:

> The Indians had in their power (as the missionaries in Veracruz gave in written testimony to the celebrated Fray Gregorio García) the entire Bible in images and hieroglyphic figures, they confused them with the passage of time, they put into practice the Scripture's histories, and confused their own history and their religion. What was the Mexican's religion, but Christianity confused by time, and the mixed-up nature of the hieroglyphics?

The testimony of early Catholic missionaries, evidences that the native Mexican people had hieroglyphic scriptures of the Bible before the Catholic missionaries landed in Mexico. Torquemada's account of the Otomi people of Mexico burying their doctrinal books of Jesus Christ to hide them from the Spaniards supports the theory that the eradication of America's Christianity was a guiding principle of Spain's greedy conquest of Mexico.

The Book of Mormon lists records that comprise the major part of the Bible's Old Testament taken by emigrants from Jerusalem to the New World about 600 B.C., and the New Testament teachings of Jesus when he visited America:

> And he beheld that they did contain the five books of Moses, which gave an account of the creation of the world, and also of Adam and Eve, who were our first parents; And also

a record of the Jews from the beginning, even down to the commencement of the reign of Zedekiah, king of Judah; And also the prophecies of the holy prophets, from the beginning, even down to the commencement of the reign of Zedekiah; and also many prophecies which have been spoken by the mouth of Jeremiah. (*Book of Mormon*, 1 Nephi 5:11-13)

And now there cannot be written in this book even a hundredth part of the things which Jesus did truly teach unto the people; But behold the plates of Nephi do contain the more part of the things which he taught the people. (*Book of Mormon*, 3 Nephi 26:6-7)

VIII. THE TEMPLE OF SOLOMON

Fray Mier testifies that ancient Mexicans had the Bible Scriptures: they practiced scriptural history, tradition, and religion even to the building of a temple like unto Solomon's Jerusalem Temple in ancient Anáhuac, now Mexico City.

Chapter 5, "Farewell Letter to the Mexicans" Fray Mier writes:

In the building and services of the temple, the Mexicans wanted to imitate Solomon's temple. From there came the famous pillar of Mexico City, which dominated the lake's seven cities or lagoon as they incorrectly say. Thus, was the pillar of Solomon's temple, which according to the Second Book of Paralipomenon, had a height of 130 cubits beyond the roof's 40 cubits. When they say that in the dedication of Mexico's Temple, 22 thousand human victims were sacrificed, it is an equivocation with the 22 thousand oxen that Solomon immolated according to the Scripture in the dedication of Jerusalem's Temple. And it is to be admired, that to put the Indians in disfavor someone believes to the letter, an absurdity as large as the peaceful beheading of a city or army of 22 thousand men in order to dedicate a temple, when nobody believes to the letter the Mexicans' famous journey via the wilderness with the same mansions and wonders, which lasted 40 years, and which is no more than a literal copy of that of the Israelites.

The Book of Mormon draws a parallel to the Judaic Temple of Solomon.

And I, Nephi did build a temple; and I did construct it after the manner of the temple of Solomon save it were not built of so many precious things; for they were not to be found upon the land, wherefore, it could not be built like unto Solomon's temple. But the manner of the construction was like unto the temple of Solomon; and the workmanship thereof was exceedingly fine. (*Book of Mormon*, 2 Nephi 5:16)

IX. THE LAW OF MOSES AND JUDAIC-CHRISTIAN PRACTICES

Fray Joseph de Acosta, a Jesuit Professor of Theology, traveled to New Spain and Mexico City the years 1586 and 1587. Returning to Spain, in 1590 he published (Historia natural y moral de las Indias) Vida Religiosa y civil de los Indios ("Natural and Moral History of the Indies: The Religious and Civil Life of the Indians"). Fray Acosta's book, Chapter 27, "Of Other Ceremonies and Rites of the Indians, Like Ours," begins with the following observations:

The Indians had other innumerable ceremonies and rites, and in many of them there is resemblance to those ancient law of Moses; in others they resemble those that the Moors use, and some take something from those of the Evangelical Law, such as washings or what they call opacuna, that were to bathe themselves in water to stay clean from their sins. The Mexicans also had their baptisms with this ceremony, and it is that they sacrificed the ears and male member of newborn children, that in some way imitates the circumcision of the Jews. [13]

Bishop Bartolomé de las Casas in *Los indios de México y Nueva España, Antología* ("The Indians of Mexico and New Spain, Anthology") extracted from a work published in 1552 writes that the native priests of New Spain grew their hair in the manner of the Nazarenes of the Old Testament. He describes the act and ceremony of anointing Indian priests as the true God ordered Moses to do to Aaron in Leviticus 8. Bishop de las Casas's Anthology, Chapter LVI, "Customs of Yucatan, Origin of the Indians" [14] evidences Law of Moses practices. Yucatan was part of the Chiapas Bishopric of which he was Bishop from 1545 to 1546. Extracts, of his study of the Yucatan culture, give historical insights into the ethnic identity of the Yucatan people that are not found in archeological studies. Bishop de las Casas's writes:

> Because with the provinces of Vera Paz part of its boundaries the large kingdom of Yucatan, within which are included many and large provinces, because it has around about three hundred leagues, and all of only one tongue or language, a thing not a little amazing, in that firm land that had such an immense number of people as that kingdom, to have no more than one language; says something about its nations, and this would be very little, for my great warning, that when I was in that kingdom, and It was part of my bishopric, that I could be informed from their roots, in all I would want to know about those people, and even after many times dealing with priests that had been there and knew the language, I did not think of asking about it and informing myself. [15]

Here is what Bishop de las Casas learned about the people of Yucatan. They were a very political and prudent people. They had their kings and great lords, who many vassals obeyed. The number of people in that kingdom was immense. They had no more than one wife, whether they were lords or subjects. He certified that there were three vices the people of this kingdom lacked more than other people sodomy, eating human flesh, and human sacrifices. None of them stole. The rigor of their system of justice caused fear and put a brake on villains to not perpetrate evil. The few who they sacrificed were not to the gods but were killed for crimes. Their vaults, pyramids, grand buildings decorated with characters and signs, and their domestic beehives were found nowhere else in the Indies. The men of these nations were very hard, brave, and industrious in wars. They fought with bows and arrows, lances or long poles, shields, helmets, and protection or doublets made of cotton. "Returning to the purpose, it is said that some of them were circumcised, it is not known if they did it for ceremony or for some other regard. Circumcision was more common in the province of Nicaragua, since not all that superfluous, they were cut according to what we knew. I have not heard that they circumcised in any other part of all the Indies." [16]

Bishop de las Casas cites the Greek historians Herodotus and Strabo from a book by Alexandre ab Alexandro of Naples Italy concluding that only seven genre of people practiced circumcision: the Colchis, Egyptians, Ethiopians, Phoenicians, Syrians of

Palestine, Anatolia Syrian inhabitants on the rivers Termodon and Parthenius, and the Macrona inhabitants between these two rivers, a circle of Middle Eastern cultures near each other. He concludes that Abraham and the Jews practiced circumcision later than these seven-founding people. He then concludes: "It seems, therefore, that it will not be good to guess, because some of these Indian people have practiced circumcision in antiquity, it follows to be descended from the Judaic people. As to what the words that were and will be found among them, they will agree in sound with those of the Jews, as a certain Juris Doctor and good Christian supposed."
17

The sources of these practices, noted by Fray Acosta and Bishop de las Casas, were the early missionaries and scholars who recorded Judaic-Christian religious and civil practices and the language of the Jews found among the native Mesoamericans. Pursuing Fray Mier's shout to study these antiquities, we find historical evidence does exist which corroborates religious and civil practices recorded in *The Book of Mormon*.

The Book of Mormon cites the Law of Moses in thirty-seven verses. Fray Mier and early Catholic missionaries noted that native Mexicans practiced Judaic Law of Moses practices defined in the *Bible*: Yea, and they did keep the law of Moses; for it was expedient that they should keep the law of Moses as yet, for it was not all fulfilled. But notwithstanding the law of Moses, they did look forward to the coming of Christ, considering that the law of Moses was a type of his coming, and believing that they must keep those outward performances until the time that he should be revealed unto them. Now they did not suppose that salvation came by the law of Moses; but the law of Moses did serve to strengthen their faith in Christ; and thus, they did retain a hope through faith, unto eternal salvation, relying upon the spirit of prophecy, which spake of those things to come. (*Book of Mormon*, Alma 25:15-16)

X. FRAY MIER'S GUADALUPE SERMON, PROPOSITION ONE— ST. THOMAS THE APOSTLE PREACHED THE GOSPEL OF JESUS CHRIST IN AMERICA

In 1492, Christopher Columbus landed on territory unknown to Europeans that lay to the west of Spain. The New World discovery was believed by early European explorers to be a new-found western route to India. It came to be known as the West

Indies, inhabited by Indians, later to be called American Indians. Catholic missionaries were puzzled to find Judeo-Christian practices in the New World. Doing their historical research, they learned that Jesus Christ's Apostle, Saint Thomas, had preached the Gospel of Jesus Christ in India where he was martyred and buried. This was the basis of the Apostle St. Thomas hypothesis. (1) The Spanish and Portuguese believed they had discovered a new route to India. (2) The native Indian people they met knew the Hebrew-Christian religion. (3) St. Thomas had taken the Gospel of Jesus Christ to Asia as far as the land of India. Therefore, the common conclusion was that the American hemisphere had been evangelized to the Christian faith by St. Thomas. Fray Mier was not the inventor of the St. Thomas hypothesis. It had been set forth three hundred years before his Guadalupe Sermon.

Fray Mier's frequent reference to slavery in his writings and the theory stated in Chapter 3, "The Mier Paradox," is that the conquest and enslavement of a Christian people was in flagrant violation of Papal Bulls prohibiting enslavement of Christians. This sets-up a hypothesis on why the St. Thomas theory was hidden prior to Fray Mier's Sermon. By the early 1500's the West Indies became known as America, a continent separated from India by the Pacific Ocean. Fray Mier in his writings sets forth other theories on the Gospel in America mostly fixed on an ancient Mexican historical character that he speculates to be a different person than Apostle St. Thomas. Saint Thomas in Spanish is Santo Tomás. However, in Chapter 5., Fray Mier's "Farewell Letter to the Mexicans," and in Dr. Mier's speech the day he takes his seat in Mexico's First Constituent Congress, July 15, 1822;[18] he insists that the Saint who brought the Gospel to America was Santo Tomé. Tomé is the Portuguese/Galician spelling of Tomás. Chapter 5, "Farewell Letter to the Mexicans." Fray Mier writes:

Mexico's main temple or teo-cal-li (a word entirely Greek and with the same significance) was built, says Torquemada, in the district of the Lord of the Crown of Thorns upon the sepulcher of Saint Bartomé, martyr in Tula, disciple of Saint Tomé, who was very venerated says Acosta and Torquemada, until the conquest. This is the famous Cópil, of course it means son of Tomé, and this signifies in Hebrew Bartomé, whose head was ordered cut off by Huémac, it was tossed into the Lagoon at the site that since then was called Cópilco, where

Cópil or Bartomé is.

Bartomé is a variant spelling of Spanish Bartolomé, English Bartholomew, English translation, "Son of Talmai." The *Bible*, Numbers 13:22 notes that Talmai was a son of Anak. The name Talmai is found in the Biblical books Joshua, Judges, II Samuel, and I Chronicles, recording Talmai as king of Geshur, and another Talmai was noted as the father of King David's wife Maacah mother of Absalom. These Biblical records would have been found in the brass plates of Laban noted in *The Book of Mormon*, which later in the *Book* identifies Alma and his son Alma as prophets and founders of the Church of Christ in America circa 173-73 B.C. The history of Alma and his son Alma comprises some 224 pages, 42 percent, of *The Book of Mormon*. With the evolution of time the Hebrew names Talmai could have evolved to Tomé in the native languages of Mesoamerica, and then further to Spanish Tomás and English Alma in *The Book of Mormon*. Another example of the evolution of a common *Book of Mormon* name is "Nephi." "There were giants in the earth in those days; and also after that, when the sons of God came in unto the daughters of men, and they bare children to them, the same became mighty men which were of old, men of renown." (*Bible, King James* Genesis 6:4)[19] The same verse in the Hebrew Torah reads: "It was then, and later too, that the Nephilim appeared on earth—when the divine beings cohabited with the daughters of men who bore them offspring. They were the heroes of old, the men of renown." (*Torah*, Genesis 6:4). Giants and Nephilim are underlined for emphasis. The "im" at the end of Nephilim is the Hebrew equivalent of plural, like English "s" at the end of giants. *The Book of Mormon* 1 Nephi 5:31 in part reads: "And now I, Nephi, being a man large in stature, . . ." Knowing the Hebrew word Nephilim translates to giant, and that *The Book of Mormon* describes Nephi as "large in stature" suggests that at the time of birth Nephi was a large baby, which caused his parents Lehi and Sariah to name him "Giant", Hebrew "Nephi." Nephi is another example of a *Book of Mormon* historical evolution of a Hebrew biblical name like the cited Talmai to Alma.

Chapter 5, "Farewell Letter to the Mexicans," Fray Mier writes: "Torquemada says that it is apparent that four generations before the conquest there was already in our America clear knowledge of the Christian Religion and of the future arrival of the Spaniards. To this epoch it appears, belong the four renowned prophets of

Yucatán, whose remarkable prophecies Montemayor relates."
Father Francisco Javier Clavijero (1731-1787) born in Veracruz,
Mexico, corroborates Fray Mier's writings. Father Clavijero, a
Jesuit, was exiled upon the expulsion of the Jesuit Order from
Mexico in 1767. Father Clavijero spent the rest of his life in Italy.
Fray Mier was born 1763 in Monterrey, Mexico. Even though Fray
Mier, most likely, never met nor read the writings of Father
Clavijero; they studied the same historical accounts coming to
similar conclusions; however, Father Clavijero did not provoke the
revolution and scandal Fray Mier fomented. Only because the
Jesuit Father Clavijero was exiled from Mexico before he began to
write; and, he wrote in Italian with the earliest Spanish translation
being 1826. In *Historia Antigua de México*, "Book VI, About the
Religion of the Mexicans: Their Gods, Temples, Priests, Sacrifices,
and Obligations; about their Fasts and Austerities; about their
Chronology, Calendar, and Fiestas; about the Rites on the Birth of
the Children, on their Marriages and Funerals,"[20] Father Calvijero
writes that Quetzalcoatl was consecrated God by the people of
Cholula:

> After having been twenty years in that city (Cholula) he
> (Quezalcoatl) decided to continue his journey to the imaginary
> Kingdom of Tlapalan (district of Mexico City), taking with him
> four noble and virtuous youths. From the maritime province
> of Coatzacoalco (port city of Veracruz State) he bid them
> farewell charging them that they should tell the Cholultecans
> that they could be certain that he would return some day to
> console them and govern them. To these youths the
> Cholultecans later charged the government of that city out of
> respect for their venerated Quetzalcoatl, of whom some say
> that he disappeared and others that he died in the same coast.[21]

The four prophets cited by Torquemada, and the four noble
and virtuous youths referenced by Clavijero fit the image of the
four noble sons of King Mosiah who accompanied the son of Alma
recorded in *The Book of Mormon*:

> And now it came to pass that Alma began from this time
> forward to teach the people, and those who were with Alma at
> the time the angel appeared unto them, traveling round about
> through all the land, publishing to all the people the things

which they had heard and seen, and preaching the word of God in much tribulation, being greatly persecuted by those who were unbelievers, being smitten by many of them. But notwithstanding all this, they did impart much consolation to the church, confirming their faith, and exhorting them with long-suffering and much travail to keep the commandments of God. And four of them were the sons of Mosiah; and their names were Ammon, and Aaron, and Omner, and Himni; these were the names of the sons of Mosiah. And they traveled throughout all the land of Zarahemla, and among all the people who were under the reign of king Mosiah, zealously striving to repair all the injuries which they had done to the church, confessing all their sins, and publishing all the things which they had seen, and explaining the prophecies and the scriptures to all who desired to hear them." (*Book of Mormon*, Mosiah 27:32-35)

Father Clavijero writes that Quetzalcoatl had a dark beard, wore full-length garments, smelted metal, and above all that he was a man of a very austere and exemplary life. From Father Clavijero's and early Catholic Fathers' writings on Quetzalcoatl it is unclear who Quetzalcoatl was. Was he a high priest or a god? Here Father Clavijero also cites Dr. Carlos de Sigüenza y Góngora, mathematician, author, and Catholic Priest. Sigüenza Y Góngora inherited the records of Fernando de Alva Ixtlilxóchitl, a direct descendent of the Aztec kings; which are among the few pre-Columbus records surviving the Spanish conquest of Mexico. Father Clavijero writes:

Dr. Sigüenza y Góngora believed that Quetzalcoatl, who those nations consecrated was none other than the Apostle Saint Thomas, who announced the Gospel to them. He exerted this thought with a large scholarly copy that like others from his learned pen had the disgrace of perishing for the negligence of those who possessed them. In this work he drew a parallel of the names of Didymus[22] and Quetzalcoatl, of his clothes, his doctrine and his prophecies, and he examined the places where he traveled, the signs that he left and the wonders that his four principal disciples made known. For lack of said manuscripts we abstain from the censuring of an opinion, to which except for the respect that we owe to the lights of the author we cannot agree. Various writers of that kingdom have had as certain that some centuries before the arrival of the Spaniards the Gospel had already been preached in America. The motives that they had for this belief were various crosses that in diverse times and places were found that appear to be carved before the Spaniards. The fast of 40 days that various people of that New World observed, the prophecies that they had of the future arrival of a strange and bearded people and human traces stamped in some stones that they believed to be of the Apostle Saint Thomas. I have never been able to agree with these authors; but the research of their fundamental beliefs, especially regarding the cross, demands another very diverse work from what we now write.[23]

Fray Mier writes in his "Farewell Letter to the Mexican":

What was the Mexican religion, but Christianity confused by time, and the mixed-up nature of the hieroglyphics? I have made a great study of their mythology and in its depth, it comes down to God, Jesus Christ, his Mother, Saint Tomé, his seven disciples called the seven Tomés *chicome-cohuatl* and the martyrs that died in the persecution of Huémac.

A parallel between Fray Mier's historical writing on Tomé and *The Book of Mormon* history of Alma is a note from Chapter 5, Mier's "Farewell Letter to the Mexicans," on the "seven disciples" of Tomé and *The Book of Mormon* account of the seven disciples of Alma: Ammon, Aaron, Omner, Amulek, Zeezrom, Shiblon, and Corianton:

And now, as the preaching of the word had a great tendency to lead the people to do that which was just—yea, it had had more powerful effect upon the minds of the people than the sword, or anything else, which had happened unto them—therefore Alma thought it was expedient that they should try the virtue of the word of God. Therefore, he took Ammon, and Aaron, and Omner; and Himni he did leave in the church in Zarahemla; but the former three he took with him, and also Amulek and Zeezrom, who were at Melek; and he also took two of his sons. Now the eldest of his sons he took not with him, and his name was Helaman; but the names of those whom he took with him were Shiblon and Corianton; and these are the names of those who went with him among the Zoramites, to preach unto them the word. (*Book of Mormon*, Alma 31:5-7)Fray Mier's December 12, 1794 sermon was on Judeo-Christian culture in America before Christopher Columbus. In his later writings he expounds on how early Spanish conquistadors and priests sifted through surviving written and oral traditions transposing Mexican culture, religion, events, names, practices, and pronunciations into their European culture and Catholic religion. Fray Mier, Fray Sigüenza, Alva Cortés Ixtlilxochitl, Fray Torquemada, Father Clavijero, Bishop de las Casas, and other Catholic scholars of ancient Mexican history spread the history of Apostle Saint Thomas's missionary preaching to Asia's India as their theory on how Judeo-Christian vestiges came to the new-found West Indies, later to be called America. Their written histories on Saint Thomas have many close similarities to the history of Alma recorded in *The Book of Mormon:*

And now, Alma was their high priest, he being the founder of their church. And it came to pass that none received authority to preach or to teach except it were by him from God. Therefore, he consecrated all their priests and all their teachers; and none were consecrated except they were just men. (Book of Mormon, Mosiah 23:16-17)

And now, as I said unto you, that after king Mosiah had done these things, he took the plates of brass, and all the things which he had kept, and conferred them upon Alma, who was the son of Alma; yea, all the records, and also the interpreters, and conferred them upon him, and commanded him that he should keep and preserve them, and also keep a record of the people, handing them down from one generation to another, even as they had been handed down from the time that Lehi left Jerusalem. (Book of Mormon, Mosiah 28:20)

Fray Mier and earlier Catholic missionaries and scholars recorded ancient Christian traditions and history of Mexico, which are analogous to *Book of Mormon* accounts of Alma and his son Alma. Fray Mier's theory on the preaching of Saint Thomas and his brief narrative on Tomé and Bartomé gives reason to believe that traces of *Book of Mormon* history were recorded in the ancient folio histories archived in the libraries, temples, and sanctuaries of

Mexico, which were translated to the Spanish Santo Tomás, Santo Tomé, and Santo Bartomé, the Apostle Thomas of the New Testament.

XI. FRAY MIER'S GUADALUPE SERMON PROPOSITION TWO—TONANTZIN, THE MOTHER OF THE TRUE GOD, GIVEN TO BE KNOWN TO THE INDIANS BY SAINT TOMÉ, HAD FROM THOSE TIMES A TEMPLE AND WORSHIP ON THE HILL TEPEYAC IN THE IMAGE OF THE VIRGIN OF GUADALUPE.

In his "Farewell Letter to the Mexicans," Fray Mier writes:

And in the understanding of the Mexicans what did *Mexî* mean? Again, it is history which must tell it to us with certainty. *Mexî* was a man God, called by other names the Lord of the Crown of Thorns, *Teohuitznáhuac*, Lord of Paradise *Teotlaloc* &. &., who a virgin called Saint Mary *Malintzin*, conceived by a work of heaven, and she gave birth to him, already a perfect male, without injury to her virginity. *Foemina circundabit virum*. So, Father Torquemada tells it.

Saint Tomé was who gave them news of son and mother, so they also called her for this *Cilma-cóhuatl* the Tomé Woman, and *Coatlantona*, Mother of the Tomés or disciples of Saint Tomé, who wearing the hair cut in the shape of a crown, *sénchon-huitznáhuac*, made three vows, of poverty, obedience, and chastity, and served in the Temple of the Lord of the Crown of Thorns: *huitznáhuac-teocalli*.

To this virgin the Mexicans celebrated two principal festivals. One, the 2nd day of February, Day of the Purification of Our Lady, and they presented children to her as she presented hers at the temple, and they had to be precisely purchased: *omne primogenitum pretio redimes*. And, they made sure that they must be blondes or fair little ones in memory of Saint Tomé having been the one who instituted the festivals.

The other they had on Tepeyácac the day of winter solstice another day of Apostle Saint Thomas, and they offered her flowers and images that they had of her that they worshipped there with the name of *Tzenteotinantzin*, which is to say, Mother of the true God, or *Tonantzin*, Our Lady and Mother, because they said that this virgin Mother of their God was mother of all the people of *Anáhuac* which we now call New Spain. Her figure was that of a girl with an encircling white and resplendent tunic, to whom for this they also called her *Chalchihuitliche*, with a sea-green blue robe, *Matlalcneye*, star studded, *Citlacui*.

Tzenteotinantzin or *Tonantzin* whether translated as "Mother of the true God," "Mother of God," "Mother of the Son of God," or "Our Lady and Mother" bears witness that Mary the mother of Jesus Christ was conserved in the ancient traditions and celebrations of Mexico. Fray Mier's Guadalupe proposition was that an ancient reverence and love of Tonantzin, the virgin mother of God existed in Mexico before the European conquest. Spain's conquest brought about a transfiguration of Tonantzin into Spain's Virgin of Guadalupe hastening the evangelism of Saint Tomé's Christians to Catholic Christians. Tonantzin and Guadalupe is a memory of Mary, the mother of Jesus Christ, the son of God recorded in Mexico's antiquities, the *Bible*, and *The Book of Mormon*:

> And he said unto me: Behold, the virgin whom thou seest is the mother of the Son of God, after the manner of the flesh. And it came to pass that I beheld that she was carried away in the Spirit; and after she had been carried away in the Spirit for the space of a time the angel spake unto me, saying: Look! And I looked and beheld the virgin again, bearing a child in her arms. And the angel said unto me: Behold the Lamb of God, yea, even the Son of the Eternal Father! (*Book of Mormon*, I Nephi 11:18-21.)
>
> And he shall be called Jesus Christ, the Son of God, the Father of heaven and earth, the Creator of all things from the beginning; and his mother shall be called Mary. (*Book of Mormon*, Mosiah 3:8.)
>
> And behold, he shall be born of Mary, at Jerusalem which is the land of our forefathers, she being a virgin, a precious and chosen vessel, who shall be overshadowed and conceive by the power of the Holy Ghost, and bring forth a son, yea, even the Son of God. (*Book of Mormon*, Alma 7:10.)

XII. HONEYBEES

The honeybee is a high-profile image of Mormon culture. The western territory settled in 1847 by Mormon pioneers was called

Deseret, which by interpretation is a honeybee. The State of Utah is known as the Beehive State with a beehive on the Utah State seal and flag. Deseret Book, *Deseret News,* and Deseret Industries are entities of the Church of Jesus Christ of Latter-day Saints. Hugh Nibley, a historian and prolific author on *Book of Mormon* topics addresses a letter "Concerning Deseret" to "My dear Professor F.:" which concludes with the following statement.

> As a naturalist you will no doubt protest at this point that the bee was unknown in ancient America, having first been introduced into the New World by the white man in the seventeenth century. There are seven references to bees or honey in the *Book of Mormon,* and without exception they all belong to the Old World. Lehi's wanderers, starved for sweets, gloried as Arabs always do in the discovery of honey–but that was in Arabia. The Jaredites carried hives of bees from Babel into the wilderness for a journey of many years, but there is no mention of bees in the cargo of their ships (*Book or Mormon,* Ether 6:4)–a significant omission, since our author elsewhere goes out of his way to mention them. The survival of the word *bee* in the New World after the bees themselves had been left behind is a phenomenon having many parallels in the history of language, but the *Book of Mormon* nowhere mentions bees or honey as existing in the Western Hemisphere.[24]

The *Deseret News,* March 17, 1991, published a brief article titled, "Beehive State has Long History, High Regard for its Honeybees," which asserts:

> Beekeeping as an occupation and a hobby originated centuries ago in Asia and Europe, says Dr. James Tew of the Apiculture Extension Service, U. S. Department of Agriculture. In the 1600's, the American colonists apparently longed for honey, a sweetener they had enjoyed 'back home.' Thus, they imported honeybees from Europe to Jamestown, Va. Because the American Indians had never seen bees and did not know what bees could contribute, they simply thought the strangers had brought in a new kind of 'fly', Tew said.

Mexican history contradicts the Nibley-Tew account on honeybees in the Americas. In a letter addressed to the Queen Lady

Juana and to the Emperor Carlos V, dated July 10, 1519, Hernán Cortés tells of his arrival on the island of Cozumel, twelve miles east of Mexico's Yucatán Peninsula. He writes: "The said island is small, and there is neither river nor stream on it, and all the water that the Indians drink is from wells, and on it there is not another thing but rocks and stones and hills, and the farming that its Indians have is colonies of beehives, and our attorneys take to Your Royal Highnesses the sample of the honey and soil of the said colonies of beehives sent in order to see it.[25] This account by Cortés of his exploration of the island of Cozumel nullifies the statement of Naturalist Professor, Apiculture expert, and historian Dr. Nibley "(T)hat the bee was unknown in ancient America, having first been introduced into the New World by the white man in the seventeenth century" July 10, 1519 was not ancient time, but the Cortés diary indisputable evidences that bee apiaries were cultivated in Mexico, before the arrival of "the white man." Cortés's naïve account of honeybees raises questions. Why was the discovery of beehives so important that Cortés solicited his attorneys to take a sample of "honey and soil," a honeycomb, to the Emperor Carlos V? Was it that honey was known, but caring for beehives and the extraction of honey from a soiled, membrane covered, honeycomb was unknown in 1519 Spain?

Fray Diego de Landa (1524-1579) preserved valuable information on the pre-Columbia Maya civilization in *Relación de las cosas de Yucatán* (*"Account of the Things of Yucatán"*). Sadly, when called to be the second Bishop of Yucatán, he forced the conversion of the Maya people to the Catholic faith by forcibly destroying ancient Mayan records, history, and traditions. Chapter XLVII of *Relación* is a short paragraph titled: "Of the Bees and Their Honey and Wax."

There are two breeds of bees and both are much smaller than ours. Most of them are raised in beehives, which are very small; they do not make honeycombs like ours, but certain tiny blisters like kernels of wax, all together one to another, filled with honey. To sap them they do no more that open the beehive and burst with a little stick these blisters and thus the honey flows, and they take out the wax when it pleases them. The rest are raised in the wild, in tree and stone hollows, and there they look for the wax and honey, of which this land abounds very much, and the honey is very good except that the fertility of the bees' produce is too much it comes out a little watery and it is necessary to boil it and by doing so it stays very good and for a long time. The wax is good except that it is very smoky, and it has never been found out what may be the cause, and in some provinces, it is much more yellow by reason of the flowers. These bees do not sting, nor do they do (anything) even when they are badly sapped. [26]

Bishop Bartolomé de las Casas served 1546 to 1546 as Bishop of Chiapas, which included Yucatán. He writes of the "Customs of Yucatán, Origin of the Indians." One custom was keeping domestic honeybees.

Not a small indication of their prudence and good policy is the admirable and ancient buildings of vaults and quasi pyramids, at least as regards the greatness, and upon mountains or mountain ranges made of earth collected and carried, built by hand, and the characters and signs that also have been found in them. Item, the multitude of beehives and large apiaries of domestic bees that give an infinite quantity of honey and wax has never been seen anywhere else in the Indies, there where one finds and uses only wild and not domestic honey and wax, because the bees produce it and work, some in holes in the earth and others in the trees. [27]

Bishop de Landa describes two breeds of bees, both smaller than "ours," presumably Old-World bees. Dr. Hugh Nibley writes: "The Jaredites carried hives of bees from Babel into the wilderness for a journey of many years, but there is no mention of bees in the cargo of their ships;" and then goes on to say: "The *Book of Mormon* nowhere mentions bees or honey as existing in the Western Hemisphere." Clearly, Nibley had never read the writings of the Catholic Bishop Landa nor Bishop Casas. *Book of Mormon* Jaredites may not have brought bees from the Old World, but they did bring their apiary skills, which would have facilitated their domestication of the small breed of bees, native to the Yucatán peninsula. Bishop de las Casas writes that the only place in the West Indies where domestic beehives were found was Yucatán, twelve miles from the island of Cozumel where Hernán Cortés first found beehives in the New World. Bee keeping of these small American species of bees is still practiced today in Central America.

Honeybees can be added to the list, along with geographic descriptions, and a written language as topics that fix *Book of Mormon* history to Mesoamerica. Honeybees also evidence a dilemma exemplified by the writings of Hugh Nibley and James Tew. If historical authenticity is to be brought to *The Book of Mormon*, scholars need to move from their exclusive Anglocentric *Book of Mormon* perspective and begin to study the historical writings of Spanish and Mexican Catholic missionaries and scholars, who preserved traces of ancient Mexican history and culture, which survived Spain's conquest of the New World. Honeybee is not a religious doctrine, but like a germ cell or a DNA sample, the honeybee is a defining, fundamental, and distinctive feature that brings location and historical authenticity to *The Book of Mormon*.

> And they did also lay snares and catch fowls of the air; and they did also prepare a vessel, in which they did carry with them the fish of the waters. And they did also carry with them deseret, which, by interpretation, is a honey bee; and thus, they did carry with them swarms of bees, and all manner of that which was upon the face of the land, seeds of every kind (*Book of Mormon*, Ether 2:2-3).

XIII. WINE

Wine is a fermented juice of many varieties of grapes usually having an alcohol content of 14 percent or less. Wine can also be the fermented juice of any of a variety of other fruits and plants. Researching the history of wine in the New-World before 1492, one discovers alcoholic drinks were fermented from tree bark, plants, fruits, and honey throughout North and South America. But, nowhere in the Americas were fermented alcoholic beverages as pervasive a habit as they were in ancient Mexico.

In Chapter 6, "Alexander von Humboldt's Contribution to Mexican Anthropology," PLATE VIII, Genealogy of the Princes of Atzacapotzalco," Humboldt describes how paper was made from the maguey plant, a vital asset to a civilization with a written language. The maguey plant, of the genus agave, was also the source for pulque, a fermented milky drink, which in modern times is refined to mescal and tequila with higher alcohol content than wine. Pulque, described by Catholic missionaries as "maguey wine," was the wine of the Maya and Aztec people in the Pre-

Columbian Era. Two other "wines" indigenous to Mexico are balché a honey wine brewed by the Maya from tree bark and honey, and tepache, a very mild wine fermented from pineapple, which grow wild in southern Mexico. As discussed in topic XII. Honeybees, the Maya had domesticated native honeybees.

Evidence of the pervasiveness of wine in ancient Mexico, were the ancient Mexican laws regulating the consumption of alcohol. Bishop de las Casas wrote a summary, "On Some Crimes and Their Punishments," which includes laws regulating the consumption of wine in Mexico before the conquest:

Among the people of New Spain to get drunk had great shame and was a vile vice and disgraceful, and for this those who drank it used the wine, not as one wishes, nor all those who wanted it, except with the license of the lords and judges, who gave it only to the old men and women of fifty years and above or a little younger; and the reason that they gave was that those had a need for it as a remedy for their blood getting cold, so that they could warm up and sleep. These drank two or three or four small cups, of the wine which they made, if it is not of much quantity, one cannot get drunk. In their wedding feasts and other festivities, they can drink two or three cups, those who were of a manly age, and no more. The doctors gave many medicines in a cup of wine, and to the women who have just given birth it was a most common thing in the first days of her delivery to give them a little wine for health and not for vice. There were many persons that so hated wine, that neither healthy nor sick did they want to taste it. The laborers and workers, when they hauled wood from the mountain and when they brought down large stones, drank to temper the cold, and to better endure the work; some drank more and others less, as they felt it was necessary for them. The lords and chiefs had as a point of honor, and the people of war, to not drink wine. Their common drink was cocoa and other brews make of toasted corn meal that does not intoxicate but gives strength and refreshes the whole body. The punishment that was given to those who got drunk or for having drank much began to become drunk and gave voices or sang were taken to the market, were they, man or woman, and they publicly sheared them, that is no less an affront among them than among us to give someone a hundred lashes by the usual way, and later they sent him to knock down his house, giving the person that became drunk to understand that voluntarily losing the justice of reason, he is not worthy to have a house in the town nor to count himself as one of the neighbors.

This was the custom and the law and the punishment that was had and was given throughout the times that those people lived without Christians seeing, which all the monks, especially the Order of Saint Francis and by the way they have, and they had, searched, examined, and verified. After the Christians had conquered that land and the native lords and judges, and there being cause that they not use their ancient laws, there are so many excesses of drunkenness that they have done and the Indians when they can do it, especially if they can have Castilian wine, that the same monks that said, they cannot believe they did not use them in the ancient times; but after much and very well investigated, and as I said, looked into and examined, they confess to having been deceived, and it is true this that I say here is all from their writing, and from their writing I have taken it. [28]

Fray Mier in his "Eleventh Note of the Second Letter from an American," writes:

The goodness of the Mexican laws exists in the testimony of the Code of the Indies, where the King of Spain orders they should keep and live according to them, because, having examined them, they have seemed very good. Wine or pulque, for example, was not allowed among them except with great precautions, and he who became drunk, if he was noble his hair was shaved, and his house was demolished, if a plebeian, he had the penalty of death. The Spanish to the contrary, in the interest of a sordid profit, opened everywhere free temples to Bacchus, and the Indians, filled with oppression and bitterness, gave themselves over without limit to drunkenness, to stun their pain. In vain the parish priests have opposed this with the liveliest zeal: The King's Administrators who take from that innumerable perennial criminal fountain, a substantial income, closed their mouths with the embezzlement passed on to the Royal Household. Thus, the demoralization of the Indians, as is their ignorance, was the work of the Spanish.

The making and consumption of wine, in ancient Mexico, was so culturally pervasive that the Catholic Fathers recorded the laws and rules governing drunkenness and the rules allowing a person to legally consume wine. The unregulated drunkenness, which followed Spain's conquest of Mexico, was a major contributor to the complete collapse of native Mexican civilizations. The consumption of wine was a cultural habit recorded in The Book of Mormon and was a Mexican custom recorded in the histories of the early Catholic missionaries. Drinking wine was a religious ritual; and more commonly, wine was a social custom consumed to the point of "drunk with wine" as recorded in The Book of Mormon. Wine, like the honeybee, geography, written language, and religious history adds another parallel between Mexico and *Book of Mormon* historicity:

> And it came to pass that Jesus commanded his disciples that they should bring forth some bread and wine unto him. And while they were gone for bread and wine, he commanded the multitude that they should sit themselves down upon the earth. And when the disciples had come with bread and wine, he took of the bread and brake and blessed it; and he gave unto the disciples and commanded that they should eat. And it came to pass that when he said these words, he commanded his disciples that they should take of the wine of the cup and drink of it and that they should also give unto the multitude that they might drink of it. And it came to pass that they did so and did drink of it and were filled; and they gave unto the multitude, and they did drink, and they were filled *(Book of Mormon, 3 Nephi 18:1-3, 8-9)*.
>
> And it came to pass that they did take of the wine freely; and it was pleasant to their taste, therefore they took of it more freely; and it was strong, having been prepared in its strength. And it came to pass they did drink and were merry, and by and by they were all drunken. And now when Laman and his men saw that they were all drunken, and were in a deep sleep, they returned to Moroni and told him all the things that had happened. And now this was according to the design of Moroni. And Moroni had prepared his men with weapons of war; and he went to the city Gid, while the Lamanites were in a deep sleep and drunken, and cast in weapons of war unto the prisoners, insomuch that they were all armed; *(Book of Mormon,*

Alma 55:13-16).

XIV. ETHNICITY

Chapter 6, "Alexander von Humboldt's Contribution to Mexican Anthropology, PLATE IX, Azteca Hieroglyphic Manuscript, Conserved in the Vatican Library."

Humboldt writes: (T)his belief, universally spread, that white men and of long beards, practitioners of a great quantity of customs, had transformed the political and religious system of the people: all these circumstances, the monks, who accompanied the Spanish army at the moment of the conquest, were led to believe that in a very remote age Christianity had been preached in the new continent.

Fray Servando Teresa de Mier: Writings on Ancient Christianity and Spain's Evangelism of Mexico, Chapter 2, "Antecedents and Consequences of the Sermon up to the Opening of the Process."

Mier writes of an ancient Mexican festival: The Virgin Mother of this true God was the beloved mother of all the peoples of Anáhuac, and for this they called her *Tonantzin*, or Our Lady and Mother, they much enjoyed raising temples to her, for her ancient and grand beneficence, and they were such devotees of her image on the hill Tepeyac, that no one passed without going up to pour upon her altar the flowers that were found there, an offering which was pleasing to her, because she detested and prohibited human victims, the same as Saint Tomé, and for this they called her *Cihuacohuatl* or Tomé woman. The figure in which they venerated this Virgin was that of an Aztec child or little girl, dressed in a white resplendent and belted tunic, and with a sea-green blue mantle studded with stars. Various fiestas celebrated her, the principal one being the 2nd day of February or the Purification of Our Lady and the presentation of the Child Jesus in the temple, with the circumstance by which children were presented to her, and they had to be precisely purchased with money *omne primogenitum pretio redimes* (*"Redeem all the firstborn"*); and they made sure that part of them were white and blond, in memory of it having been *Quetzalcohuatl* who instituted the fiesta.

Mier's "Farewell Letter to the Mexicans," Chapter 5, reiterates the message that blond, white (fair little ones) children must be chosen for a sacred religious celebration.

To this virgin the Mexicans celebrated two principal festivals. One, the 2nd day of February, Day of the Purification of Our Lady, and they presented children to her as she presented hers at the temple, and they had to be precisely purchased: *omne primogenitum pretio redimes redimes* ("*Redeem all the firstborn*").And, they made sure that they must be blondes or fair little ones in memory of Saint Tomé having been the one who instituted the festivals.

"An Aztec child or little girl" playing the role of the Virgin Mother with children presented to her, some of whom were "white and blond," "blondes or fair little ones," is a witness by Fray Mier that vestige evidences of Christianity and a diverse ethnicity were the heritage of Mexico prior to the conquest of Mexico by Spain. The Mexican festive gathering of "white and blond" children "in memory of it having been *Quetzalcohuatl* who instituted the fiesta" is a likeness of Jesus gathering children as recorded in *The Book of Mormon*.

And it came to pass that he did teach and minister unto the children of the multitude of whom hath been spoken, and he did loose their tongues, and they did speak unto their fathers great and marvelous things, even greater than he had revealed unto the people; and he loosed their tongues that they could utter. And it came to pass that after he had ascended into heaven—the second time that he showed himself unto them, and had gone unto the Father, after having healed all their sick, and their lame, and opened the eyes of their blind and unstopped the ears of the deaf, and even had done all manner of cures among them, and raised a man from the dead, and had shown forth his power unto them, and had ascended unto the Father—Behold, it came to pass on the morrow that the multitude gathered themselves together, and they both saw and heard these children; yea, even babes did open their mouths and utter marvelous things; and the things which they did utter were forbidden that there should not any man write them (*Book of Mormon*, 3 Nephi 26:14-16).

The Book of Mormon is a religious record of ancient America. Belief in the truth of *The Book of Mormon* can lead to a "mistake of men," one of which is to believe that *The Book of Mormon* is an encyclopedic record of all the inhabitants and all the cultures of the entire ancient American continents. The belief was that Nephites, Lamanites, and Jaredites were the ancestors of all Native American people. DNA testing of Native Indians living in North and South America evidence this is not so. An article published in the October 26, 2015 journal *Proceedings of the National Academy of Science* reports a DNA study of two babies buried in Alaska as early as 11,500 years ago. The article connects the genes of these early immigrants crossing the Bering land bridge to the American Indians who now inhabit North and South America. There are numerous DNA studies connecting North and South American Indians to the Bering Strait emigrants from Siberia.

The topics of this Chapter are geography, written language, natural paper source, honey, wine, and the ethnicity of white bearded men and white and blond children, that tie *Book of Mormon* history to a small area in the vast continents of North and South America – Mesoamerica. Mesoamerica extends from central Mexico south to Belize, Guatemala, El Salvador, Honduras, Nicaragua, and northern Costa Rica. Though not noted in the *Book* itself , the people of the *Book* had to have cohabitated with ancient Bering Strait emigrants now known as American Indians. So, where is the ethnic identity, the DNA gene pool, of *Book of Mormon* people, identified as Nephite, Lamanite, and Jaradite immigrants from ancient Babel and Jerusalem? What caused the gene pool and ethnicity, of the *Book*'s ancient Middle East emigrants to ancient America to be lost? What happened to those white men of long beards, the white and blond children, and those traces of Judaic heritage that the early Catholic Fathers discovered? National Geographic Channel's documentary film, "America before Columbus," estimates the population of all the Americas at the arrival of Columbus to be equal to that of Europe, about 100 million inhabitants. The documentary gives a conservative estimated death toll in the Americas of 50 percent after discovery but goes on to say that the loss was more likely 90 percent of the America's population. Studying the writings of Catholic Priests, this devastating destruction of America's people had two crises as its root. First, was the catastrophic death toll of infectious diseases the Europeans and their domesticated animals brought to the New World; and, second was Spain's reckless conquest of natural resources, the destruction of civilizations, and enslavement.

Fray Mier In his "Eleventh Note of the Second Letter from an American," and Bishop de las Casas in his *Brevísima relación de la destrucción de las Indias* ("A Very Brief Account of the Destruction of the Indies"), [29] written 1552, describes the depopulation of Spain and the Americas and reads like the 20th Century Holocaust, the World War II genocide of the European Jews and other Groups, between 1941 and 1945, across German-occupied Europe. Bishop de las Casas's "Brief Account" writes of enslavement, reckless killing, and butchery of native Indians to feed herds of Spanish attack dogs. He tells of passing through villages where the streets were littered with dead bodies due to the European contagious diseases with no survivors to bury the dead. The 10 percent of Native Americans who survived disease and a brutal conquest were forced into a vicious encomienda system of slavery with no regard for human rights.

The United States of America celebrates Columbus Day to commemorate the discovery of the New World by Christopher Columbus October 12, 1492. Mexico celebrates October 12, 1492 as Día de la Raza, ("Day of the Race"), the founding of the mestizo race, a mixed ethnicity of European and Native American people. The death toll, the Spanish conquest's immoral treatment of the native people, and the founding of a mixed race are the painful memories of Día de la Raza—a very different remembrance from the simple day of discovery celebrated in the United States.

The few American natives who survived the European invasion became known as American Indians. With no protection of human rights, the 10 percent who survived the Conquest became victims of Spain's slavery under the encomienda system in violation of Catholic Papal Bulls, and the immoral rape of the surviving native women creating the Mexican Mestizo race. Thus, began the repopulation of Mesoamerica with mixed race Mestizos, today commonly called Hispanics, Latinos, Mexicans, and other Mesoamerican nationalities. In Mesoamerica, pure blood American Indians are a minority. From evidence set forth here, the mixed-race mestizos are the most likely survivors of the ancient Nephite, Lamanite, and Jaredite immigrants to the Americas. A DNA study of a Mesoamerica Latino/Latina could show in the majority evidence of Middle Eastern Judaic genes. However, this does not solve the conundrum of Latino DNA. Jews were early immigrants to ancient Spain. [30] DNA studies in Spain have estimated that 75 percent of Spaniards have Jewish roots. Yes, Latinos have Middle East/Judaic roots; but, with no surviving genealogy records the question is: Are their Judaic roots from Spanish Jewish ancestors or from American Nephite, Lamanite, or Jaredite ancestors? DNA studies in search of descendants of *Book of Mormon* people should be done on the people of Mesoamerica, the Mestizo Latinos.

DNA studies have shown that pure blood Native American Indians are not descendants of *Book of Mormon* people. Nevertheless, it is very likely that mixed race Mestizo Latin-Hispanic Americans have Jewish DNA heritage from one or both of their Spanish and ancient Mexican ancestors.

The Book of Mormon "Introduction" begins with a description of the ethnic identity of the "ancient inhabitants of the Americas." Underlining is not included in the "Introduction." It is included here to clarify a change in descriptive words:

> *The Book of Mormon* is a volume of holy scripture comparable to the Bible. It is a record of God's dealings with the ancient inhabitants of the Americas and contains, as does the Bible, the fulness of the everlasting gospel.
>
> The book was written by many ancient prophets by the spirit of prophecy and revelation. Their words, written on gold plates, were quoted and abridged by a prophet-historian named Mormon. The record gives an account of two great civilizations. One came from Jerusalem in 600 B.C. and afterward separated into two nations, known as the Nephites and the Lamanites. The other came much earlier when the Lord confounded the tongues at the Tower of Babel. This group is known as the Jaredites. After thousands of years, all were destroyed except <u>the Lamanites, and they are the principal ancestors of the American Indians.</u>

Carrie A. Moore wrote an article, "Debate renewed with change in the Book of Mormon introduction," published in the *Deseret News* November 8, 2007, which begins with the following statement.

> A one-word change in the introduction to a 2006 edition of

the Book of Mormon has re-ignited discussion among some Latter-day Saints about the book's historicity, geography and the descendants of those chronicled within its pages. The book is considered scripture by members of the Church of Jesus Christ of Latter-day Saints, and many lifelong members grew up believing that American Indians are direct descendants of ancient people in the book called Lamanites, who the book says built a civilization in the Americas between about 600 B.C. and 400 A.D.

The Book of Mormon "Introduction" word change, underlined and bolded here, is in the phrase: "the Lamanites, and they are **the principal** ancestors of the American Indians;" which was changed to "the Lamanites, and they are **among the** ancestors of the American Indians." The understanding in the Church of Jesus Christ of Latter-days Saints, since The Book of Mormon, 1830 publication, was that American Indians were descendants of *The Book of Mormon* Lamanite people. DNA studies of American Indians have not found Hebrew or Middle East DNA. The studies link Native American Indians to Siberian/Asiatic DNA origins. DNA studies was most probably the reason for the one-word change. The writings of Fray Mier, Baron von Humboldt, Bishop de las Casas, and other missionaries identify ethnic qualities, groups, and historical heritage in Mexico that evidence Judaic culture, like the Mexican practice of the" Law of Moses, "and "blond, white (fair little ones) children" in Mexican traditions discovered by early Catholic missionaries that connect the Mexican Mestizo race to *Book of Mormon* history.

XV. ELEPHANTS

Now for the elephant in the room. Alexander von Humboldt, in *Aportaciones a la Antropología Mexicana* ("Contributions to Mexican Anthropology"), writes of finding an Aztec hieroglyphic in Velletri, Italy, known as the Codex Borgia, which is now in the Vatican Library, and gives a brief discussion on the animals portrayed on the Mexican folio, including what appears to be elephants. Humboldt writes:

> The Aztlán people originally from Asia, may have conserved some vague notions on elephants? Or, what appears to me even less probable, were their traditions back dated to

the time when America was still populated by these gigantic animals whose petrified skeletons are found immersed in marly soils, on the same backs of the Mexican mountain ranges? Is it probable that there exists in the northwest part of the New Continent, in regions that have not been visited by neither Hearne, Meackenzie, or Lewis an unknown pachyderm that, by the configuration of its trunk, occupies a happy medium between the elephant and the tapir? [31]

Baron von Humboldt finding elephant references in Mexican manuscripts predating the Spanish conquest, is surprising and opens a dialogue on how and why the evidence and history of elephants, horses, and Christianity recorded in *The Book of Mormon* is hidden even in our modern time when information is so accessible? *The Book of Mormon* as an ancient history of the Americas and sacred scripture is not accepted as verifiable by the mainstream academic community. There are moments of doubt even for faithful believers to acknowledge. Where is the evidence of elephants, horses, Hebrew-Christian culture, and secular history? This Chapter provides historical authenticity to these questions. Elephants are spoken of in *The Book of Mormon* (Ether 9:19) "And they also had horses, and asses, and there were elephants and coreloms and cumoms; all of which were useful unto man, and more especially the elephants and cureloms and cumoms." *The Book of Ether* is a record of the Jaredites who immigrated to the Americas from the destruction of the great tower of Babel. The Jaredite occupancy in the Americas could have been between 4000 B. C. to 2000 B. C.

Senator Robert F. Bennett in his 2009 book *Leap of Faith: Confronting the Origins of the Book of Mormon* applies his expertise on forgery to test *The Book of Mormon*; and it passed his forgery tests but leaves unanswered the criticism that there is no historicity. Bob Bennett and I were friends. Our last meeting was 2013 when he signed my copy of *Leap of Faith, Confronting the Origins of the Book of Mormon*. In his book Bob wrote:

> The critics say the book fails the external test for the following reasons: *There is no evidence of an ancient Israelite presence in Central or South America.* Modern DNA analysis says that pre-Columbian Indians all came from Asia, not the Middle East. Although some believers insist that Book of Mormon sites

have been found in pre-Columbian America, no non-believing archaeologist agrees with them. There are no signs of Hebrew Influence in any of the religious rites of the pre-Columbian tribes. There are no traces of Old-World linguistics in any of the languages of the American aboriginal tribes. [31]

We briefly discussed the issues in the quoted paragraph. I told him of my research, and that I had answers to the critics' doubts. Bob told me that he and Joyce, his wife, had just returned from a trip to Guatamala. From what he learned on his trip; he agreed with me, and said: "Gary, when I edit my Book, I will consult with you." Bob's bout with cancer made it impossible for us to meet again.

Baron von Humbold's discovery of an ancient folio featuring elephants, referenced in *The Book of Mormon*, puts an elephant in the room, giving cause to speculate that if the Mexican archives had not been destroyed by the Spanish conquistadors in 1519 and 1526, today we would have access to ancient American folios with the scriptures and ancient evidence of Hebrew-Christian heritage discovered by the early Catholic missionaries in the Americas, later to be abridged and unveiled by Fray Mier.

CHAPTER 7 SUMMARY

The audacity of Fray Mier revealed by his December 12, 1794 Guadalupe Sermon; and, his proud demeanor, obvious in his writings, gave him the strength to carry onward and upward for the rest of his life. Across the Atlantic Ocean, across continents and national boundaries, he conveyed his theological research on ancient Christianity in The Americas. His research was his study of the writings of his antecedent Catholic Missionary Brothers. In his "Apologia, Antecedents and Consequences of the Sermon up to the Opening of the Process," Fray Mier writes:

And, who does not know of the blasphemies of the incredulous against the Christian religion, whose Divinity, they say, was testing them sixteen centuries, up to crushing their bones, with its expansion into all the world by only twelve men, and with the universality of the Church; and in the end a New World was discovered where nothing was known of it? It is false. Throughout America, monuments and vestige evidences of Christianity were found, according to the unanimous testimony of the missionaries.

Fray Mier's writing mirrors this verse from *The Book of Mormon*:

And the Lord God hath sent his holy prophets among all the children of men, to declare these things to every kindred, nation, and tongue, that thereby whosoever should believe that Christ should come, the same might receive remission of their sins, and rejoice with exceedingly great joy, even as though he had already come among them. (*Book of Mormon*, Mosiah 3:13)

Fray Mier died December 3, 1827. *The Book of Mormon* was first published in English the year, 1830. Fray Mier's writings are an abridged history of Christianity in the ancient Americas. The many sources he cites are a hidden prologue and witness to the truth of *The Book of Mormon*.

CHAPTER 7 NOTES

1. de Cervantes Saavedra, Miguel., *El Ingenioso Hidalgo Don Quijote de la Mancha*, Editorial Ramón Sopena, S. A., Barcelona, Spain, 1962. Second Part, Chapter III, p. 466.

2. de Humboldt, Alejandro., trans. from French and study by Jaime Labastida, *Aportaciones a la antropología mexicana*. Mexico, D. F.: Editorial Katún, S. A., 1974, 63.

3. de Humboldt, Alejandro., *Aportaciones a la antropología mexicana*. loc. cit., 33.

4. Diamond, Jared. *Guns, Germs, and Steel, The Fates of Human Societies*. New York & London: W. W. Norton & Company, 1997, p. 215 and p. 218.

5. de las Casas, Fray Barolomé, ed. Prologue, Appendices, and Notes by Edmundo O'Gorman, with collaboration of Jorge Alberto Manrique. *Los indios de México y Nueva España, Antología*. Mexico, D. F. Editorial Porrua, S. A., Sixth Edition 1987, first published 1552, p. 95.

6. Clavijero, Francisco Javier. *Historia Antigua de México*. Mexico D. F.: Editorial Porrua, S. A., Fourth Edition 1968. First published 1780 in Italian, p. 1.

7. de Alva Cortés Ixtlilxóchitl, Fernando. *Historia de la nación chichimeca*. Linkgua ediciones S.L., Barcelona, 2008. Original written circa 1640, p. 170-171.

8. Bataillon, Marcel, trans. by J. Coderich and J. A. Martínez Schrem. *Estudios sobre Bartolomé de las Casas*, Serie Universitario, Historia/Ciencia/Sociedad 127. Barcelona: Ediciones Península, First Edition: 1976, p. 230.

9. Cortés, Hernán, Edition annotated by Dr. Julio Le Riverend. *Cartas de relación de Hernán Cortés*. Mexico, D. F.: Editorial Concepto, S. A., 1983, written 1519-1529, p. 95.

10. de las Casas, Los indios de México y Nueva España, Antología. loc. cit., p. 91-92.

11. de Humboldt, Alejandro., *Aportaciones a la antropología mexicana*. loc. cit., 40.

12. de las Casas, Batolomé, Prologue Olga Camps. *Brevísima relación de la destrucción de las Indias*. Mexico, D. F.: Editorial Fontamara, S. A., 1984. First edition 1552, Sevilla.

13. de Acosta, Joseph, Prologue and selections by Edmundo O'Gorman. *(Historia natural y moral de las Indias) Vida Religiosa y civil de los Indios*. Biblioteca del Estudiante Universitario No. 83. Mexico, D. F.: Universidad Nacional Autónomoa de México, 1963, published in Spain, 1590, p. 70.

14. de las Casas, *Los indios de México y Nueva España*, *Antología*. loc. cit., p. 190-194.

15. Ibid., p. 190.

16. Ibid., p. 192.

17. Ibid., p. 193.

18. González, José Eleuterio. Juan Peña, ed. *Biografia del benemérito mexicano D. Servando Teresa de Mier Noriega y Guerra*. Monterey, Mexico: José Saenz, published, 1876. Commemorative Edition, Facsimile of the Original, Government of the State of Nuevo Leon, Autonomous University of Nuevo Leon, Sesquicentennial of the Death of Father Mier, 1827-1977, 1977., pp. 340-348.

19. The Bible Dictionary of *The Holy Bible* published 1960 by the Church of Jesus Christ of Latter-day Saints lists "GIANTS, or Nephilim," R.V., Gen 6.4; Nu 13.33.

20. Clavijero. *Historia Antigua de México*. loc. cit., p. 151-153.

21. Ibid., p. 152.

22. Didymus is the Greek equivalent of the Aramaic name Thomas.

23. Clavijero, op. cit., p. 152-153.

24. Nibley, Hugh. *Lehi, in the Desert, The World of the Jaredites, There were Jaredites*. Salt Lake City, Utah: Deseret Book Company;

and Provo, Utah: Foundation for Ancient Research and Mormon Studies, 1988, pp. 189-194.

25. Cortés. *Cartas de relación de Hernán Cortés*. Mexico, loc. Cortéz. loc. cit., 38.

26. de Landa, Fray Diego. *Relación de las Cosas de Yucatán*. Merida, Yucatán, Mexico: Ediciones Dante, S. A.,1983. Previous editions 1864, 1881, 1900, 1928-29, 1937, 1938, 1938, 1941. An abridgement of Landa's writing, believed to have been first published about 1660, p. 138.

27. de las Casas, *Los indios de México y Nueva España, Antología.*, loc. cit., Chapter LVI, p. 191.

28. de las Casas, *Los indios de México y Nueva España, Antología.* loc. cit., Chapter XL, p. 134-135.

29. de las Casas, Batolomé, Prologue Olga Camps. *Brevísima relación de la destrucción de las Indias*. Mexico, D. F.: Editorial Fontamara, S. A., 1984. First edition 1552, Sevilla.

30. de los Rios, José Amador. *Historia social, politica y religiosa de los judios de España y Portugal*. Madrid, Spain. Aguilar, S.A., 1960 Edition, republished 1973. Original text first published 1848.

31. de Humboldt, Alejandro., *Aportaciones a la antropología mexicana.* loc. cit., 112-113.

32. Bennett, Robert F. *Leap of Faith, Confronting the Origins of the Book of Mormon*. Deseret Book, Salt Lake City, Utah. Copyright and published 2009. p. 213.

CHAPTER 8

A Sermon on Fray Servando
Teresa de Mier

One would expect that accepted academic standards, valid research sources, and an author's recognized honors would validate an author's writings, but such is rare with Fray Servando Teresa de Mier. A rare example of honor given Fray Mier in our time is the publication of his letters "Eleventh Note of the Second Letter from an American," "Farewell Letter to the Mexicans," and his Memoirs published 1945 by the Universidad Nacional Autónoma de México ("Autonomous National University of Mexico"). It is a public research university rated highly in world rankings based on the university's extensive research and innovation. The published book is titled: Biblioteca del Estudiante Universitario, 56, *Servando Teresa de Mier escritos y memorias*, ("University Students' Library, 56, Servando Teresa de Mier Writings and Memoirs") with selection of Fray Mier's Letters and Memoirs and Prologue written by Edmundo O'Gorman. The following is a translation of Dr. O'Gorman's Prologue Introduction:

> Fray Servando Teresa de Mier is one of the most interesting characters of our modern history. The process of his political thinking, that begins and manifests itself with large abundance during his stay in London, and that culminates with Mier's vigorous action as a Deputy to the first two Constituent Congresses of Mexico, is the process of the ideological struggles surrounding the movement for Spanish America's Independence. To study Father Mier is like doing a small study, but with large authenticity, of this momentous event.
>
> On the other hand, his difficult and picturesque life has left us, with his *Memoirs*, the impressions that the old Europe at the end of the 18th century could have left on the soul of a

Mexican Creole as Father Mier was.

For these reasons, Mexico's Autonomous National University, has wanted to devote to Father Mier one of the volumes of this Library, in which it had reserved a place of honor for a long time.[1]

A second rare example is the publication of *Biografía del benemérito mexicano D. Servando Teresa de Mier Noriega y Guerra*, ("Biography of the Distinguished Don Servando Teresa de Mier Noriega y Guerra") with biographical writings by José Eleuterio González, published 1876 by the Mexican State of Nuevo Leon and the Autonomous University of Nuevo Leon. With a Commemorative Facsimile Edition of the Original by the Government of the State of Nuevo Leon and the Autonomous University of Nuevo Leon on the Sesquicentennial of the Death of Father Mier, 1827-1977. González writes what could be called Fray Mier's obituary:

> In addition to this pension [three thousand pesos annually] that was always religiously paid to him [Mier], the President of the Republic, Don Guadalupe Victoria, assigned him a very decent abode in the National Palace, where he went to live and there passed the remaining years of his life. Three years of a peaceful and tranquil life loved and respected, in contact with the best society of Mexico and in relations with the most notable men of the nation, were the last of his life. It is to say, he had three years of rest for thirty of outrageous persecutions, jails, labors, and sufferings. He was very highly respected by President Victoria and his ministers, as well as by Vice President Don Nicolas Bravo who consulted with him on their gravest concerns. From all the States, or as he says in his letters, from the entire kingdom, inquiries were directed to him, and he came in this time to be the most popular man in Mexico.[2]

The preamble to Dr. Mier's "Apologia," in defense of his Guadalupe Sermon, noted in *Fray Servando Teresa de Mier: Writings on Ancient Christianity and Spain's Evangelism of Mexico*, is his homily revealing his personal audacity, the pains he suffered, and his final desire that Eternal Father in Heaven pardon his enemies for their errors.

Powerful and sinners are synonymous in the language of the Scriptures, because power fills them with pride and envy, it facilitates their means of oppression, and ensures their impunity. Thus, the Archbishop of Mexico, Don Alonso Nuñez de Haro achieved it in the persecution by which he ruined me for the Guadalupe Sermon that then being a monk of the Order of Preachers, I recited in the Sanctuary of Tepeyacac the 12th day of December 1794. But *I saw the unrighteous man exalted on high and lifted up like the cedars of Lebanon. And I passed by, and behold he was not.* It is time to instruct the posterity upon the truth of everything that happened in this affair, in order that you might judge with your accustomed impartiality that you might take advantage and do justice to my memory, since this *Apologia,* cannot now serve me in this life that naturally is near its end at my age of fifty-six years. I owe it to my very noble family in Spain and in America, to my Mexican University, to the Order to which I belong, to my character, to my Religion and to the native land, whose glory was the object that I had proposed in the sermon. I will follow in the *Apologia* the same order of the events. I will first tell for your intelligence what preceded the sermon and followed it up to the opening of the process. I will then prove that I did not deny the tradition of Guadalupe in the sermon; I will explain it with some proofs, and it will be seen that far from contradicting it, its theme was all calculated to sustain it against the arguments, if it were possible; and if not for that it takes away from the native land a glory more solid and greater without comparison. From there the passions appeared in a conspiracy prosecuting the innocent, slandering it under the disguise of censors, defaming it with a libel called Pastoral Edict, incriminating it with a public prosecutor's indictment that the same is no more than a horrific crime, and condemning it with a sentence worthy of such a tribunal; but with the cruel derision of naming the most absurd and atrocious penalty, piety and clemency. And I left for exile, but always under the tremendous escort of the false testimonies disguised with the title of confidential reports. Always the oppression accompanied me, always the intrigue, and I found nothing in all my resources but venality, corruption and injustice. Even with twenty-four year of persecution I have acquired the talent of painting monsters, the discussion will show that I do no more here than copy the originals. I have nothing now against who bloodied me; all my enemies disappeared from this world. They have already given their account to the Eternal; I desire that He has pardoned them.

Gathering lost memories of Fray Mier's motives is a necessity before delving into the thesis of his Guadalupe Sermon. His life story gives credence to his personal testimonial of the truth of his writings. Fray Mier quotes the italicized language of St. Clement's Epistle to the Corinthians 14:5, as he begins his written *Apologia* in defense of his Guadalupe Sermon. He uses the scripture to define his adversaries, while adhering to the overarching counsel of Saint Clement's Epistle.

It is therefore meet and right, men and brethren, that we should be obedient unto God rather than follow them that in pride and disorderliness are leaders of detestable sedition. For we shall incur no slight harm, but rather a great danger, if we rashly give ourselves up to the wills of men who launch out into strife and sedition so as to estrange us from that which is good. Let us, therefore, show kindness towards them according to the mercy and sweetness of him that made us. For it is written, the men of kindness shall inherit the land. The innocent shall be left upon it; but they that be lawless shall be destroyed out of it. And again, he saith, *I saw the unrighteous man exalted on high and lifted up like the cedars of Lebanon. And I passed by, and behold he was not;* I sought his place and found it not. Keep innocence, and regard righteousness; for there is a remnant that remaineth to the man of peace (St. Clement's Epistle to the Corinthians 14: 1-5).

The verses, "Let us, therefore, show kindness towards them according to the mercy and sweetness of him that made us,"and, "Keep innocence, and regard righteousness; for there is a remnant that remaineth to the man of peace;" tell us how Fray Mier chose to respond to the exalted cedars of Lebanon. Fray Mier's style of unrest was a forerunner to modern peaceful dissenters such as Mahatma Gandhi, Martin Luther King, and Nelson Mandela. Gandhi compounded Sanskrit words coining "Satyagraha" to describe his non-violent resistance. "Satyagraha" translates to

"Truth and Persistence." Fray Mier's Sermon and Inquisition preceded Gandhi, but he trod the road of Persistent non-violence sharing of Truth.

To fully appreciate the significance of Fray Mier's audacious attempt to raise ancient American Christianity from myth to the light of history, we must come to know his personal history and how the entire world viciously fell upon him after he preached the Guadalupe Sermon from the pulpit of the Collegiate Church of Guadalupe, Mexico City, December 12, 1794. The Guadalupe Sermon is his legacy to Mexico and the World. A legacy which sadly plagued him for the rest of his life.

Spain's conquest of America was a quest for exploitation and sovereignty of land, wealth, and slavery. In its Mesoamerica conquest, Spain discovered inexplicable, vestiges of Hebrew-Christian practices and symbols that predated Spain's arrival. After Spain's successful conquest, the Virgin of Guadalupe appeared December 12, 1531 to Juan Diego on Tepeyac hill, now central Mexico City, in the image of a native Mexican woman, thereby merging Mexico's ancient Christian religious belief in Tonantzin, Mother of the True God, into Spain's Extremadura Virgin of Guadalupe, bringing Mexicans to accept the Catholic faith in a symbolic fusion of New and Old-World Christianity. John Francis Maxwell in his book, *Slavery and the Catholic Church,* outlines 1434 to 1526 Catholic Church and Spanish Royal edicts on slavery, writes: "It was a custom of war in Christendom that no Christian prisoner of war should ever be enslaved." Finding traces of Christianity in Mesoamerica would have been probable cause for Spain's reckless destruction of Mexican culture, to knowingly and willfully destroy any evidence that could be construed as the practice of Christianity in the New World. Consequently, Spain undertook aggressive evangelism of the native people of the Americas to European Christianity justifying a brutal conquest. Destruction and evangelism erased traces of New-World Christianity and hid Spain's violation of Catholic Church doctrine against enslaving Christian prisoners of war.

December 12, 1794, in the presence of Viceroy Miguel de la Grua Talamanca y Branciforte, Marques de Branciforte, Archbishop Manuel Omaña y Sotomayor and the members of the Royal Judiciary of New Spain, Fray Mier preached his infamous Guadalupe Sermon, warmly received by the lay audience but giving rise to Church Hierarchy accusations that he denied the apparition of the Virgin of Guadalupe on the 263rd anniversary. His alleged denial of the Virgin of Guadalupe gave causes for Archbishop Nuñez de Haro to exile Fray Mier to Spain; to perpetually ban him from teaching, preaching or hearing confessions; and the loss of his doctoral degree. Fray Mier's Guadalupe Sermon was the cause for subsequent multiple confiscations of his library, doctoral insignias, and personal documents; multiple incarcerations; suspension of his ecclesiastical authority; multiple deportations, investigations, and judicial actions; his secularization, impoverishment; and personal humiliation. The actions taken by New Spain's appointed Church, Royal Court, and Viceroy hierarchy were motivated by fear of a political revolutionary and religious apostasy. Fray Mier was perceived as a religious rebel, agitating for religious freedom and liberty of Mexico from Spain's civil and religious rule. Fray Mier's Guadalupe Sermon set forth two "Propositions." First, the ancient people of Anáhuac already had knowledge of the Gospel of Jesus Christ brought to America by the Apostle Saint Thomas; and, second, the Virgin of Guadalupe, was a symbolic intermingling of Spain's Catholic Virgin of Guadalupe with the holy Anáhuacan image of Tonantzin, Mother of God. Fray Mier summarizes the Sermon's message in the closing admonition of his "Farewell Letter to the Mexicans" written and sent twenty-six years later while imprisoned in Castle San Juan de Ulúa: "My fellow countrymen stop howling and go study this issue. Today the ancient preaching of the Gospel in America is beyond doubt."

Even today after nearly five hundred years, Mexico celebrates the festival of the Virgin of Guadalupe as a religious holiday as prominent as are Christmas and Easter. Fray Mier's sin was to unveil hidden history before a crowd of common Church members gathered to celebrate the December 12th festival of the Virgin of Guadalupe. He violated his Catholic vows by publicly preaching religious history well known to Church hierarchy, but unknown to lay Church members. His trials became more complex, while an exile in Europe, he was granted secularization by the Pope; then later, named a domestic prelate of the Pontiff.

An anomaly I title, "The Mier Paradox," is found in Mexico's Fourth Grade Primary Education textbook, "My Book of Mexico's History, Lesson 10, The 19th Century Revolution of Independence." Featured with a picture and brief introduction are Fray Servando Teresa de Mier, Priest Miguel Hidalgo y Costilla, and Priest José

María Morelos de Pavón. Hidalgo and Morelos were leaders in the war for Independence. Both were captured and executed. Both are well known for their contribution to Mexico's War of Independence from Spain. Mier was incarcerated numerous times in Mexico and Spain, but never threatened with execution. Despite his inclusion in "Lesson 10," Mier is virtually unknown to the citizens of Mexico be they Fourth Grade students, the student's parents, or even teachers and members of Mexico's modern Congress. The conclusion is that Fathers Hidalgo and Morelos fought for Mexico's freedom from Spain, while Fray Mier preached that we might know the truth of Mexico's ancient Christian heritage. Fray Mier's Sermon was centuries past the time when it may have harmed the kingdoms of Spain and New Spain; thus, his incarceration in Mexico and Spain was always under the jurisdiction of the Catholic Church. The legacy of suppressing Fray Mier's Mexican religious history continues even into the 21st Century.

Fray Mier's bold 1794 Guadalupe Sermon unveiled Mexico's ancient Christianity hidden to hasten Spain's conquest of America. In 1830, thirty-six years after the sermon and three years after his death, *The Book of Mormon* was published. Fray Servando Teresa de Mier lived the life of a true "Mexican," which he writes is the same as to call one a "Christian." Fray Mier's audacity reveals authentic historical evidence that Christianity, the virgin Mother of the Son of God, and the Messiah were known in ancient Mexico; bearing witness to history and Hebrew-Christian practices recorded in *The Book of Mormon*.

CHAPTER 8 NOTES

1. O'Gorman, Edmundo. *Servando Teresa de Mier, escritos y memorias, Biblioteca del Estudiante Universitario 56.* Prologue and Selection by Edmundo O'Gorman, Ediciones de la Universidad Nacional Autonoma, Mexico, D.F., 1945. pp. v-vi.

2. González, José Eleuterio. Juan Peña, ed. *Biografía del benemérito mexicano D. Servando Teresa de Mier Noriega y Guerra.* Monterey, Mexico: José Saenz, publish.,1876. Commemorative Edition, Facsimile of the Original, Government of the State of Nuevo Leon, Autonomous University of Nuevo Leon, Sesquicentennial of the Death of Father Mier, 1827-1977, 1977. P. 364

BIBLIOGRAPHY

de Acosta, Joseph, Prologue and selections by Edmundo O'Gorman. *(Historia natural y moral de las Indias) Vida Religiosa y civil de los Indios.* Biblioteca del Estudiante Universitario No. 83. Mexico, D. F.: Universidad Nacional Autónomoa de México, 1963, published in Spain, 1590.

de Alva Cortés Ixtlilxóchitl, Fernando. *Historia de la nación chichimeca.* Linkgua ediciones S.L., Barcelona, 2008. Original written circa 1614.

de Alva Ixtlilxóchitl, Fernando. *Obras históricas de don Fernando de Alva Ixtlilxóchitl.* Volume 1 and 2. Reprint from the collection of the University of Michigan Library. Original written circa 1608-1611.

Bataillon, Marcel, trans. by J. Coderich and J. A. Martínez Schrem. *Estudios sobre Bartolomé de las Casas*, Serie Universitario, Historia/Ciencia/Sociedad 127. Barcelona: Ediciones Península, First Edition: 1976. The original French edition, *Études sur Batolomé de las Casas*, published by Centre de Recherches de l'Institut d'Études Hispaniques, Paris, 1965.

Bennett, Robert F. *Leap of Faith, Confronting the Origins of the Book of Mormon.* Deseret Book, Salt Lake City, Utah. Copyright and published 2009.

The Bible. King James translation. Distributed by The Deseret Book Company, Salt Lake City, Utah, U.S.A.

The Book of Mormon. The Church of Jesus Christ of Latter-day Saints, Salt Lake City, UT, U.S.A. First edition published in 1830.

Bowen, Gary. *Christianity in The Americas Before Columbus: Unfamiliar Origins and Insights and Fray Servando Teresa de Mier: Writings on Ancient Christianity and Spain's Evangelism of Mexico.* Salt Lake City, UT. 2019. Elite Online Publishing de las Casas, Bartolomé, Prologue Olga Camps. *Brevísima relación de la destrucción de las Indias.* Mexico, D. F.: Editorial Fontamara, S. A., 1984. First edition 1552, Sevilla.

de las Casas, Fray Bartolomé., trans. from Latin Atenógenes Santamaría 1942, Forward by Agustín Millares Carlo and Introduction by Lewis Hanke. *Del único modo de atraer a todos los pueblos a la verdadera religión.* Mexico, D. F.: Fondo de Cultura Económica, 1942, 1975.

de las Casas, Fray Barolomé, ed. Prologue, Appendices, and Notes by Edmundo O'Gorman, with collaboration of Jorge Alberto Manrique. *Los indios de México y Nueva España, Antología.* Mexico, D. F. Editorial Porrua, S. A., Sixth Edition 1987.

de Cervantes Saavedra, Miguel., trans. Edith Grossman and Introduction by Harold Bloom. *Don Quixote.* New York: HarperCollins Publishers, Inc., 2003.

de Cervantes Saavedra, Miguel., *El Ingenioso Hidalgo Don Quijote de la Mancha*, Editorial Ramón Sopena, S. A., Barcelona, Spain, 1962.

The Church of Jesus Christ of Latter-day Saints. *The Book of Mormon, Another Testament of Jesus Christ.* Salt Lake City, Utah, U.S.A. 1992, First published 1830.

Clavijero, Francisco Javier. R. P. Mariano Cuevas, Prologue and Editor. *Historia Antigua de México.* Mexico D. F.: Editorial Porrua, S. A., Fourth Edition 1968. Published from the original Spanish text 1945, 1968. First published title: *Storia Antica del Messico.* Cesna, Italy, 1780, Original Spanish text translated to Italian by the author; *The History of Mexico.* Translated from Italian, published London 1787; Richmond, Virginia 1806, London 1807, and Philadelphia, 1817. Translated from Italian to Spanish; *Historia Antigua de México.* London 1826; Mexico, D. F. 1844, 1853, 1861-62, Jalapa 1868, Mexico, D. F. 1833, 1917, 1944.

Cortés, Hernán, Edition annotated by Dr. Julio Le Riverend. *Cartas de relación de Hernán Cortés.* Mexico, D. F.: Editorial Concepto, S. A., 1983.

Diamond, Jared. *Guns, Germs, and Steel, The Fates of Human Societies.* New York & London: W. W. Norton & Company, 1997.

Frost, Robert. *The Poetry of Robert Frost.* Edited by Edward Connery Lathem. New York, Chicago, San Francisco: Holt, Rinehart and Winston, 1969.

González, José Eleuterio. Juan Peña, ed. *Biografía del benemérito mexicano D. Servando Teresa de Mier Noriega y Guerra.* Monterey, Mexico: José Saenz, published, 1876. Commemorative Edition, Facsimile of the Original, Government of the State of Nuevo Leon, Autonomous University of Nuevo Leon, Sesquicentennial of the Death of Father Mier, 1827-1977, 1977.

Herring, Hubert. *A History of Latin America from the Beginnings to the Present.* New York: Alfred a. Knopf, 1961.

de Humboldt, Alejandro., trans. from French and study by Jaime Labastida, *Aportaciones a la antropología mexicana.* Mexico, D. F.: Editorial Katún, S. A., 1974.

de Landa, Fray Diego. *Relación de las Cosas de Yucatán.* Merida, Yucatán, Mexico: Ediciones Dante, S. A.,1983. Previous editions 1864, 1881, 1900, 1928-29, 1937, 1938, 1938, 1941. An abridgement of Landa's writing, believed to have been first published about 1660.

Lane, Helen., trans., and Susana Rotker., ed. and Introduction. *Fray Servando, The Memoirs of Fray Servando Teresa de Mier.* New York and Oxford: Library of Latin America, Oxford University Press, Inc., 1998.

Maxwell, John Francis. *Slavery and the Catholic Church.* Chichester & London: Barry Rose Publishers in association with the Anti-Slavery Society for the Protection of Human Right, 1975.

Mills, Kenneth and Taylor, William B. ed. "José María Morelos, "Sentiments of the Nation," Chilpancingo, Mexico (1813);" reprinted in *Colonial Spanish America: A Documentary History*, (Wilmington, DE: A Scholarly Resources Inc. Imprint, 1998), pp. 341–44.

Motolinia, Fray Toribio de Benavente or Motolinia. Edmundo O'Gorman. Critical Study, Appendix, Notes & Index. *Historia de los indios de la Nueva España*. Mexico D. F.: Editorial Porrua, S. A., Fourth Edition 1984, Previous editions 1858, 1969.

Nibley, Hugh. *Lehi, in the Desert, The World of the Jaredites, There were Jaredites*. Salt Lake City, Utah: Deseret Book Company; and Provo, Utah: Foundation for Ancient Research and Mormon Studies, 1988.

O'Gorman, Edmundo. *Servando Teresa de Mier, escritos y memorias, Biblioteca del Estudiante Universitario 56*. Prologue and Selection by Edmundo O'Gorman, Ediciones de la Universidad Nacional Autonoma, Mexico, D.F., 1945.

Paz, Octavio. *El laberinto de la soledad*. Mexico, D. F.: Fondo de Cultura Economica, First Edition 1950, 1983.

Paz, Octavio. *Sor Juana Inés de la Cruz o Las trampas de la fe*. Barcelona: Editorial Seix Barral, S. A.1982.

de los Rios, José Amador. *Historia social, politica y religiosa de los judios de España y Portugal*. Madrid, Spain. Aguilar, S.A., 1960 Edition, republished 1973. Original text first published 1848.

Secretaría de Educación Pública de México. *Mi libro de Historia de México*. Mexico D. F.: Comisión de los Libros de Texto Gratuitos, 1992.

Vickery, Paul S. *Bartolomé de las Casas Great Prophet of the Americas*. NewYork/Mahwah, N. J.: Paulist Press, 2006.

ABOUT THE AUTHOR

Gary Bowen earned degrees in Economics and an MBA from the University of Utah. His career began in egg marketing, when hired by Jon M. Huntsman Sr. His experiences included agricultural wholesale marketing, financial consulting, a Utah State Division Director, and Securities Examiner. Before his 2011 retirement, he met Dr. Paul Y. Hoskisson, Director of the Laura F. Willes Center for Book of Mormon Research and The Foundation for Ancient Research and Mormon Studies (FARMS) at Brigham Young University. They discussed Gary's studies on Mexican history and its evidence of the authenticity of The Book of Mormon. At the end of the meeting, Dr. Hoskisson said: "Gary, you have to get this written. No one else in the Church studies what you study." *Christianity in The Americas Before Columbus* and *Fray Servando Teresa De Mier Writings on Ancient Christianity and Spain's Evangelism of Mexico* were written upon Dr. Hoskisson's wise counsel.

Gary's studies began 1962-64 as a Church of Jesus Christ of Latter-day Saints Missionary to West Mexico, where he learned Spanish and Mexican culture. In 1964, he married Herlinda Briones-Vega, who introduced him to Mexico's hidden history. Reading Spanish history books, coincidental meetings over decades with a member of Mexico's Congress, Mexican Jesuit Priests, etc.; he came to know a history of Mexico that other than Herlinda and Mexican Catholic Priests is largely unknown. Gary likens his historical research to the idealistic dreams of Don Quixote of La Mancha for a better world.

ABOUT THE AUTHOR

Gary and Herlinda are parents of 4 children, 10 grandchildren, and one g-grandchild. In 2017, he was elected to the Emigration Canyon Metro Township Council, which keeps him very involved in community activities in Salt Lake County, Utah.

Follow Gary

Twitter.com/GaryBowenAuthor

fb.me/GaryBowenAuthor

Linkedin.com/in/garybowenauthor

Look for Gary's other book:
Fray Servando Teresa De Mier:
Writings on Ancient Christianity and Spain's Evangelism of
Mexico

CPSIA information can be obtained
at www.ICGtesting.com
Printed in the USA
LVHW021102090520
654944LV00004B/293